CHASING RUTH

CHASING RUTH

A CENTURY LATER

A FAMILY DISCOVERS ITSELF

Holly J. Pierce

with

Katherine P. Chinelli

Elizabeth A. Pierce

and

Ruth Crapo Johnson

Photographs by Holly J. Pierce

iUniverse, Inc.

Bloomington

Chasing Ruth
A Century Later a Family Discovers Itself

iUniverse books may be ordered through booksellers or by contacting:

iUniverse
1663 Liberty Drive
Bloomington, IN 47403
www.iuniverse.com
1-800-Authors (1-800-288-4677)

ISBN: 978-1-4502-9782-0 (sc)
ISBN: 978-1-4502-9784-4 (hc)
ISBN: 978-1-4502-9783-7 (ebk)

Printed in the United States of America

iUniverse rev. date: 11/10/2011

For Ruth

We shall not cease from exploration
And the end of all our exploring
Will be to arrive where we started
And know the place for the first time.
—T.S. Eliot

Nothing is more revealing of character
than the experience of travel.
—Paul Theroux

TABLE OF CONTENTS

Prologue

"ARE YOU WILLING to risk alienating your daughter over this?"

The therapist peered at me gravely through her bifocals. Katie leaned forward from her chair across the little room. Richard sat next to Liz, who was dabbing at her teary eyes with a tissue. I looked resolutely back at the therapist.

"Yes," I said.

IT STARTED WITH THE little red book, the one that had been tucked away on a dusty bookshelf in my parents' house. I discovered it one Sunday afternoon in the front bedroom. About six inches tall, it had a dark, dried-blood-red leather cover, soft and malleable, and fit perfectly into the palm of my hand. The edges of the pages were rounded and a dull gilt, darkened by age. The cover of the little book was scuffed and battered with use, revealing the tan leather beneath the dye. The spine shifted in my hands, and while the pages were once firmly stitched in, use and the passage of time had stretched and loosened the threads. It was so fragile, I had to be careful handling it.

Holding the book in my left hand, I eased the pages apart, only allowing them to partially reveal themselves. The book was a diary; perhaps half the pages were filled with dull-tipped penciling. The writer's handwriting was spiky, firm and slanted, and very, very tiny, as each page held twenty-six pale blue lines.

Inside the front cover, the left was inscribed with "R.K.C./269 Ridgewood Avenue/Glen Ridge, N.J." while on the right in dark pencil was written "R.K. Crapo/Sept. 1st 1907." Then in a loose, clear hand the admonition, "Private," underlined for good measure.

R.K. Crapo—that would have been my paternal grandmother, Ruth Kelsell Crapo (my middle maiden name was Ruth in her honor, a name my mother resisted but grudgingly capitulated to when the time came around to fill out my birth certificate). I remembered family legends about Ruth being given the choice of four years of college or two years abroad. In my hand lay evidence of her choice. But 1907? That would mean she was twenty-seven when she wrote this diary, quite a while after she would have graduated from Dana Hall, her boarding school in Wellesley, Massachusetts, and faced the choice apocryphally given her.

Who could answer the questions beginning to fill my mind about this little journal? Surely not my dad. While he was proud of his Crapo heritage, such mundane details as those of my grandmother's girlhood would hardly have interested him. As for siblings, my dad had only his brother, Sam, who was deeply into the family's genealogy but not the stories that would bring these ancestors alive. There was no sister who might have remembered the stories that her mother might have told her while working in the kitchen or sitting together sewing.

Peeking out from the pages was the very edge of some sort of note different from the diary's ivory pages. Pulling it out, I saw written on a cut-out piece of lined white paper in my mother's hand: "Sept. 20—shopped, rode bus." Hmm, so my mother had paid some sort of attention to Ruth's diary. But how much? What did she know?

Diary in hand, I found my mother sitting in her swivel chair in the living room working on one of her eternal knitting projects. Holding out the little book, I asked her what she knew about its contents.

"Well, it's not very interesting. It covers Ruth's trip to Europe, but all they seemed to do was shop and go to the American Express office," she sniffed.

"'They?' Who were 'they?'"

"That would have been Ruth and her younger sister, Lucy, and 'Dearo,' their mother. Edith didn't go; she was already married to Martin."

Of the Crapos, only these three women made this six-month Grand Tour of Europe plus the Holy Land and the Nile, as I later discovered. Ruth's father had died four years previously, but this didn't stop them.

"So you read all of it?"

"Well, I did skim over some parts."

I could understand her disinterest in the diary; after all, this wasn't *her* mother's journal. My mom's head was already full of the vivid tales of her grandmother's Midwestern life: of her hiding the twins, Julia and Julius, amid the rustling corn stalks when Indians passed through and her own mother's husband's ban on her driving when she ran over a pig. And she held a certain resentment for Ruth and the Crapos. They were the wealthy ones who lived in the big white house on New York Avenue, complete with a Chinese cook, while my mother's family was genteelly impoverished, suffering the embarrassment of her well-married and wealthy sister's weekly bestowal of a bag of groceries and an angel food cake from Van de Camp's. Then, once the Crash of 1929 stripped the widowed Ruth of her share of the family fortune, any remaining cash went to Sam, the firstborn, and his Caltech education, while my dad stayed home in the little stucco house on Mar Vista Avenue in Altadena, California, entrusted with caring for his mother and her phlebitis leg.

Looking at the little leather-bound book, I couldn't imagine that it was boring. I was sure there were plenty of tidbits between the shopping and visits to the American Express office that would help me see my grandmother as a vibrant young woman. I recalled Grandma Ruth was the active one, proud of her silver loving cups won in tennis and golf tournaments, remembering with pleasure her palomino horse, Sally Ann; according to memory, she was the first woman in her county to "ride astride" a horse, as she put it, rather than sidesaddle like any other proper young woman. We had sepia photos of her trip west to a dude ranch, including one picturing Ruth and a group of others, rifles in hand, surrounding a dead bobcat.

My own memories of her and her life on Mar Vista included her prized cactus garden and the lemon tree which provided the fruit for the seed-y lemonade she squeezed for us. Above the fireplace on the mantel stood a large, black statue of an elephant, trunk raised. She never complained when my sister, Nancy, and I banged out "thunder and lightning" music on the mahogany upright piano in the dining room.

Best of all was the trunk in the closet of the back bedroom. The strong smell of old leather and odors unknown overpowered us as the dusty lid was thrown back to reveal a trove of American Indian treasures Ruth had collected in her youth. There were beaded purses, leggings, moccasins, even an elaborately decorated war club. These all provided great show-and-tell fodder for school when she allowed my brother, sister and me to borrow them, we little knowing just how valuable they were.

When she came to visit at our house in the town next over, I only have memories of her being outside. She must have been close to eighty and still hampered by her phlebitis, requiring her to wrap her right leg in heavy, flesh-colored bandages and to use a light brown wooden cane. Yet she would check out my bird feeder and stump out into the orchard to admire my two rows of scrawny sweet peas of which I was so proud. Most vividly I remember her standing by the cement back step, suit skirt tight over her spread legs, her hair backlit in a white halo, as she got ready to underhand me my red punch ball in a lame game of catch. Was this the picture of a woman who in her youth was only interested in money and shopping on a trip through Europe?

What a gold mine this journal had to be: a six-month trip with every day accounted for in tremendous detail! Undoubtedly some of it would prove mundane, but the seed was planted. "Would you mind if I borrowed this? I want to try typing it out," I asked.

"Go ahead," Mom responded, "but it's awfully hard to read. You may need a magnifying glass," she foretold.

SHE WAS RIGHT. A magnifying glass did come in handy at times, and even then some words were simply indecipherable despite repeated tries. Ruth's spiky handwriting had always been somewhat difficult to read, but rendered in an unsharpened pencil in tiny script, reading it became a grueling task. And there was always the matter of treating the book as delicately as it demanded.

But the months it took to transcribe the diary were worth it. For a photography class in college, I had spent whole days in a darkroom watching as my photos slowly came into focus, resolving themselves from vague shadows into sharp black and white clarity. So it was with the diary. From the pages arose that image of the young Ruth that I was sure was there, a girl with the candid voice of youth, aware of the beauty and humor to be found in the most magnificent to the dingiest of settings. In contrast to her more timid and careful sister, she was an optimist and unafraid (" . . . we visited the famous aquarium [with] an electric eel that gave me a shock when I pressed him up by the middle. No one else would be shocked.") yet had a temper that would flash from the page: "Mad." Even then she suffered the effects of the phlebitis that affected her leg, yet seldom allowed it to slow her down.

She included details that would help a reader of this "private" document place her in context with her times. She noted that her camel was named "Mark Twain" and blithely remarked with obviously little understanding on Wall Street's Panic of 1907: " . . . [I] suppose we are paupers, but what care we? As long as we have a few American Express checks left." She spoke unselfconsciously about how increasingly better she was getting at "Jewing down" merchants. Long-forgotten idioms and sayings perplexed me: "Now we are holding our thumbs." Sewing and repairing clothes and stockings, cleaning clothing with ether and celebrating Thanksgiving by washing her hair gave me insight on the day's habits of personal hygiene and sartorial care.

The puzzle, however, was how the diary ended. From what I gleaned from my mother, the plan had been for Ruth and Lucy to remain behind in France for another six months outside Chenonceaux in the Loire Valley with a Monsieur and Madame Garreau to perfect their French. Where Dearo must have dug up this couple, I will never know. All Ruth offers once she reached the Garreaus was less than a week of entries, and those generally ones of wet, misery and hard lessons. In the blank half of the diary are notes from a botany lecture given by Monsieur Garreau in August, so she must have stayed there for at least four months. But why she quit writing in her diary after six months of diligent entries remains a mystery.

As RUTH'S LIVELY VOICE continued to rise from the pages, I couldn't help thinking of my own two daughters. Katie, the elder, would be twenty-six a century after Ruth's grand adventure, while Elizabeth would be twenty-two—perhaps Lucy's age? The idea of taking the two girls and following in Ruth's footsteps couldn't help bubbling up. Six months would be impossible, but perhaps an abbreviated version was feasible? And even though the three women traveled without a male companion, we could hardly leave my husband, Richard, behind; as he put it, he would be more than happy to be the "hod carrier," or the Cook's man on the trip. Traveling as fast as it began to appear we would have to, he would be a crucial member of the party.

But the expense! Lodgings, meals and travel costs for four people would require a deep pocket, especially with the euro up above $1.60. But the chance to make this journey exactly a hundred years later was too good to pass up, no matter into how deep a hole we'd dig ourselves.

Mapping out a rough itinerary, I figured we could compress the trip from Plymouth all the way to Aswan and back into five weeks. It would require intense planning, rock-solid reservations and close connections, something I would have to begin arranging that September, 2007, if we were to leave nine months later, right on the heels of Liz's graduation from U.C. Berkeley in June, 2008.

The timing was perfect; Liz wouldn't have a job yet that would block our plans, and Katie's massage practice was flexible enough to allow for the missed five weeks. Richard had enough vacation time, and being a writer and editor, I could make my own hours. Even though my one condition for the girls' participation was that they keep their own daily journals, they seemed enthusiastic about the venture, especially when told that out of my own inheritance we would pay their expenses—a promise we paid for dearly later. But we couldn't know that then. The trip was on.

IT WASN'T UNTIL after I'd sent a copy of the diary to my ninety-year-old uncle, Sam Johnson, that I learned about "Lucy's postcards" from my aunt Fran. A century ago cameras the size of a pack of cards and easy enough to slip into a shirt pocket didn't exist. Instead, travelers collected postcards depicting their destinations—and in the case of my grandmother's sister Lucy she collected two albums full. Apparently Ruth had collected cards as well, but as the diary seemed to reveal, she was adept at losing them as quickly as she bought them. Whatever the truth was, no postcards of Ruth's remained.

Aunt Fran still kept in touch, albeit tenuously, with Sandra Goodson, Ruth's sister Lucy's granddaughter. Fran was pretty certain that Sandra had the albums stashed away at her home in Oklahoma. On the last page of a letter from Sandra dated 1996 Fran had scribbled out several phone numbers, one of which led me to Sandra herself. Yes, she had the albums, but they were up in the attic, and it might take some time for her to dig them out, especially as she was acting as live-in fulltime nurse for her 96-year-old mother. I wondered if I would ever see them.

Yet several months later a heavy cardboard box landed on my doorstep with a thud: the postcard albums. They were an amazingly meticulous record of the journey, a real coup that promised to add an entirely new dimension to our trip. I was so excited at the challenge of taking pictures from the same vantage point of these hundred-year-old tinted postcards.

Yet I wasn't about to take these precious cards with me; I'd have to take scans of them. Unfortunately, a century later the heavy, black construction paper pages with precut slits for holding cards were now as fragile as cobwebs, and trying to balance these albums whole on my scanner risked ripping the spines. So scanning each card individually entailed painstakingly arching it out of its slots without tearing the page, a process at which I was only moderately successful. Eventually, though, I had my collection whose increasingly tattered pages both acted as a free pass to an island in Egypt and an occasion in Rome for a nasty family fight.

THERE WAS A HUGE amount of planning to do, with plane reservations first on the agenda. Here it was, September, 2007, and I felt so smug with all the miles we'd totted up on our Visa card. But I was in for the first of many unexpected surprises in this planning process.

"May 31, 2008?" said the customer service lady on the other end of the line. "I don't know if that'll be possible. Most people make their reservations a year in advance."

A *year* in advance? I thought I was doing pretty good checking in nine months early. In the end we all flew out on the same plane on May 31, but the return flight left us with Richard leaving on June 28 while we women came home almost a week later.

These dates gave me our starting and ending points. I began with three legal-sized pieces of paper Scotch-taped together to create a large, five-week calendar, one big enough to hold lodging and travel plans for each day. This I stuck up on the closet door next to my computer. Then came plotting what days would be spent where. I immediately realized that half, if not whole days would have to be devoted to traveling from one place to the next.

Some places would have to be dropped altogether, like the Blue Grotto in Naples and the Aswan Dam in Egypt. I was especially sorry to lose "Ghirginta," Ruth's spelling, or Girgenti, a town on Sicily's coast, because I had looked for it in vain for weeks, only to find it serendipitously in a map shop on a piece of gift-wrap paper depicting a century-old map of Italy. Apparently it was renamed Agrigento by Mussolini in 1927, an Italianized version taken from the Sicilian Girgenti. No wonder I couldn't find it; Ruth had preceded the Fascist "Il Duce."

So where did that leave us? In theory each destination would receive the end of a travel day, one whole day, then the beginning of the next travel day. This meant that as news got out about our planned trip, a person might gush, "Oh, you're going to Rome! How romantic! How long are you going to stay?" and I would have to answer, "One day," and no, I wasn't kidding.

After firming up dates, I started in on transportation. While we bought them, RailPasses could only take us so far, and then we were on our own. England would require a rental car. EgyptAir was frustratingly expensive until one sharp soul on TripAdvisor.com told me to log in as an Egyptian. What a surprise! That eighty-dollar fare suddenly fell to thirty dollars.

Only one destination presented a serious snafu, and that was Israel. The original idea was to fly out of Tel Aviv on a Saturday. Oh dear, there were no modes of transportation in or out of Israel on the Sabbath, and I mean none, save for a private taxi to Egypt's border, then a nine-hour bus ride to Cairo. Talk about grueling! We finally had to settle for flying out of Israel on Sunday, stopping in neutral Amman, Jordan, on the way, thus losing a day in Egypt and even then arriving at dusk. But if we hadn't been forced to stay that extra day, we might have missed our seriously memorable adventure with Muhammad in the West Bank.

Lodgings: one way or another I was going to have to make us nineteen reservations in what? hotels? hostels? YMCAs? yurts? Two in two rooms or four in one? If it hadn't been for TripAdvisor and an armload of library books, I could never have made intelligent choices. My respect for travel agents rose exponentially each time I found myself on the phone with a hotel's night clerk who spoke only the most broken English. And even though many of the hotels Ruth had stayed in still existed in some form, the price was always astronomically out of reach.

Ultimately, I simply had to make some reservations on faith; even though one couple griped on TripAdvisor about the noisy bar at Taormina's two-star Hotel Condor, it turned out to be one of our favorite hotels of all. We heard no noise from the bar, and the front desk clerk was a charming young woman who helped us out at every turn. No one had mentioned that the ritzy cookie-cutter resorts were down at the beachfront, while the little Hotel Condor was located high on the Sicilian hillside, just outside of Taormina proper, and with a to-die-for view of the Bay of Naples. Only a day later, however, was the hotel in south Bari, located just steps away from the train station. A good idea for a weary traveler, except that southern Bari had been flattened during World War II and had not included any restaurants or cafés when the town was rebuilt, opting instead for business buildings and opulent clothing stores. At the end of an exhausting day, having to walk to the far side of town with two cranky, argumentative daughters for something to eat was grim.

As THE WEEKS and months of planning passed, I began to notice events I hadn't before. Headlines started grabbing me that I would have ignored before. Had these calamities been taking place all along while I ignored them in a state of blissful uncaring? Naples was in the grip of a garbage crisis, and the streets were filling with uncollected garbage. A Boeing 777 crash-landed at Heathrow airport, while cabdrivers in angry protest brought traffic to a grinding halt in Paris. In Gaza, land mines blasted through the barrier at the border town of Rafah—the town an Egyptian guide we were considering suggested we travel through to get from Israel to Egypt. And that was just in January.

February was full of its own stories. A fire ripped through London's Camden Market, noted in the article as one of the city's top tourist attractions. In Switzerland masked gunmen stole paintings from a museum, while in the middle of the month Hezbollah's chief threatened an open war with Israel, noting that they might press Hamas to send suicide bombers into the Israeli state. By then I knew we were planning three days in and around Jerusalem. I'd laughed at the possibility before, but *should* we be concerned about terrorists?

April was the month for the Middle East: "Thousands of demonstrators torched buildings, looted shops and hurled bricks at police" in Egypt, while five days later the country was setting up roadblocks and checkpoints due to reports that terrorists planned to bomb a tourist site. On Palm Sunday in Jerusalem Greeks and Armenians thrashed police with palm fronds when they attempted to break up a fight instigated by questioned religious rights at the Church of the Holy Selpuchre, the site of Jesus' burial and resurrection. Violence over a holy site? I couldn't help thinking of the saw, "What would Jesus do?"

Practically speaking, the worst came with the headline "Cruel Summer Ahead" above a photo of a thicket of jet planes awaiting departure. A travel expert warned travelers to stick an extra day into each stop on their itineraries due to the threat of "schedule chaos." One extra day for each stop was something we did *not* have. We would just have to trust in the travel gods that we would not be affected.

San Francisco International
Liz, Richard and Katie

The day of departure closed in, still with a host of last-minute details to attend to. Elizabeth's graduation from Berkeley with a degree in Physical Anthropology was a proud moment, especially with her red, green and yellow sash indicating that she had spent a semester in Ghana. But then came getting her packed up, her earthly belongings stored and out of her apartment in the two weeks prior to our May 31 departure. A tight squeeze, considering the rest of us were still wrestling with paring down our "must-take" lists. But then the day arrived, documented with photos of Richard wedging our bags into the trunk of the car. It was too late to consider if this expedition was total insanity. We were on our way at last.

Across The Atlantic

Diary of Ruth K. Crapo, 1907-1908

Blue Ridge, New Jersey, September 1, 1907

I washed my hair and packed the steamer trunk. Martin [Ruth's sister Edith's husband] left for Chicago to be back in time to see us off on Thursday. The *S.S. Kaiserin Auguste Victoria* arrived in New York yesterday, and it looks as if we are to get off.

Blue Ridge, New Jersey, September 2, 1907

Labor Day. I sewed all day, as it rained too hard to do anything else. Mother tried trimming "the steamer hat" but failed to please the family. I packed my big trunk and sent a box off to New Bedford. My birthday was today [she turned twenty-seven] which was celebrated by an extra nice dinner and money from Mother and Lucy. I received letters from Bill [possibly Ruth's fiancé] and Maude.

Blue Ridge, New Jersey, September 3, 1907

I had an osteopathy treatment and then spent the day in New York. I lost my umbrella, and it's too late to get another before we sail. I spent two hours with Cliff [Ruth's brother] and Henry Clews and had a good scolding from Cliff for not being more of a businesswoman.

Cliff came out to dinner and discussed "when and where a young woman should drink wine, if at all." I made a big break at Righters when I tasted my first cocktail.

The trunks have gone to the steamer.

Blue Ridge, New Jersey, September 4, 1907

I finished my pongee waists and put on finishing touches to everything.

John Cameron came out at eight P.M. and stayed until nine P.M. We had a good, long talk about his trip and got lots of pointers on European traveling, including places we must be sure to see. He explained English and French money to us.

Blue Ridge, New Jersey, September 5, 1907

I cleaned my room after a lecture from Edith and called on Mrs. Speel. I packed my dress suitcase and started for the steamer.

It rained hard all morning. Edith and Mother got soaked. I broke my glass watch face and had it mended in Bloomfield.

Then and Now
Across the Atlantic

Aboard *S.S. K.A.V.*, September 5, 1907

At the ship, Mrs. Crapo and son, Edith, Cliff, Mr. Sinclair and John Cameron saw us off. We got lots of flowers, fruit, books and candy from friends; great excitement. The ship is a monster, and the state rooms are very comfortable. I have fifteen steamer letters to read.

Aboard *S.S. K.A.V.*, September 6, 1907

There are only 103 first-cabin passengers. Our places at table are not very good, but the food is excellent. I saw three whales and spent the day reading and walking. No one in our party is seasick. I spent the evening writing letters to Bill, Maude and Bud. Lights out at eleven P.M. with all hands to bed at that time.

Our greatest danger is from overeating.

Aboard *S.S. K.A.V.*, September 7, 1907

There was a big storm last night, and waves were high this morning. Lucy felt queer and has been walking all day. I made the acquaintance of a Mr. Minasian from Blue Ridge, a lawyer—quite a coincidence. He speaks French well, I find.

We have been off the coast of Newfoundland all day and have had lots of fog. Fishermen were sighted early this morning and also a Swedish Man-of-War that dipped its flag for us three times. Still, no one has been seasick.

Aboard *S.S. K.A.V.*, Sunday, September 8, 1907

We were awakened this morning by the band playing "Nearer My God to Thee." There was more fog, and with the fog horn blowing and the band playing sacred music, some passengers thought the ship was sinking. We're making good time, though, in spite of the fog.

I started to read some French books besides guidebooks, books on architecture, etc., and am all in a muddle. We planned our route for England. Mr. Minasian gave us pointers.

There was a very nice concert by a stringed orchestra this evening. It wasn't like Sunday at all.

Aboard *S.S. K.A.V.*, September 9, 1907

We discovered today that we were racing with White Star Line's *Baltic*. We're now ahead of her, but we could see her smoke several times.

Mr. and Mrs. George Vanderbilt and party are aboard—very exclusive, but they attract much attention. Love affairs are thick as leaves on bushes. Many nice men are going over, and also many unattached girls. I played shuffleboard for the first time and exercised in the gymnasium.

I'm reading *Tom Sawyer* in French; very clever. I gave up on Maupassant, though.

Aboard *S.S. K.A.V.*, September 10, 1907

I was on deck about 10:30; I'm getting lazy. I had a long talk with a girl just getting over typhoid and was quite excited to meet the German I've been flirting with. I took a walk and talked French with Mr. Minasian.

We passed *R.M.S. Lusitania*, and she is three hours ahead of the arrival time expected of her. Marconigrams were received from *R.M.S. Lusitania* and *S.S. Amerika* by passengers aboard. We're due in Plymouth on Thursday. One more day of grace.

There was another concert this evening in which passengers took part, this to benefit poor American artists in Dresden. It was a grand old night out of doors.

Aboard *S.S. K.A.V.*, September 11, 1907

Got up at 10:30 in time for the band and bouillon.

This afternoon we saw two sailing schooners, some gulls (a sign we are near land) and a school of dolphins.

Tonight was the captain's dinner with twelve courses and many decorations. I've received so many souvenirs my trunk will hardly hold them. I must make my will and dispose of them to friends. I had a long talk with a fascinating English architect who sits at our table and ate with the young man Lucy has been making eyes at. Tomorrow at this time will find us in England.

I have my friend with me tonight. Hard luck.

Aboard *S.S. K.A.V.*, September 12, 1907

Stunning day, clear and sunshiny. We passed the Isles of Scilly about four P.M., the first land we have seen for six days. After dinner we watched the lights of England appear.

We arrived in Plymouth Harbor at ten P.M. We had our trunks examined in the custom house with help of our English friend, the architect, and got completely taken in by a wordy porter who took us to a busy hotel in Plymouth. Good joke.

S.S. K.A.V. was a gorgeous sight as we left her in the harbor, and we almost wept to have to leave. We have arranged to meet Mr. Minasian in London.

We had one candle to go to bed by. Lucy thinks the hotel is not even decent.

Diaries of Holly, Katie and Elizabeth Pierce, 2008

Santa Rosa, California—Plymouth, England, Saturday, May 31, 2008

Katie

The parents wanted me to check my bag but I didn't want to—paranoid about it getting lost. We waited in the lobby for about 1½ to two hours. I read gossip magazines, and I couldn't resist getting another. We finally boarded the plane twenty minutes later than we were supposed to.

They're showing "The Bucket List," a movie about boring old guys—bleh. I don't care if Morgan Freeman used to be hot, he's old now!

ONCE INTO HEATHROW, we discover that American Airlines has somehow lost Richard's bag. Poor man; of all the bags that could have gone missing, it has to be his. If it were one of the rest of ours, we could at least have shared clothes. But we have forgotten to "cross-pack," so he is stuck in the same clothes until we get back to London, which unfortunately will be a day later than we'd planned. But at least we've been told the bag is there waiting for him at the St. Athan's.

England

Diary of Ruth K. Crapo, 1907-1908

Plymouth, England, September 13, 1907

After checking our baggage, we took a long drive in Plymouth and saw the Mayflower Tablet, Plymouth Harbor, the Royal Citadel's famous barracks, and statues of Drake and Raleigh on the site from which the Spanish Armada was first seen.

This morning we arranged for Clovelly tomorrow and Lynton on the same day. I'm getting quite used to English money. Tonight we had Devonshire cream on our prunes; great.

Lynton, England, September 14, 1907

This morning it was down to Clovelly, the prettiest place I've ever seen. The main street was of cobblestone in steps. Donkeys carried merchandise up and down. Dear little houses were covered with vines and flowers. We had a lunch of fruit, tea and Devonshire cream. It was lovely on the Bristol Channel with fishing there.

At 3:41 P.M. we took the train for Lynton, arriving at eight P.M. We were cold and hungry, and Lucy was not feeling well. I had claret and biscuits and am now ready for bed.

Lynton, England, Sunday, September 15, 1907

We walked down this morning along the shore and sat on the ocean wall. Lots of jolly tars were enjoying Sunday on the rocks. There were also people in bathing.

I washed my hair this afternoon and read *Westward Ho!* Before dinner I walked and explored the side streets of town and the hotel grounds.

At dinner the menu was in French, and I couldn't make out anything. When the waiter mumbled, we all said, "Yes," and had a queer meal. Some Englishmen picked at their teeth with knives. They looked nice and rural like farmers, and I was glad they had teeth to pick.

We had cider twice today, but no one has been affected so far.

Lynton-Wells, England, September 16, 1907

We left by coach for Porlock and Minehead, dear little villages of thatched roofs, flowers, vines, etc. From Minehead, we took the train to Wells. On the way we had our first Bath buns; delicious.

At Wells we stayed at the Swan Hotel across from the cathedral, which was magnificent and considered by some the finest as a whole in England. The cathedral has an old clock with machinery that runs the clock both outside and inside the walls, fascinating in every detail.

We had dinner with friends from the coach. I started on Apollinaris water and received much good advice about Continental traveling.

Warwick, England, September 18, 1907

It's been fine weather so far. We drove to Kenilworth Castle this morning with its fascinating and grand old ruins. On the way we stopped at Guy's Cliffe and saw an old mill five hundred years old. A nice old man at Guy's Cliffe, a poet, recited for us.

I found I haven't been putting enough postage on letters. We're in too big a hurry.

Warwick-London, England, September 19, 1907

We left Warwick at 9:45 and went up to Stratford-on-Avon. At the station we took a carriage and drove first to Anne Hathaway's cottage, a fascinating old place with a queer bake oven, candle box, candlesticks, linsey woolsey hangings, etc., and with an open chimney and seat upon which Shakespeare wooed Anne. On the windows in Shakespeare's house we saw the names of Carlysle and Scott written with diamonds on the windowpanes.

Tonight we are in London, 26 Montague Place, tired but happy to be settled.

London, England, September 20, 1907

We left the house at 10:30 to see about our trunks and mail. We had a funny time hailing our first bus and then modestly taking seats inside.

The first person we met was Mrs. Coulter. She went with us for the rest of the day. We took three bus rides (this time on top) during the day, one to Paddington Station where we found our trunks. We hunted up a hat for Mother. The first purchase for me was a wristband for my watch. Next was a soda water, horrid and flat.

We took the wrong way home and were just in time for dinner. I was tired and hungry, and to clap the climax, I found my trunk with the lock broken, so I can't get into it tonight. No clean clothes for Ruthie tomorrow. Mrs. Coulter is to get a room here, too.

London, England, September 21, 1907

We met Mrs. Coulter at 10:30 at the American Express office and proceeded to the Houses of Parliament. Lucy lost her letters, and Mrs. Coulter left the Westminster book behind, so lots of waiting around, but we finally reached our destination. Westminster Abbey is a great mix-up in my mind. It would take weeks to see it all.

Had a lunch of Bath buns, lemon squash and tongue.

London, England, Sunday, September 22, 1907

Mrs. Coulter and I went to Westminster Abbey for the three o'clock service. On our way there and back, we found out much more about buses, the terror of our lives at present. We paid an extra fare to ride one block!

We had supper Sunday night at 8:45, a weird hour but to make it possible for members of the household to go to evening services.

London, England, September 23, 1907

My luck deserted me today. I woke up in awful pain and discovered that indigestion was to be my company for some hours. After taking the usual remedies and talking things over, we decided that it wasn't exactly indigestion but a slight case of food poisoning that was troubling me, and we laid it to some very queer-looking cheese I ate for supper last night. I spent the day in bed and finished reading *Westward Ho!* but didn't have a good time.

London, England, September 24, 1907

The Tower was our goal starting out this morning, and after much ado we managed to reach it. We saw inscriptions on the walls put there by prisoners, among them the names of Lady Jane Grey and the Earl of Warwick and his coat of arms. We also saw the spot where the guillotine stood—ghastly.

From the Tower we went back to Charing Cross for lunch, then Lucy and I went shopping in the leather stores. I bought a pigskin bag and other pocketbooks. We found Cheapside to be very expensive.

I would have enjoyed the day more if I hadn't had any insides.

London, England, September 25, 1907

We spent all day shopping, the most strenuous time so far. Lucy, Mother and I each ordered a suit from the first tailor we saw. Now we are holding our thumbs. We went to Liberty's where I got a dress and party coat, Lucy, a dress.

I bought a green bag with the money that was a birthday present from Mother and Lucy. We had a very funny time getting hats, but finally got great bargains. I tried "Jewing," but was not overly successful. It took Mrs. Coulter to call down the talkative clerk in there.

I had two letters from Bill tonight; he doesn't seem so far away after all. I was told at dinner by some Englishwomen that they sometimes put copper wire in cheese to make it look like the one that poisoned me. Beware of the English.

London, England, September 26, 1907

After lunch we went to St. Paul's church. The statuary was the most impressive we've seen, and for dignity and splendor found it to surpass Westminster. Also went into the Whispering Gallery and were whispered to.

We found a good fruit store today, and we all filled up on grapes, pears and plums. I am beginning to like London very much.

London, England, September 27, 1907

After lunch in the jewelry shop's tea room, the nicest and cleanest we've found yet, we went to Westminster and were in time for the afternoon service.

Afterward, we asked to see the effigies made in wax we'd heard of. We were taken up a steep, winding staircase, dark and dusty, and then suddenly came upon the ghastly figures, with Queen Elizabeth's the worst. Lucy and Mrs. Coulter almost had hysterics.

I discovered today that English cakes are our rolls or biscuits, and sweets are the cakes as found in the United States. Also, if you want lemonade, you must ask for "lemon squash" or "natural lemonade," or you get the kind made from pellets.

London, England, September 28, 1907

Windsor Castle is not nearly as pretty or pleasing in appearance as Warwick but is of much more historical interest. We saw the window in which, on the anniversaries of the battles of Waterloo and Blenheim, the flags must be hung before noon, or the heirs of Marlborough and Wellington will lose their estates.

Got home at four o'clock and after a rest went to see Maxine Elliot at the Lyric Theater in "Under the Greenwood Tree." Well received, considering the audience was English.

London, England, Sunday, September 29, 1907

Sunday is always welcome, as we actually get time to take a long breath. Mrs. Coulter and I went church-hunting and managed after a long walk to find one that was not Episcopal. Even the Baptist church was a relief, and we enjoyed a fine sermon.

After dinner while closing the window (or trying to), I managed to get my elbow mixed up with the glass, smashed things and got some fine cuts on my arm. It was a gory sight but not painful.

Lucy, Mother and Mrs. Coulter have gone to church to hear one Mr. Campbell, a "socialist" or "New Thought" preacher. I read *Kenilworth* until the late hour of eight P.M. There is a musician nearby, for I've been listening to some fine piano playing for an hour.

London, England, September 30, 1907

This morning we made up our minds about our next move. It's straight to Paris now and Switzerland later.

We went to the American Express office for money, postage, etc., then up to the tailor's and from there to lunch and more hat-hunting. We then ambled on to the National Gallery.

I had to stand up in the bus on the way home and was bent double. I found the pane of glass repaired in my window but broke my bracelet. That's the fourth thing since coming here. It's expensive at this rate.

London, England, October 1, 1907

A beautiful, bright morning today. First on the list was a ride through the Tube. After much hustling around we got into it and went down to The Bank of England. My! but it was smelly and horrid (the Tube, not the bank).

We took a train to the Kew Gardens, which were perfectly lovely. We visited the famous Blue House, nearly three hundred feet long and wonderfully kept up, with thousands of tropical plants on exhibit. We also saw the cacti houses and three filled with orchids of marvelous beauty and coloring.

My suit came back, and the skirt was a mess. Another day on the run, it means. Why can't we go without clothes?

London, England, October 2, 1907

We were wild to see a play at Drury Lane Theatre. After a long hunt for the theatre through back alleys and markets and a long wait at the ticket office, we were able to get in and certainly got our money's worth. Blood and thunder from start to finish, but beautiful clothes and scenery, and the theatre is a beauty in every respect. Mother and Lucy were not overpleased at the performance itself.

Once home, we started packing. It is now towards morning, and my packing, thank heavens, is almost done. I wish we were to stay here longer. London's all right.

Diaries of Holly, Katie and Elizabeth Pierce, 2008

London—Plymouth, England, Sunday, June 1, 2008

Katie

Since both parents have control issues, we've decided Mom will do the driving and Dad will handle the money. Both want to have control over it all.

TIME TO CLAIM the rental car, and what with my obsessive volume of maps which I've printed out, highlighted, and penned and penciled upon, we manage to find the Auto Europe counter. We have already decided that I will drive while Richard will navigate. After settling the paperwork, a nice gent takes us out to a parking lot, waves his arm and says, "Take your pick!" Oh my goodness, here's a BMW!

"We'll take this one!" I announce gleefully.

"Oh no," the gent responds immediately. "I meant anyone in *those* two rows," he points out.

I take a look. They're all manual Ford Focuses and VW Passats. Well, I know how I feel about U.S. cars, and I did have great luck with the VW Derby in Baja, so definitely we'll go with the Passat. But I'd kind of hoped we could get an automatic; after all, this will be my first experience with driving on the right, which also means shifting with the left hand.

Somehow this wish gets lost in the shuffle as the man helpfully narrows our choice to two cars. Okay, let's take blue; it's my favorite color. We cram all of our luggage into the trunk, pile in, and we're off to Plymouth.

Liz

Mom drives, as we are afraid the driving stress might burst a blood vessel in Dad's forehead. In fact, it isn't long before he had to sit in the back seat because he was stressing out too much. I took over as family navigator and did a decent job.

Now, HOW LONG have we been awake? By now we're so jacked up on adrenaline that it doesn't matter. Driving on the highway is a snap. Rain is intermittent. We haven't seen a patrol car (and never do), and people seem to drive with this in mind. So I gun the Passat westward, screaming past Stonehenge on the way.

Stonehenge? Why, there it is, not a hundred yards north of the interstate! With what care and respect do the English cherish this worldwide treasure! We don't take the exit, though, as it's on the itinerary for tomorrow.

Katie

Lovely English hillsides. We pulled over into a tiny lane and all ran into the bushes to hide and pee since we'd been driving around in circles and getting lost. Land just as expected. Lush green fields—good thing no rain—with cute brick houses and narrow-ass streets that seem ever-so-perilous the way the cars park and block the road. Quaint shops. Still haven't brushed my teeth today.

IT'S NOW LATE afternoon, and the girls are hungry. Where we can find food, however, is a mystery; all there seems to be out here are rolling green hills with little copses and not-so-quaint-looking outbuildings. We eventually spot what looks like a tiny mall nearby, and we pull off. A single covered walkway leads us into the center of a rectangle of stores. A sign reminds us that skateboarding is not allowed.

The odd thing is, though, that it seems deserted. Despite its considerable size, there's hardly a soul within its cobbled perimeter. A few people have walked in to stop off at a shuttered post office, but otherwise, *nada.*

This is not funny. I'm suddenly overwhelmingly tired. Then we realize: it's Sunday, and everything is closed. Of course! At the south end of this suddenly-huge arena a middle-aged man in a dark windbreaker appears from around the corner of the farthest building. I want to fall at his feet, weeping with hunger and despair, and beg for compassion and respite.

Instead, Richard asks him the obvious question. "Hey, is there somewhere around here where you can get some food?"

The man waves his arm vaguely in a southwesterly direction. "Yeah, you might try the garage over there. I think they're still open."

The garage? (That's "*gare'* aghe" hereabouts.) What kind of automotive repair shop has food? But at this point I don't care who dishes it up, as long as it's edible. But man, that archway out seems impossibly faraway. I don't feel I could make the walk all the way back. But it's the only way out.

I've begun to plod when the girls excitedly announce they've discovered an alternate exit quite nearby, and quite close to the garage as well. They lead us around the corner of the end building, and I see that behind it is a six-foot wall. Easy! All we have to do is scale the wall!

I can't believe that Richard is all for it. Somehow I picture us being apprehended by one of those until-now invisible bobbies and being held for trespassing or suspicious behavior of some sort. Wouldn't *that* be the icing on this endless cake.

But slogging through the rampant ivy I see that with a little boost from Richard, Katie is already atop the wall, and she is assisting his ascent. Hah, hah. Everyone is laughing at this crazy adventure except me. Katie and Richard have disappeared over to the other side. I'm practically delusional from fatigue, and I'm supposed to hie myself over this cement wall.

"C'mon, Mom, I'll help you over. Here, just stand on my hands, and I'll boost you up," Liz directs, linking her fingers into a sling.

No choice. I stick my foot into her hands.

"One, two, *three!*" I throw myself at the wall as Liz puts her back into hoisting me upwards. I manage to get my elbows, then my boobs, onto the wall's capstones. There, I'm stranded.

"Push her foot up!" yells Katie from the other side, and Liz rams my leg upward. I throw it sideways atop the wall, and suddenly I'm up there. Wow, uh, it feels pretty high up here. And so, just as ungracefully as I got up, I fall awkwardly over the wall like a sack of potatoes into Richard's fumbling arms. Meanwhile, Katie manages to get the nimbler Liz up and over.

And there in the not-so-far distance is the "garage." For crying out loud, it's a gas station! And—it has a little convenience store attached. With a sudden renewed vigor, we hustle over.

Inside we find a refrigerated case with little triangular plastic boxes holding boring-looking sandwiches, except—wait a minute: smoked salmon and cream cheese with dill? Unbelievable. And it looks passably fresh. Everyone greedily picks over the sandwiches, drinks and chips. We are revitalized.

BY THE TIME we get into Plymouth it is dark, and the Google map murky. So we begin what I come to call the "Hotter, Colder" game: ask someone directions, follow them until you feel lost again, then ask another person; repeat. Somehow I'd imagined Plymouth as a little more quaint and manageable; at least the maps make it look that way, but trust the roundabouts and one-way streets to squash that expectation. There is one time we definitely go in a circle, seeing the same buildings over again, but it isn't until we pull up alongside the older, white-haired gent wearing a turquoise sweatshirt out walking his dog to ask directions that we finally find our street.

Is it the zoning or just me? Here is our hotel, St. Rita's, in the middle of what looks to be a residential section of town. Raining still, but we manage to haul our bags up the steps (oh, the curse of steps and wheeled luggage!), and I am sent around back with the damned car to park it in the free hotel parking.

Right. Down the narrowest of rutted, damp alleys to a little rectangle of cement exactly the length of a car which, were there room to maneuver and we were all driving Mr. Bean cars, one might have gotten three cars in, door handle to door handle. Opposite the "car park" is a steep verge of grassy hillside, not to mention other cars that have managed to get there before us and have been able to parallel park on a 45-degree angle. Thankfully, Liz is there to direct my feeble efforts. First, a try to parallel park in a dubiously small space. No way is that going to work. So it is the little cement rectangle for me.

I do try to park responsibly, leaving room for another vehicle that later might show up (a motor scooter perhaps?). But in the dank darkness, wedged in between the verge, the wall I was to nose into and the distinct possibility of incurring a costly metal abrasion, I finally just jam the car in there with nary a scruple for "the other driver." I've had enough for one day, and so to hell with courtesy.

A round-headed, squarely-built teenager with dark eyebrows and a red T-shirt stands behind the front desk. He has already directed the others upstairs to our room, and considering the doggy accommodations we were to encounter later, it is a sweet little room with space for the four of us in which to move around. Richard and I can hardly wait to hit the sack, but amazingly the girls have mustered a second wind, intrigued as they are by the teenager and his brother, sons of the hotel owners. As Richard and I fight through our exhaustion into sleep, we can hear the yakking and guffaws of the kids downstairs. Well, at least they're having a good time.

Later, at midnight, we awake briefly when Katie comes in for bed. But at 3:00 A.M., we all awake to find that Liz is still not in bed yet. Oddly enough, Katie feels responsible for leaving Liz downstairs and so goes down to fetch her.

Katie

I finally decided to go to bed about quarter to midnight. I left my sister and her fake British accent to keep drinking the (second) bottle of wine the boys bought for us. I woke up at three in the morning to see that my sister had not come to bed yet. The parents awoke, too, and so I wandered down to collect her. Snookered.

Liz

Asked for some wine glasses from the hosts and ended up having a nice chat with the two sons who live in and help run the place for their parents who own it. I learned some interesting new things about the Brits and London. Minimum wage is about 5.75 pounds or roughly eleven dollars.

Flats can cost anywhere from 400-800 pounds in Liverpool for a two bedroom to 1,000-2,000 pounds in London. "Fags" actually can come in ten packs and cost almost twice as much as in the U.S. Beer is about the same. Different English accents have different connotations. Stayed up late, but I finally went to bed.

Plymouth—Wells, England, Monday, June 2, 2008

THE NEXT MORNING we arise to what England must call sunshine: a somewhat opaque, ivory light slanting through the lacy white curtains. Even though Liz has had only five hours of sleep, she is game to get up and get going, particularly for the hearty English breakfast awaiting us. After airplane food and packaged sandwiches from the gas station the night before, this meal is truly one fit for a king, English or whatever nationality. I start with a creamy oatmeal ("porridge") which I think is the extent of the meal. Oh no; then come the eggs and "rasher" of bacon, which is more like a big slab of ham than the thin, crispy strips to which we're accustomed. In retrospect, this is surely the largest and most sumptuous breakfast we enjoy on the entire trip. I guess it's best we don't know that now.

Before heading out, I have to check our e-mail, still chasing and confirming our guides in Israel and Cairo, plus send a stern note to the Winter Palace in Luxor asking that we get rooms in the old section of the building and not in its soulless new wing. St. Rita's computer is in the reception nook right next to the kitchen where the missus is cleaning up the dishes, and Chris, slender with delicate features like his mum and dressed in a freshly-pressed, long-sleeved dress shirt, is slicking up his hair and getting help tying his tie for a job interview that morning. I don't gather what the job is he's applying for, but we all join his family in a chorus of "Good luck!" as he rushes out the side door.

Liz

The four of us drove, then walked nearby to "the Hoe," an area in Plymouth that is by the waterfront. Lucy and Ruth walked along the promenade there, so it was exciting to know we were in the same place as they had been one hundred years ago.

BREAKFAST IS OVER, and after extricating the Passat from its little stable out back, it is off to the Hoe for us. The Hoe is the historical center of town, a vast, grassy slope down to the bay with its statue of Sir Francis Drake and the Royal Citadel (check off those postcards), built in 1666 by Charles II as a military installation and still in use as such. Walkways crisscrossing the Hoe lead both up to a stone installation with benches placed for enjoyment of the sweeping view high above the town and to the Promenade, a broad walkway skirting the cliffs along the bay. A sign prohibiting "tombstoning" puzzles us until an elderly local informs us of the number of people who have taken their lives by swan-diving off the Promenade's low seaward wall onto the rocks below—hence the term "tombstoning." How someone dead can be fined for such an infraction is not explained.

While searching for the Sir Francis Drake statue, I trudge to the top of the slope to the stone benches where I come upon an ordinary-looking, middle-aged man in a slope-shouldered suit and with a briefcase at his side, sitting in the pale warmth of the sun. I stop to ask him where the statue might be. So commences a chat that wanders on, and I understand that he is simply lonely and wanting for someone to talk with. Finally excusing myself, I feel guilty leaving this soul in need, but there are statues to find and views to locate, not to mention a family that will eventually grow bored with the Hoe scene.

I did find Sir Francis farther on and took a correctly-positioned shot, now featuring a Holiday Inn prominently set in the background. When I begin to look for the gate to the Royal Citadel, though, instead of circling on maybe a hundred feet more to the sought-for gate around the corner, I end up walking the other direction, all the way down, then up the entire way around the installation. I finally find the gate manned by some rather jolly men in uniform who are more than happy to have me stand square in the middle of the driveway into the installation to take my picture. Whatever happened to the prohibition against taking photos of military bases? I imagine I don't look sufficiently dangerous to arouse suspicion.

Now I just have to find the rest of the family. So, striding along faking an outward sense of purpose, I walk *yet again* around the entire Citadel, hoping to see a familiar face. Somehow I know that the longer I walk, the madder they are all going to be.

Meanwhile in its usual British way the sky has become overcast, and the wind off the sea is turning chilly. It begins sprinkling off and on. At one point Richard and I actually agreed to meet at the Barbizon, a section of town directly east of the Citadel. So I am wandering back and forth along the eastern side of the promenade, trying to look purposeful, not lost, when I spot the nose of a blue Passat in a parking lot on the cliff above me. Climbing up on a railing, I can just make out "TUP" on the license plate. Yes! For some reason I remember that combination; it has to be our car. I have just found my way into the "car park" above when I hear a chorus of accusing voices. There is my darling family, spilling into the lot from the opposite end, the girls hurling invectives, pissed as all get out. Mom has blown it again.

Katie

Spent the whole morning touring around. Everyone split up for a while until Dad and my sister found me. Then we spent forty-five minutes looking for Mom. My sister used her loud voice to call for her, but when we found her finally, she acted as if she'd been looking for *us* forever. I know she planned this trip, but we're all on it together and to wander around for forty-five minutes looking for her sucked.

THE GIRLS ARE ravenous as usual, and so once everyone's spleen is vented, we eat at the first place we can find with indoor seating. How fortunate; it turns out to be the pub that claims to be built on the real Plymouth Rock, not the would-be rock across the street. At least we girls get to view the site, as the Rock is deemed to be located directly below the women's loo. Okay, it's just a bathroom, but we dutifully take photos of the sacred spot.

Our plan is to reach London by that evening, but it is already early afternoon. Hmm. Looking at the map, we foolishly feel it's still possible. We made it to Plymouth yesterday; why not back to London today? Okay, maybe I feel we need to see at least a few of the quaint little villages Ruth raved about in her diary; Clovelly really isn't that far away, is it? That little foot of land, sticking out into the Atlantic? Surely that isn't but a skip and a hop? So off we go, north through Eggbuckland, then Tavistock.

Katie

Now driving to Clovelly. My sister is still not off her fake accent. It gets old fast. Mom's driving seems terrifying but somehow I don't think Dad's would be much better. I had to take a Xanax because my bladder keeps getting full every five minutes. The driving in general is quite precarious.

WHAT I HAVEN'T counted on are the road conditions once one is off the main thoroughfare. Yesterday had been freeway all the way with nary a police car in sight. We flew. But now: nice little two-lane roads, but interrupted regularly by odious roundabouts. Roundabouts quickly become my nemesis, what with driving on the left side of the road in a car with an intransigent stick shift and filled with family members who each loudly and in their own special way express their terror and impatience each time the Passat jerks to a halt while I am trying to downshift in the midst of circling traffic. This rental car can be counted on to die in these traps, at which point I will it to drift to the verge while frantically trying to get it back into gear.

There is a protocol to the two-lane-wide, clock-wise roundabout, one which I suppose I could've caught onto eventually: stay on the outside if you are turning left or going straight ahead, but move to the inside, then once past the straight-ahead, to the outside if you are turning right. Our particular problem is that in the midst of all this uproar, we are never sure which way we need to turn, a difficulty that persists all the way back to Heathrow.

Liz ponders the useless map.

After about two hours of jerking our way through roundabouts and stopping along nameless country roads to try to orient ourselves, we reach Clovelly. By now it is gray and raining off and on. Ruth has found this little village hanging on a cliff's edge overlooking the Irish Sea to be sweetly captivating and endearing. She has "yet to see a prettier place," an apt description if we could trust Lucy's picture postcard watercolor rendering.

And indeed, one hundred years later it is still charming with its narrow cobblestone path winding down toward the sea between still-inhabited houses prettied up with window boxes full of flowers.

Liz

In Clovelly you had to walk down to the village at a very steep incline on quite slippery cobblestones. Absolutely charming little town, and the people extremely friendly. It felt straight out of a fairytale! Lush trees, quaint cottages with rose gardens, narrow, winding streets and a lovely view of the water. Fog all curled snugly against the curving coast.

UNFORTUNATELY, ENGLAND seems to have latched onto these quaint, picturesque places and designated them as "Heritage Sites," meaning people must pay through the nose to see them. Now Clovelly is touted as England's "car-less village" where you first must pay to park up top, then pass through a huge gift shop disguised as a ticket booth and pay yet more for the privilege of walking down the steep (and now wet with rain) path to see the village that Ruth had so loved. Quaint and sure-footed little donkeys no longer carry the residents' loads in large baskets (although you could certainly buy dear little basket-laden donkey models for an equally dear price). Now the villagers use wooden sledges dragged up and down over the cobbles into the "car-less village" from their autos parked up top or at the bottom of the cliff by a large, white, jolly-looking hotel at ocean's edge.

It is late in the day; the parking attendant even gives us a break on the price. The footing is slippery and dangerous as we pick our way down through the little village. Few other tourists are around. But determined to see what must be a spectacular view, we finally arrive at a landing overlooking the cliff's edge. It sure must be gorgeous when there isn't a whole mess of fog obscuring the coast. We take a glance at the hotel on the shore, then start up again.

Then and Now
The village of Clovelly

I find the spot from where Lucy's postcard painter must have set up his easel. Surprisingly, everything still looks much the same. But I find there is a rather nasty "Heritage Site" ambiance.

By this time we know we will not be reaching London this day and so will be forfeiting our night's prepaid charge at St. Athans (and Richard will go yet another day in the clothes he's worn since leaving Santa Rosa). Where to stay, then?

About halfway up, I spot a grizzled older man in a pea coat and captain's cap, a pipe clenched picturesquely between his teeth. He is sitting above me in a rustic chair on the miniscule front porch of a wee hotel, looking like something out of a Thomas Kincaid painting. I guess he is the hotel's owner.

"Hello!" I call out cheerily. "Have you got any vacancies?" I am already setting up for the upcoming negotiations with my smiley, non-threatening demeanor.

"E-yep," he answers.

Great, I think. It's late in the day and the hotel isn't full.

"Would you have a room for four people by chance?"

"Got room, but you'd have to take two rooms. No room for four," he sing-songs.

Hmm, a small snafu. But if he has two empty rooms at five P.M., surely he'll be eager to fill them.

"How much?" I call up to him.

"Sixty-five sterling."

"For both?"

"For each."

After some quick figuring, I realize he is saying the rooms are about a hundred dollars each. Come on, two hundred for the night? I'm thinking he might come down this late in the day.

Keeping on my happy face, I ask, "Would you come down on that price? It's late. How about one hundred pounds for both?"

"Nope. One hundred thirty sterling the both," he replies obstinately with nary a twitch of his whiskers.

Greedy old man. I hope you choke on your damn pipe.

"Okay, then. Have a good evening," I call as I start up the steep path. I'm not going to let him know what I think of him; then *he'd* win.

"E-yep," he states laconically. So much for Ruth's enchanting vision.

When we reach Wells, it is almost dark. Because we are farther north than at home, it stays lighter later; lucky for us. And at last we find a truly worthy landmark, the Wells Cathedral, a huge and magnificent Gothic wonder, all deeply carved towers and needle-like spires. Not surprisingly, in this misty gloom few people are around. Liz grabs her Handycam and is out of the Passat in a flash, seemingly determined to capture this edifice digitally at every possible angle.

Liz

At the first sighting of poke-y towers in Wells, we headed toward them and found the church. It was rather run down, but we were snapping photos happily when we realized it wasn't the Wells cathedral at all but just a local church—oops.

When we reached the cathedral I realized just how wrong we were! Well, the cathedral nearly knocked me over with its splendor. I shouldn't even try to describe it because there's no way I could capture its beauty in words. Went through a lovely gate called the "Palace Eye" and into the grounds, a long expanse of lush green grass. The cathedral was absolutely massive and had a lovely little arch that crossed the road. I was really blown away by the amazing detail included in the façade, everything so delicate and carefully constructed. Must have taken ages.

RICHARD AND KATIE are content to mosey around together, while I explore beyond The Palace Eye, an arched passageway through a portion of the cathedral. I think I will find a match for one of Lucy's postcards but am disappointed when I get to the spot; what was once tidy and complementary shrubbery a hundred years ago has grown into an obscuring thatch of leafy trees. I wait for a picturesque cyclist to come wheeling up before taking the picture.

Never mind. I walk the length of the Vicar's Close to get another postcard shot, this one successful due to its lack of foliage. This narrow lane built perpendicular to the cathedral is lined on each side with a row of two-story flats. It is quiet and peaceful, save for a practicing oboe player. The oboe's archaic tones spill out of a lit practice room and into the echoing gloom of the close. The cathedral looms ahead of me.

Katie

It's already quarter to eight. We finally made it to Wells so Mom and my sister could get their pictures of the cathedral. After an hour or so of wandering I was quite hungry, but Dad was concerned about our hotel situation since we couldn't make it to London. He sent me across the green to the White Swan Hotel. A luxurious four hundred dollars later (two hundred and four British pounds) I secured us two rooms, gotten at a discounted rate because of my charming personality alone. Felt good about that. Mom was ecstatic because apparently our relatives Ruth and Lucy stayed there, too, in 1908!

In Mom and Dad's room there was a big blowup to the point where my sister refused to join us for dinner at a Bangladeshi restaurant.

Liz

I stopped and said, "What did you say?!" thinking all I'd been trying to do lately was help. Upset Dad told me, "Shhhhh! Shut up!" So I promptly went back to my room and slammed the door. I refused to speak with either of them for the rest of the evening. Skipped dinner and took a hot shower instead.

Katie

Tears from both of us on the unfairness of the situation, which really got blown out of proportion. We were all hungry and tired. I cried more when I thought we were eating Indian food, but then the food was actually pretty good.

After dinner my sister and I went down to the dining room/sitting room, and I attempted to order claret à la Ruth, but they had none, so we drank red Australian wine instead. In the room we shared we rehashed the day until the night porter knocked on the door and told us we'd gotten a noise complaint from the neighbors.

Wells—London, England, Tuesday, June 3, 2008

So TODAY WE STOP to see Stonehenge. The girls are wild to see it, so we make the effort to wind our way down to the site after leaving Wells. By now it is raining pitchforks, so Richard and I buy clear plastic rain ponchos for four dollars apiece in the gift shop before paying thirty-six total (and that with the student discount) to walk under the highway, then emerge in the blowing rain along with tourloads of people to walk around the site at a respectful forty feet away. There is a little boy from Baton Rouge looking rather forlorn and wearing the same gift shop rain poncho as ours but with his orange baseball cap holding the rattling plastic in place. I can't help saying, "You came to Stonehenge, and all you got was this crummy raincoat?"

"Yeah," he said, staring indifferently at the stones in the rain.

I dutifully take pictures, but somehow can't resist taking shots appropriate to the mood—"Stonehenge with Freeway," "Stonehenge with Korean Tourists," that kind of thing. It is a waste, but also rather sad. I buy a Stonehenge mug to the tune of ten dollars that will go nicely with our mugs from Turkey and Cuba, but with us so early into the trip, I fear it will be broken before we get home.

Katie

Stonehenge was as wet as could be, though I got nice pictures all around it. Cost too much for how long we stayed, but I did get a build-your-own Stonehenge kit for my desk.

Liz

Then we drove in the crazy-backwards car to Stonehenge. It was raining quite hard, but I was positively thrilled to see it—so excited. I fashioned an umbrella contraption so I could videotape in the rain. Got bloody wet but came back elated. Amazing to think I was that close to such an incredible historical feat.

We continued driving, Mom in an absolute rage at the car.

AFTER STANDING IN the drenching rain to pay respects to Stonehenge, our next task is to return the effing car to Heathrow. By now it is 5:15 P.M. in London, and I feel as if I haven't even seen England yet, and it has been three days. This is because I was the one with the task of driving the VW Passat that got foisted off on us. I say "foisted" because somehow we ended up with the stick shift, and I will say that that car was a piece of shit. The clutch was extremely sensitive, and I stalled out on more roundabouts than I care to remember. The stick has very little leeway between gears, making it so easy to put it into the wrong gear. And the key! Have you ever driven a car where you push in the key to start it? And of course there was the matter of driving on the left-hand side of the road. How many curbs did I run over? Enough, I'm sure, to put the left wheels out of alignment.

And then there was the matter of the little dead animal (a pheasant, I believe) that I ran over and the left front wheel well of the car that I took out on one of those precious little stone bridges. And the intersections in the country, those roundabouts I mentioned that leave you no time to think which direction you're supposed to go—to Bonehead or Knook Village?—and the fact that there are no shoulders on the roads, just stretches where you are driving through those tall hedgerows that looked so romantic on the BBC James Herriott episodes but which are in fact like driving down a narrow hallway with no leeway, and there's a huge hedge mower or moving van headed straight at you. What to do? Many times it was close my eyes and pray—not very Buddhist (my faith of choice), but certainly appropriate to the moment. Hours we drove that way, winding through bitsy towns that were on no one's map, probably not even Google's satellite maps.

My hands ache from clutching the steering wheel in a death grip. I am harried and snappish from total fatigue and exhaustion.

Katie

Missed home the most when the family fight erupted after we finally landed back at the airport and took the tube into London. Mom was upset about the big ding and scrape along the wheel well because it will cost her between six hundred and twelve hundred dollars.

WE COME OUT OF the tube station, and because it is raining, Richard is insistent on taking a taxi despite the fact that we have our cheesy Stonehenge ponchos, and the Hotel Athans (harboring Richard's suitcase) is just around the corner a couple of blocks. I get into trouble, though, because I decide to walk, feeling I have made that clear to Liz who later *insists* I did not. These crossed wires are only the beginning of a looming, huge foursome blow-up and confrontation, complete not only with initial recriminations directed at me but an airing of everyone's grievances so far and flight to a pub by the girls ending with Katie incapacitated by a panic attack.

But walking right now in London is wonderful, my first "alone" time in England, strolling along in the rain, asking friendly people along the way to set me straight (I'll take my compass from now on), finally getting my photo of the camera placard that doesn't mean "scenic view" but rather "speed checked by radar." Strange, but we maybe saw three police in all of England. Speed on the freeways is incredibly variable, with people poking along in the fast lane and speeders blinking their lights at me when I am going a good 120 kilometers an hour. I finally decided I could go just as fast as I wanted, which I did. Hum-dee-dum.

Katie

Mom was frazzled from driving the car, so when we got through the tube station and realized we'd left our map somewhere, Mom took off on her own. Dad, my sister and I panicked because we didn't know if she was coming back. Dad searched the streets for her while we waited just out of the rain. He came back in fifteen minutes looking quite upset and without her. We were enraged by that point since we felt we had to search and search for her.

Liz

Then all hell broke loose. It was raining hard, so I didn't want to walk with the luggage. While Dad and Katie tried to find a taxi, Mom simply walked off on her own. I told her to come back or we would all be lost, but she didn't listen.

Dad and Katie came back, only to find her gone. Anger was rising quickly. All were upset that she would leave with no clear explanation, but Dad started absolutely losing his mind. He went to look for her while we waited, but he couldn't find her, and instead came back threatening to leave for home immediately because he thought Mom was off her rocker and in danger.

Shouting ensued. He was absolutely determined to continue looking for her. Katie and I convinced him to take a taxi to the hotel first to see if she was there. Dad was nearly crying during the ride, he was so worried. Of course she was there, all Holly-jolly.

Katie

Finally we three caught a taxi to the hotel where we were all on the verge of tears. When Mom greeted us at the front desk with a cheerful hello and a smile, I felt that if I were a different person, I might have slapped her for all the trouble and fright we went through looking for her and worrying about her safety.

Liz and I stepped into a nearby pub where Dad tried to explain away Mom's behavior, but we told him he was just a conduit for her, and we didn't think it was fair for him to bear the brunt of our anger. I started crying in the middle of the pub and then had a panic attack where I couldn't breathe.

So we went back to the St. Athan's hotel where our room for four was smaller than the room my sister and I shared at the Swan. There was a double bed and a bunk with an impossibly low head space underneath the upper bunk. I felt on the verge of going home completely.

Liz

Dad came and found us at the pub and had a good talk about our feelings. Katie and I felt Mom didn't respect ours or Dad's opinions or voices and refused to say sorry for mean things she did. Dad admitted he was also hurt, but kept trying to take the blame and responsibility for her. We told him he couldn't apologize for her.

To PUT IT MILDLY, family relations are rocky so far. Before dinner we have a family meeting, using Katie's hairbrush as a "talking stick," and we work out many of our grievances. Everyone has their own view of how they are being maligned. Richard and I learn the first of many unexpected things about our daughters as we move along. Katie *must* have food about every three hours, or she goes ballistic. And the more ballistic and tense she gets, the more often she has to pee. To these needs she is very susceptible, and in a way I feel the trip so far has been controlled by these two needs.

Elizabeth's susceptibility to obsessive behavior is full blown, through railroad stations, along the sidewalks and through the car parks. It is acceptable for Katie to tell her to "Let it go, Liz," but not I; if I do, I get called on it.

Katie

We had a family meeting in calm voices after I took my Xanax so I could breathe normally again. Looking back, what started it all was when Mom scoffed when I had to pee for the millionth time due to anxiety. It is a response I can't help, but it comes up and makes trouble at the worst times. I may have overreacted, but I am quite sensitive about the issue.

Liz is roundly criticized for affecting a fake British accent; we all find it irritating to the max, and yet she persists: "Having trouble repressing an uncontrollable fake British accent. Luckily none of the Brits notice, though my family is thoroughly annoyed." As for myself, I think the family finally appreciates just how grueling and fatiguing driving that car was, and so my audible sigh when Katie said she had to pee for the fiftieth time is forgiven as my "not being myself," an apt description; I am a mess. And though I don't open my mouth about it, I am finding Katie's new addiction to trashy gossip magazines totally irritating. *Who cares if Angelina Jolie has a cold sore?* And the argument about whether or not Tom Cruise is gay or not—do I need to listen to this while driving between those damn hedgerows? My patience was minimal with this inane chatter while under these most trying circumstances. Yet I couldn't say anything.

But once our meeting concludes, I uphold Liz's wish to go out by herself in the fading day to take in Parliament and Westminster Abbey all by herself. Poor Richard; he is so afraid for our daughters' welfare, despite the fact that Katie has been on her own for four years, and Liz was in Ghana on semester abroad, and we were amazed by her competence and independence in such an alien environment. She comes back around ten o'clock in a triumphant state, having navigated London and its tube by herself and snapping a number of good shots in the rain with my camera. I think she is also proud that an older man approached her and asked if she'd like to go for a drink with him, but she responsibly refused.

Liz

It felt so refreshed to be walking in the streets of London on my own—couldn't stop smiling. Got scared to take the tube all by myself at first, but was really proud when I managed to get to Westminster on my own. When I arrived, my breath was quite literally taken away. I was so overwhelmed by what I saw I could barely stand up. Walked up subway stairs to see the Houses of Parliament right in front of me next to the Thames river which calmly flowed under Westminster Bridge. Across the water was the "Eye," a giant Ferris wheel floating gently in the dimming evening light. My spirits were high even though it was raining, and I had only just made it before it got dark. What luck!

How to even describe what I saw? Parliament surprised me because it was absolutely huge, and yet every square inch had incredible, carefully carved detail. No idea how old it is. I saw Big Ben and thought the gilding at the top was indescribable. Went on to see Westminster Abbey right around the corner; particularly loved the colorful rose window. I can't believe the history involved with this place.

Katie

Squished into the room at night. All packed together like sausages or pigs in a blanket.

France

Diary of Ruth K. Crapo, 1907-1908

London, England—Paris, France, Thursday, October 3, 1907
A bright, sunny day for the channel. We got up at 6:30 and finished packing, then breakfast and a race for the train. On the road to Dover it was dirty, and there were many tunnels. We were all dreading the channel, but the water was fairly smooth, and no one of our party was sick.

At Calais we heard enough French to set us guessing, so all the way to Paris I devoured my dictionary.

There, trouble. We drove around for two and a half hours before we could find a bed to sleep in. We went to six different pensions and hotels, and finally after much "parleying," we got into Hotel Richmond, 4 Rue Helder at twelve francs per day each. There was no kick from us. We were glad to get in anywhere.

Diaries of Holly, Katie and Elizabeth Pierce, 2008

London, England—Paris, France, June 4, 2008

IT IS 9:30 IN THE morning, and we are now on our way to Paris via the Eurostar which takes us through the Chunnel. The trip is 3¼ hours, quite a bit shorter than when Ruth traveled across the channel. The ride is incredibly smooth, and though in second class, I feel very comfortable and snug. My seat faces backwards, but it isn't weird at all. We go in and out of tunnels that make my ears pop. Richard goes off on his quest to find coffee in the dining car, although the Englishwoman wearing a black puffy-paint-sparkle T-shirt who just passed us informs us she is on the way back to get champagne. I thought this was a non-stop train, but here we are, pausing to pick up a few more passengers on the outskirts of town.

The weather is clearing up a little, and I see a few bits of blue between the overcast. Perhaps it will be sunny in Paris! Right then we are all in a cheerful, anticipatory mood. Perhaps Paris will mark a new beginning for us all.

In the Gare Du Nord—Northern Train Station—the silver trains pull in side by side under a high, misty-glassed roof ribbed with metal and full of echoing Gallic voices talking and yelling, trains hissing and sighing, whistles blowing, all ricocheting and amplified by the *gare's* acoustics. It is much as I remembered it thirty-five years ago when I passed through after graduating from college and taking the requisite trip to Europe, except for a few significant changes. There are now the sexy, beautiful trains with their smooth, scooped noses, of course, but it is the armed military presence that is new. The powers that be must pick their soldiers for their youth and good looks here at the station to wow the new arrivals like my daughters.

Katie

Here there were cute cops or military with red berets and giant semi-automatic machine guns. French men are ever so flirtatious. One mouthed to me that he loved me as he went past, despite the appearance of an engagement ring on my left finger, the fake one my sister lent me.

Liz

Quite upset upon arriving in Paris. I had to get into the bathroom quickly, but I had to pay in coins to get through a wicked-confusing turnstile. I couldn't figure it out, and the woman attendant only spoke French. I finally figured out how to get enough money into the machine, but I didn't get through in the allotted time. At that point I just crawled under the turnstile arm. A bad way to start a visit to Paris, and I'm not amused. Nonetheless, the cute soldiers patrolling the station just put a smile on my face. Thank God for cute men.

NOT A PEEP of protest from the girls when we head for the metro. The map immediately outside the station shows the metro's main line coming up right next to our hotel.

Katie
Mom tried to disappear on the Parisian streets when I stopped to get a mini Eiffel tower, but my sister stopped her. We made it in one piece.

NOT SURPRISINGLY, our hotel is named The Esmeralda, as it is just across the Seine from Notre Dame. I discovered this little gem in my research months ago, and while readers were warned that the place is a little funky, it has a loyal clientele—just my kind of place, I think resolutely as we haul our thumping luggage up a steep, dark and very narrow circular stairway to the fourth floor, the girls half-heartedly bitching all the way.

Liz
After arriving in Paris, we left the station, took the metro and walked to our little hotel, the Hotel Esmeralda. We were exhausted by wrestling with our boxy luggage while climbing four narrow flights of stairs to our room, but found it all worthwhile, for our single window opened out right onto Notre Dame, with the Seine flowing right in front of it. Worth every stair for such an amazing view.

The room itself was quite quaint, covered with various old mismatched floral wallpaper.

Katie
Peeling wallpaper covered the walls. Print is as if a bad paisley LSD trip threw up all over the ceiling.

THE DÉCOR IS "ECLECTIC," but who is looking at the room? Since I'd requested the quad eight months ago, we have the coveted top floor (otherwise known as an attic or garret) with a to-die-for view of Notre Dame and the park across the way. So everyone is content with their own bed, while outside the cathedral's magnificent bulk rises above the treetops along the riverbank.

Diary of Ruth K. Crapo, 1907-1908

Paris, France, October 4, 1907

It is wet and raining, and Paris looks so forlorn that my spirits are very low. We went out to hunt for the American Express office, where we found some mail, got some money and so our spirits rose a little.

We walked down the Rue de L'Opéra and in no time we were lost. My French finally did the business, but I was mad. Paris makes me weary.

After a good lunch and rest, we started out again, and again got lost. After a long walk we found the American Express company again and bought a guidebook and two maps. Paris has yet to impress me, though. It's London for me.

Paris, France, October 5, 1907

Lucy and Mrs. Coulter left us after breakfast and went up to Miss Woods' [their prearranged pension] to get some warm clothes out of their trunks.

Mother and I took a cab and went to the Louvre. The cabby first took us to the Magasin de Louvre, and I had some trouble explaining that we wanted to see the art gallery.

In the afternoon it rained, so we didn't do much but get lost once more, read and wrote letters in the evening. The hotel is all right.

Paris, France, Sunday, October 6, 1907

Mother, Mrs. Coulter and I started out to find a church to go to. We walked and walked but found none, so we kept on walking.

We admired the Place de la Concorde where Marie Antoinette, Louis XVI, Charlotte Corday and others were beheaded during the French Revolution. We also walked along the new Pont Alexandre III bridge erected for the Paris Exposition, and a corking affair it was.

We were driven home by the rains. We tried to get Floy Little and Frances Wyman to come to dinner, but they were off for the day. It took three-quarters of an hour to telephone them. The system here is awful, and no one uses telephones when they can help it.

Paris, France, October 7, 1907

After breakfast we took a cab and drove to 4 Rue Chevreuse to see Floy and Frances. Floy dropped a few hints, and I am certain she's engaged to Sydney Barttell. We invited them to dinner, then went back to the hotel to telephone the Peasleys. The telephone was out of order, so we started out in a cab again. We found the Peasleys in, and they accepted our invitation to dinner, too.

We had a very enjoyable evening talking about Burlington, the many engagements, etc. and exchanging European experiences. Floy was rather worried about Frances, who wants to leave her and go where she can get uncooked food.

Paris, France, October 8, 1907

Something else has disagreed with me. I've had pains for four days. I'm glad we got settled at Miss Woods' today. I was able to pack up and take the ride up here. Then I went to bed and took the medicine Lucy hunted up last night.

I got worse, so Mother had the doctor come: a typical Englishman. He talked about long women's nightgowns and other queer things and insisted I'd had a chill and gotten my feet wet. It did no good to tell him I'd done neither, so to please him I took the doses without a word—pills as big as quarters and some other vile stuff.

They did me good just the same, and I was able to sleep some after two bad nights. Bad luck seems to be pursuing me over here.

Paris, France, October 9, 1907

Rainy again, but as I spent the day in bed, I didn't mind it a bit.

In the afternoon Lucy and Floy called, and through Floy we heard of the fire in the Tausa Building and the narrow escape Bud had getting out of the building with his stenographer.

An old English lady came in during the afternoon and brought three birds for me to see. She has a collection, I believe, and keeps from twenty to thirty varieties in her home. A charming old piece, she was. The birds were wonderful: one orange, one red, one green and red, and all tiny.

Paris, France, October 10, 1907

A great old day, this, and the first real sunshine in Paris. I felt first rate this morning, so we decided to go to the Louvre. We found it closed, of course. We find it hard to see anything here.

We went to the American Express office, then went to the Louvre store, bought petticoats and then went home to lunch. After a short rest

34

we went to the Grand Palais where they were having a festival. It was a pretty thin affair, and we soon left.

We managed to find the Hôtel des Invalides open. It was built as a hospital for maimed and old soldiers. There are only five of them there now.

Paris, France, October 11, 1907

We spent this morning at the Louvre, mostly with the pictures. I loved some of Corot's, Millet's, Daubigny's, David's, Rousseau's and others. These were more modern, but beautiful.

After a few minutes' rest following lunch, we went by tram to the Bon Marché. Such a mob and so much noise and so hard to buy! Mother bought a dress, and Lucy and I, underclothes.

We got home too late for dinner, so we bought a light lunch of crackers and fruit. Mad.

Paris, France, October 12, 1907

Lucy and Mrs. Coulter spent the morning hunting for lace waists. They came back quite disgusted with Paris shops.

In the afternoon I went to a small bridge party at Gladys Hawkins Van Hooten's. The all-absorbing topic of trousseaus was discussed and other questions of dress. Gladys' baby is a dear and was much excited to have so many people around. Gladys looks fat and happy, and her husband seems nice and jolly and devoted to Baby.

In the evening I shortened my blue broadcloth suit for rainy-day wear, a big job.

Paris, France, Sunday, October 13, 1907

Pious members of our party went to church, Mother and Lucy to a Christian Science church, and Mrs. Coulter to an American one. I stayed home.

After dinner I promised Mother to stay downstairs to prayers, so I spent the time until nine P.M. with *The Texas Steer*. This a wild product if there ever was one. It comes from Waco, Texas. I enjoyed the little service very much, but I was twenty-five years younger than anyone else present.

Will we accomplish anything in Paris? I wonder. We've been here nearly two weeks and have seen practically nothing but ugly weather and the insides of cabs.

Paris, France, October 14, 1907

No, it will never clear up. The heavenly water works are in full running order now.

This morning I took Mother to the Bon Marché where she had a fitting, and we did a few other errands. After lunch and some swearing at the weather, we went to the Madeleine Church.

Floy and Frances were to call this evening, but we waited in vain for them. We finally fell to and ate up the refreshments we had purchased in their honor.

Paris, France, October 16, 1907

Mother and I hunted up a hairdresser on the Avenue Victor Hugo and had our heads shampooed. We also purchased *crepous*, or rats, for our hair, so tonight we have marvelous pompadours.

After a short rest, we all four started out for Notre Dame and Sainte-Chapelle, taking the metropolitan subway. It poured down rain. It was too dark to see much of Notre Dame, and we were too late to see Sainte-Chapelle. We came home four in a cab and were soaked to the skin with some of our new clothes spoiled. We changed our clothes and tried to get warm. Mother put her hair up in curl-papers.

Paris, France, October 17, 1907

This morning we started out for Notre Dame again and saw it in a good light. It was far more beautiful than we discerned it to be after yesterday.

We got out in the afternoon to see Sainte-Chapelle, the most lovely chapel we have seen. There were fifteen windows of 13th century stained glass which escaped the Revolution and all.

Next, we visited the Conciergerie and saw the cells in which Marie Antoinette, Charlotte Corday, Mme. du Barry, Robespierre and others were imprisoned. It's a gloomy spot filled with prisoners now. Mother was overcome at the sight of an hysterical woman whose husband was a prisoner there.

Paris, France, October 18, 1907

Starting early for Versailles, we took a cab and first drove to the Grand Trianon. I sat up on the seat with the driver, a nice old boy, and sputtered in French to him.

We took a walk in the gardens, then went to the Petit Trianon. We saw the English gardens laid out after Marie Antoinette's plans and the farm with its mill, dairy, theatre, etc. where Marie and her ladies pretended to farm.

From there we drove to the Palace of Versailles—impossible to describe! We ate lunch in the gardens on the sly.

On the whole I had a very satisfactory day. I bought thirty-six postal cards and am glad Versailles is off my mind.

Paris, France, October 19, 1907

It was a warm and sunny day, the finest we've had since we arrived. We walked over to the Trocadero, a building put up at the time of the World's Fair and surrounded by the most attractive fountains and gardens. We sat for an hour in the park sunning ourselves and getting warmed thoroughly after so many cold, rainy days.

On the way home we got lost. Lucy and I bought some tarts, which gave us some trouble by running over and were not as good as they were cracked up to be.

In the afternoon we drove for two hours in the Bois de Boulogne. We passed Longchamps where the races were, and Mother was anxious to stop and see them; in fact, we heard nothing but "races" from her all afternoon.

Paris, France, Sunday, October 20, 1907

Another fine day. After church we walked up the Champs Élysées and marveled at the wonderful costumes and turn-outs, at the cherry lips, peach-bloom cheeks, black, curved eyebrows and marceled hair. The Parisians put it on thick. Lucy called them at first by mistake "parishioners."

After lunch Lucy and I took a walk over to the Parc Monceau. It was a regular baby show. Nursemaids were most attractive in their frilled, beribboned bonnets with long streamers reaching to the ground and capes to match in color. French children were truly lovely, dainty and sweet enough to kiss. We saw some wonderfully dressed artists with long hair, big hats and ties, full trousers, long, drooping moustaches and dirty hands—the real article.

Paris, France, October 21, 1907

About ten A.M. Lucy and I went downtown to hunt for Les Trois Quartiers, a store recommended by the women at the house where we got some good bargains in silk petticoats. My French-y one created quite a furor, with Mother especially excited about it. I also purchased a much-wanted feather boa. Mater again worked up; she thinks that Paris has turned my head.

Paris, France, October 22, 1907

Lucy and I again went shopping, this time to the Galerie Lafayette. I had trouble finding a bath brush to suit me but finally bought something resembling a soup ladle. Lucy purchased an untrimmed black hat and has already turned it into a thing of beauty.

We went to the American Express office but found no money. I wrote a hot letter to Cliff, which I regretted as soon as I mailed it.

In the afternoon Lucy and I took a short walk on Rue Victor Hugo and in the Bois de Boulogne. Lucy bought chestnuts as big as buckeyes only to find that they had to be cooked before eating.

Paris, France, October 23, 1907

After lunch we went down to see the making of the Gobelins tapestries. Three men often work on one loom. They work on the wrong side and have little mirrors to show their work and coloring on the right side, but they have to squint through the threads to see the mirrors. The pattern is on the back, and the design is drawn a little at a time on the loom of threads with impression paper. Gorgeous finished work can be seen in museums.

Paris, France, October 24, 1907

This morning we went down to 200 Rue Rivoli and bought some underwear and handkerchiefs to give away at Christmas. We got some really great bargains but have been hearing awful tales of the high duty to be paid going home, so my enthusiasm for buying is growing less.

Frances and Floy had dinner with us and spent the evening. We had our first grate fire tonight, and it certainly was a fizzle. It's colder now.

Paris, France, October 25, 1907

Too much sightseeing for Sister Anne [a sarcastic reference to herself]: "Everything went to the bad at once, leg, head and 'tummence.'" I spent the day in bed until 5:00 P.M. No one went out. Millinery, dressmaking and general sewing was the order of the day. We had a pathetic little fire in our grate, and during the morning the following piece of poetry was composed by the chilly ones:

> Waiting, fondly waiting, while the fire just meanders along.
> And we find ourselves half-freezing
> As around the grate we throng.
> Waiting, fondly waiting, for the coals to get red hot,
> And I'm afraid we'll keep on waiting
> Until this world is not.

Heard of the big panic in Wall Street, and I suppose we are paupers, but what care we as long as we have a few American Express checks left?

Paris, France, Sunday, October 27, 1907

This afternoon we started off for the Théâtre du Châtelet to hear the Colonne Orchestra directed by Édouard Colonne, one of the Paris favorites. The music was perfect, and I was surprised to find Paris so music-mad. Great enthusiasm was displayed, and yelling, hissing and clapping very genuine. We'd love to hear the orchestra again and are regretting more and more that we are to leave here on Thursday.

Paris, France, October 28, 1907

Lucy and I spent the morning at the Louvre store buying heavy clothes to wear in Switzerland. I found some wonderful knitted knee caps and bed slippers which look like enormous socks. Mother was much pleased with our unusual good sense.

In the evening we spent the time tearing up letters and packing. I'm sorry we must leave this nice, rainy old Paris.

Paris, France, October 29, 1907

We did some last shopping in the rain on Rue Rivoli, then came home and roasted *marrons,* or chestnuts, in our baby grate. We had no appetite for dinner. Put the fire out.

Paris, France, October 30, 1907

We packed all morning until the American Express men came for our trunks, which are to go on to Florence while we go to Switzerland.

After lunch we bought tickets for the opera, a box, and considered ourselves lucky to get anything. The opera was "Ariane," and the music, perfect, with singers Mlles. Cheval, Rose Fiart and Lucy Arbell. Mademoiselle Cheval had a wonderful voice and was beautiful, while Rose Fiart was ugly but sang well. L'Opéra-Garnier cost six or seven million dollars, was too gorgeous to describe and well worth the price of admission.

Diaries of Holly, Katie and Elizabeth Pierce, 2008

Paris, France, June 4, 2008

ONCE WE GET our stuff all squared away, it is time once again to tie on the ol' feedbag. Yes, the girls are hungry, but it is roughly lunchtime, so out we go. Katie is ecstatic when the waiter sets in front of her a bowl of French onion soup. Now, however, we are dealing in euros, and I could roughly guess how much this repast is going to set us back. Should I dwell on a hundred dollars for lunch? I let it go.

Katie decides to return to the hotel for some "alone time" while Richard, Liz and I take the bridge over the Seine to Notre Dame.

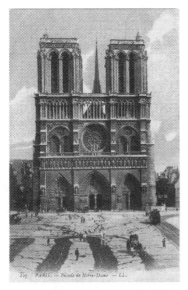

Then and Now
Notre Dame: Richard, the author and Liz

The vast square in front of the cathedral is full of visitors but not really crowded. Liz wanders off to inspect the incredible web of stone carvings adorning every square inch of the church's exterior. A small, dark woman in rags approaches me. She looks as if she could be Eastern European or a gypsy.

"Do you speak English?" she asks in a thick, indeterminate accent.

When I say yes, she hands me a rumpled piece of paper explaining how she is here to beg for money to feed her starving children. Boy, she knows how to pick 'em. I give her a euro and she is instantly gone. Only as time passes do we see there is a bunch of these women working the crowd. Liz returns, indignantly sensing a scam much more readily than her naive mother; she has scornfully turned one of the insistent "beggars" away.

We decide to check out the cathedral's interior, which is absolutely huge and dark save for the bits of colored light radiating from the two glorious rose windows. The French removed these windows and put them into storage during World War II, fearing the Germans would bomb the cathedral. This fascinates me. The South Rose window is over forty-two feet across; how do you remove something so incredibly large and delicate, the hundreds of pieces bound together only by traceries of stone and lead? I think of numbering them, making charts, then charts of charts.

The floor is an incongruous black and white marble checkerboard pattern; it reminds me of those found on 1950s bathroom floors. Stone columns soar into the darkness above, while the walls are broken into niches, each honoring one saint or another; not being a Catholic, I'm at a loss with most of this. It's incredible to realize that this is still a functioning church, that masses have been held here for almost 850 years.

Liz

Inside, Notre Dame was breathtaking. It was the first time I've been in a church like that. How to explain it? Hundreds of people constantly streamed in and out. Each of the huge stained glass windows had a story or reference. The ceiling stretched up and up. I particularly admired the arching roof sections, coming together in perfect geometric patterns. Beautiful paintings and sculptures as well. The intricate exterior façade was stunning. There was no way to describe it; it must be seen for oneself. I especially liked the young school children whose assignment was to draw the façade.

ONE THING ABOUT these Catholics, though: they don't hold back on the gory stuff. Here is a deeply carved, painted wooden relief depicting a naked first-born son held in its hysterical mother's arms while a broad sword is driven into the howling infant's stomach by an angry, white-haired old man who should know better; hard by him is a black-haired man in a red-striped tunic, arm cocked back and ready to strike, something like a black machete in his hand, ripping another naked babe by its arm out of his helpless mother's grasp. A third, bloodied baby boy lies dead on the rocks below. I find this appalling; the phrase "gratuitous violence" comes to mind.

Outside is no better. Within the pointed stone arches of the three west doors are increasingly smaller, concentric layers lavishly carved with tall, angular figures in robes and crowns and—what's that? Egad—a hairy chimera, or what might be called a gargoyle, has climbed down from his perch on the roof and is using a pitchfork to stuff some unfortunate into a boiling kettle, its sides half covered in flames, toads hanging from its rim. Above this bug-eyed creature a woman hangs helplessly upside down, next in line for the kettle. Two niches over, a wickedly horned chimera, its toothy maw stretched open in grim excitement, is using a lance to impale two poor, bearded souls, and—wait a minute, that lance looks as if it might accidentally be hitting another chimera off to the side who's looking none too happy.

Actually, in most of these tableaux it's hard to tell exactly what's going on. Figures are twisted and distorted and intertwined. Even dogs are after birds and other small creatures in spaces too small for larger horrific scenes. The rows of kings or saints are sorted out a little better—but here's an upright fellow holding his bearded head in his hands flanked by two serene angels, one with a slight smile, reassuringly patting the decapitee's elbow as if to say, "There now, that wasn't so bad, was it?"

Frankly, I'm righteously shocked at this jam-packed Catholic display of hideous brutality. I later learn the gargoyles and chimeras were relatively recent additions, the phantasms of a famous but controversial mid-nineteenth century French architect commissioned to restore Our Lady of Paris. The concept of restoration, however, is a surprisingly contentious subject; architects, art historians and others have argued about how faithful a restoration need be to the original form. In my opinion, this definitive French Gothic treasure just happened to come up for major refurbishing during an unfortunate period in history.

ENOUGH INDIGNANT photographing of egregious examples of violence. Farther out in the square Richard shows me what looks like an eight-pointed copper star set inconspicuously among the paving stones. Having graduated as a geography major, he is pleased to have discovered "Point Zéro," the starting point from which all distances are measured throughout France. Liz is hauled over to admire it, and at this point we decide to wander around the neighborhood.

Gratifyingly, Liz is wild to see Sainte-Chapelle, as Ruth has mentioned it in her diary as the "most lovely chapel we have seen," but when we get there, it's closed. So we settle for checking out the Palais de Justice where out front an old bald chap wearing a black ski glove is waving a French flag upon which he has sewn a large black square. Smiling and amiable, he in vain does his best to explain what he is protesting but is happy enough to pose, gloved fist raised, for a photograph.

Back at the Esmeralda Katie is feeling better for having had her alone time. For once and probably all we use the multicolored set of plastic dishes and utensils from Target I've hauled along to have inexpensive deli suppers.

Katie

Paris is the most expensive place so far, by far. The bathroom has a distinct urine scent. Dad is splashing around in the bathtub right now while having a conversation through the open door with my sister and me. Mom is at the Internet café. We had baguettes, cheese and salami for dinner with wine. Dad said our lunch was a hundred dollars! Paris *is* expensive. I did some Carmen Electra dance moves in front of the family, and they thought it was charming. Mom smiled.

In my dreams I ask who will win the election, and even the cat says Obama.

Paris, France, Thursday, June 5, 2008

Liz

Relaxing and pleasant to sit atop the bus in the breeze and see the sights. We saw the big square with an Egyptian-looking obelisk, where everyone was killed by guillotine in the Revolution. We alit on the street leading up to the Arc de Triomphe and enjoyed the shops. I was tickled by the groups of boys who gathered and sat all day watching women pass by and calling out to them. Greatly entertaining.

We reached the Arc de Triomphe, and I was truly amazed. I guess I hadn't really understood the grand scale of the monument. I had trouble even fitting it within my camera lens.

Katie
Saw the Eiffel tower, which was what I was really excited to see. It really made no sense for us to get out to look, though, because any pictures we took wouldn't be comprehensive and tower-evoking since it was so huge. Little did Ruth know that Paris would preserve this magnificent structure, yellow then but in a different color now.

Liz
Went on to the Eiffel Tower but didn't get off the bus because we knew it would be loads of money to ride to the top. I wasn't as impressed as I thought I would be anyway. Really, it's just all metal, and it's not nearly as pretty as these cathedrals and such.

Had another irksome family moment during which Dad became separated from the rest of us, yet Mom insisted on going into the restaurant and beginning to order instead of looking for him. I was kind of angry at Mom for this, so I kept searching and finally found him, but he was sure to be wandering forever if I had agreed to give up the search.

Katie
"Yuh nuh num num num num num num," my sister and I sang together, full of wine and Xanax. I took a Xanax outside of Notre Dame, and it made the rest of the day way more pleasant.

We saw some other stuff including the Pantheon. On our way back we ran into barricades and lots of commotion in the streets. We found out they were filming a movie with Meryl Streep! They blocked us from going through, so we had to go all the way around. Very exciting.

All in all a much better last two days than all the previous days, stress-wise. At the hotel Liz and I sang and had fun until Mom and Dad got back, and we had to stop acting so silly. I know I took more Xanax than before, but it was to keep my pee-levels at a manageable level (in consideration for the family so I don't "hijack" the trip anymore). Dad and I were on a close wavelength early on, then Mom and I when we went shopping, then my sister and I when we were being silly this evening. The parents seem to dampen our silliness even if they don't mean to.

Switzerland

Diary of Ruth K. Crapo, 1907-1908

Paris, France—Vevey, Switzerland, October 31, 1907

The French countryside is most beautiful, delicate and feathery, with the fall coloring of the foliage too lovely. We—Mrs. Coulter and I—raved and raved over it all, while Mother and Lucy made up for lost sleep.

There were two people in the compartment with us whom we supposed to be French. Our party talked some about others in English, and so we were surprised and horrified when a discussion about tickets arose, and the man spoke to us in perfect English. Will we never learn?

We got into Vevey before we were ready to get off, and it took the combined efforts of friends and trainmen to land us on the platform. The bus for the Mooser Hotel was at hand, and so here we are on Lake Geneva with snowcapped mountains in the distance. We haven't actually seen them yet, but I know they are near.

Diaries of Holly, Katie and Elizabeth Pierce, 2008

Paris, France—Vevey, Switzerland, Friday, June 6, 2008

THE DAYS GO BY in a strangely undifferentiated flow. Yesterday was a full day in Paris, and for once it was a good day for all. I think the curse of the Passat has been broken.

Katie

Got up at the butt-crack of dawn, it seemed. Really only 6:30, but we had to get to the train by eight o'clock. My sister made a comment that she and Dad had been ready and waiting for "slowpoke Mom," so I got offended for her and told my sister that she would have been down right away if she hadn't spent ten minutes cleaning up the blood my sister left on the white sheets. Mom knew my sister would be freaked, which she was, so she helped her out. I stayed back with Mom. Such early-morning drama.

Liz

So we are on the train now. The countryside is simply overflowing with lush green foliage, and there are little houses tucked away in the hills while cattle and horses are wandering in fields far from any sight of man. I particularly like that. I find that I really don't mind the trains and find them awfully convenient. Why they aren't crisscrossing America beats me. I know they used to.

OUTSIDE, THE COUNTRYSIDE streams by, a smooth smear of green punctuated by little towns, slender steeples and some fine, handsome brown and white cows. There are tunnels that make your ears pop, and off in the distance, now and then one can see the highway we would be taking if we were driving, but thank God we are not.

We have just left Dijon, so it will be awhile before we reach Lausanne. Because we are in the Schwengen Pact countries now, we do not have to have our passports checked at the borders, but I did notice a gendarme on the platform with a large German shepherd tightly on leash as the train pulled out of Paris. Not quite like the soldiers in camouflage with their semiautomatic rifles and red berets who strolled through the Gare du Nord as we arrived from London, but it still shows that watchful presence in effect.

Diary of Ruth K. Crapo, 1907-1908

Vevey, Switzerland, November 1, 1907

I got up during the night and found it bright outdoors with stars and the moon overhead. I had a glimpse of the lake and mountains and knew somewhat what to expect this morning.

It was certainly a wonderful sight: the blue, blue lake and the grand old mountains, the vineyards in their fall colors and the lovely flowers, and the quaint pink, blue and white houses and the narrow streets with high stone walls on either side. We started off after breakfast and had a lovely walk to the village and lake where we fed the swans and gulls with bread purchased by Mother (she gave us a fright by suddenly disappearing, and we were much reassured when she came out of an alley with a loaf in her hand).

Vevey, Switzerland, November 2, 1907

We went down to the village again this morning to get postal cards and books. First we visited the market, a big square near the lake where the vegetable and flower merchants sold their goods from baskets on the ground. The odor of strong cheese prevailed, and such dirty stuff it was.

From there we walked through the streets looking in windows and spooking around in general. We bought some of the Collier chocolate made near here, and it was delicious. Peter's Chocolate was originally manufactured in Vevey.

Vevey, Switzerland, Sunday, November 3, 1907

We started off early this morning for a walk and found some very pretty places. We ended up at the lake where all Vevey was promenading. Mrs. Coulter left us, saying she was too tired to walk, but ended up taking a much longer walk than we did by herself. We are all now onto her tricks.

We came home tired and hot and refreshed ourselves with some of the native wine, into which we have to put much sugar. Vineyards are everywhere, and Vevey is noted for its grape cure for consumption.

Vevey, Switzerland, November 4, 1907

Another beautiful day. After lunch we took the boat on the lake to Territet, where we took the train to the castle of Chillon, a wonderfully interesting site. Up to within five years ago prisoners, including the assassin of the Empress of Austria, were kept there but were then moved to Geneva. We saw the torture rooms, the court room, and all historic parts of the prison.

Vevey, Switzerland, November 5, 1907

More sun this morning. I washed my hair and hung it over our dear little balcony to dry. Mother and Mrs. Coulter helped me in the drying process.

We had an early lunch at 11:45 and started out for Caux, a small resort up in the mountains above Territet. First we took the train, then the funicular to Glion and cogwheel to Caux, quite an alarming trip, but a novel experience. We encountered clouds partway up, and on both sides of us it looked to me as if we were in eternal chaos.

By the time we reached Caux, we had left the clouds below us and were in the bright sunshine. All around were lovely snowcapped peaks, and the fleecy white clouds below looked like a wonderful, billowy lake.

Vevey, Switzerland, November 6, 1907

This morning Lucy and I started off to Château D'Œx. We took the Montreux-Oberland Bernois line at the station in Vevey. It was a most wonderful ride up 3,150 feet, and the scenery was marvelous.

At Chateux D'Œx we walked off north towards the mountains. We were so sorry Mother was not with us. Chateau D'Œx is entirely surrounded by mountains, and there were many lovely little Swiss chalets all over them. We saw goats feeding on the mountainsides and people in queer costumes and found milk chocolate very cheap. An ideal day.

Vevey, Switzerland, November 8, 1907

We've decided to go to Milan tomorrow, so after lunch we packed and sewed and listened to the music from the orchestra downstairs. Lucy and I have both started sewing on the pillows we bought in Geneva and find them very engrossing.

After dinner we tried to settle up our accounts with the hotel and amongst ourselves, which was a great undertaking. No two came out alike, and we finally compromised on the hotel bill by each paying the same in spite of specials by some.

Diaries of Holly, Katie and Elizabeth Pierce, 2008

Vevey, Switzerland, June 6, 2008

THIS AFTERNOON Richard and I leave the girls at the hostel (the desk person isn't due back until four o'clock) as they are both in something of a snit. We go out to take the bus line to look for the site of the Park Hotel Mooser where Ruth et. al. stayed while here. The nice woman at the tourist office tells us it had been torn down and replaced with an old folks' home and some other housing, so after plotting our route on the bus map, we rumble along with the riffraff (the man in the bank told us he'd never ridden on the bus) in search of the lost hotel.

We finally find a tiny lane called the Sentier de Chemenin that bordered the west side of the property, according to the tourist center woman. No structures are left, but after a while I start to see that the old stone wall by which I'm walking must have been left from the property. With that realization comes the logical idea that some of the ancient fir and fruit trees beyond the walls are also left from the grand grounds the hotel was renowned for. Peeling bark, bare, twisted limbs, thick, dowdy trunks all attest to their old age. I end up feeling some connection with what was once there in a former, more graceful age.

Then and Now
The Vevey waterfront

It's evening in Vevey, and we are back from dinner: pizza at The Pizza Taxi, kind of a toned-down Swiss Chuck E. Cheese with liquor. No one to speak of was in there because we were eating at such an unfashionable hour—six o'clock—but it is the cheapest place in town, fourteen dollars for a pizza Richard and I split. The rain has been following us from England; it was clouded over when we arrived in Paris and here in Vevey, but it has now finally decided to sprinkle a little unpleasantly.

Vevey, Switzerland, Saturday, June 7, 2008

SWITZERLAND GOES well tracking Ruth. The biggest surprise is taking the boat, *Le Vevey*, to Chillon and discovering that the paddle boat was inaugurated in June of 1907, so may well have been the exact one the three took along the lakeside. The steward shows me a photo of the dining room taken on that date, and beside it is another photo dated June, 2007, with men arranged in the same configuration as in the original. The stairway to the upper, first-class level rises in arced layers with brass plates embossed with "Vevey" on each step.

The *Vevey*
Was this the same boat Ruth sailed on?

Liz

Around noon our boat arrived, and we were pleased and astonished to find the boat was launched in 1907, so it's quite possible Ruth and Lucy could have sailed on the same boat. Drank a glass of white wine in honor of Ruth, as she said that is what she drank.

Katie

We took the boat to the Castle de Chillon and toured up a million stairs
to the top of the tower. We passed the torture rooms and saw breathtaking
views. Then we purchased a cheese sandwich and a Coke for eight francs
after I found a ten-euro note on the ground!

LATER, AFTER EXPLORING the romantic and gloomy Castle of Chillon,
Richard and I decide to take the funicular up the mountainside to Glion.
Afraid of heights, the girls elect to take the local bus back to the hotel.

The modern car up isn't scary at all, and a local woman points out
that the other car parked at the base of the mountainside is "an original,"
although I doubt it is a 100-year-old original.

From Glion we take the cogwheel train up to Caux, as Ruth did, and
it really does still work with cogs. A mother and her six-year-old boy sit
near the front, and the little boy peers through the window separating
the passengers from the engineer, totally fascinated. Kindly, the engineer
invites the little boy in beside him, and we can just see his little blond
head peeking above the window ledge as he and the young engineer chat
companionably. How nice to know that sort of old-fashioned kindness
still happens. Another train engineer in the making.

I decide to make my way up to the front of the car, where I compliment
the engineer on his gracious treatment of this little boy.

"Oh no!" he laughs. "I'm just along for the ride. This kind of train
doesn't need an engineer."

I suddenly realize there is no bank of controls in front of him. He's
just taken an empty seat. I compliment him on his treatment of this little
passenger anyway, then sidle foolishly back to my seat.

Above, in Caux, we get out at the foggy train station and wander over
to a café for cups of Earl Grey and espresso. Interestingly, the French and
Swiss insist that if you are not eating a full meal in a restaurant or café, you
are banished to a side, less scenic section. We have an hour before the train
comes back, and there is no town nearby to see, and it is so comfortable
just sitting there in the warmth, having our "alone time." Eventually
Richard gets up to use the restroom, and comes back completely agitated,
insisting that I must go use the bathroom! Okay, why would he be so
adamant about this?

Well, it is unlike anything I have ever seen in my life and would be the
only thing to drive me to drugs. After peeing, I flush the toilet. Nothing.

Then, a box-like projection slides with a humming sound out of the front of the tank and grasps the toilet seat. With another slight grinding noise it starts to—what? I couldn't tell at first, but then realize: the toilet seat is slowly circling around! Is the seat rubber? It seems to warp in shape as it moves, but is just an illusion. The box is sanitizing the seat. Finally it stops in its original position.

Oh, God, how I wished the girls could have seen this! It is Richard who has the brilliant idea: film it with my camera! So I sneak back into the café and its restroom and film this wonder of the modern age. We decide that it would be the perfect gift for Katie, given her germ phobia.

Katie

Mom and Dad's self-cleaning toilet video taken in Caux was akin to a drug trip but much cooler. Mom showed me the footage, and it was amazing to watch the rim spin around and around by itself.

Liz

These lovely Swiss, they are always clean and on time.

Katie

So far it's been gentle relaxation walking in the small village. I believe this is my favorite place so far. It's much calmer than Paris. Even though they speak French here, a lot of people also speak English and are truly friendly, whereas Parisians gave us a sour first impression before acting nicer.

This town is quiet and misty. It rains at night, but the day is sparkling clean; damp, but so wonderful. I could definitely live here more than any other place we've gone so far.

Liz

For dinner, the family strolled to a lovely little restaurant recommended to us for traditional Swiss food called "Café Central." I had quite possibly the best meal yet: lamb cutlets that were absolutely delectable and savory. Holy crap, they were good.

So VEVEY IS GOOD, with its cleanliness, crosswalks that drivers observe, drinkable, clean water, chic little shops, and dogs, dogs, dogs everywhere! Everyone has some well-cared-for canine, mostly small-sized, on a leash not only along the promenade but in the trains and restaurants as well. We have seen only one cat in Vevey.

Liz

Overall (so *far*) I loved being able to have splendid chats in London where the people are forever friendly, but Vevey takes the cake for atmosphere and the way it makes you feel. Paris is the one if you're looking for endlessly stunning architecture.

Katie

I was awakened at eleven o'clock by people honking their car horns and screaming in the hallway. I guess Portugal won a soccer game, and the Swiss are in support, so they were really showing it. I finally got back to sleep.

Italy: Florence

Diary of Ruth K. Crapo, 1907-1908

Vevey, Switzerland—Milan, Italy, November 9, 1907

We got off to the station by 9:10 this morning and found when we were almost there that Lucy had left her umbrella behind. By telephone and a special messenger and two francs we managed to get it before the train left.

We left Switzerland smiling in the sunshine, then came out of the other end of the Simplon tunnel into Italy and rain and cold. What we saw of the Lake District was exquisite, but the rest of the country seemed old and unattractive and tumbledown. An Italian creature on the train made himself obnoxious by taking a stand outside our compartment door and staring at us for about an hour. He was an evil-looking person, and he gave us quite a scare by his impudence.

Diaries of Holly, Katie and Elizabeth Pierce, 2008

Vevey, Switzerland—Florence, Italy, Sunday, June 8, 2008

Katie

I was awakened at seven by Dad saying, "Oh shit," and when he didn't stop making noise, rustling plastic bags and such, I gave him a tongue-lashing until he finally left me in peace so I could finish sleeping until eight.

I GUESS WE ARE now in the Simplon tunnel, as Ruth mentioned and Paul Theroux speaks of in *The Great Railway Bazaar*. I just read the section last night with his adventures with Duffill, the old Englishman with the down-at-the-heel trousers and his brown paper parcels. After Theroux leaves Vevey and Montreaux, it is light for a while, and then suddenly everything is darkness, and Duffill says, "This must be the Simplon tunnel." They are in complete darkness, and Duffill complains he can't taste his salami when eating in the dark.

While trains now more than thirty years later have lighted compartments, the feeling of closeness prevails. Richard is busy sawing up *our* salami with a plastic picnic knife (Katie notes, "Dad is overly concerned about the salami rinds"), preparing lunch even though it is only a bit past 11:30. He does like to have something to do and arrange.

We pass in and out of tunnels, but it feels as if mostly in. Across the aisle Katie and Liz sit with the two-liter bottle of Coke and leftover olives Elizabeth bought the other day that have managed to leak brine and olive oil all over lunch. We have to "hankie" all the foodstuffs with one of her graduation handkerchiefs. Today we have the usual: a baguette, salami, bananas, slices of prepackaged assorted cheeses, and a last-minute score, Collier chocolate, the brand Ruth speaks in her diary of eating in Switzerland.

Liz
Finally, finally got to taste Swiss chocolate, just the same kind as Ruth noted in her diary, and it certainly lived up to its reputation.

Diary of Ruth K. Crapo, 1907-1908

Milan, Italy, Sunday, November 10, 1907
Today we managed to see a good deal of Milan. The cathedral was only a block away, so we spent the morning there.

In the crypt we saw the tomb of St. Ambrose of Milan. Inside the glass case you could see the body of the saint dressed in great splendor. His face and head, with the skull and dried skin stretched over it, was exposed to view—a ghastly sight.

Milan—Florence, Italy, November 11, 1907

Last night while at dinner in the Hotel Europe in Milan, Edith Hungate Wardell and her husband gave us a big surprise by walking into the room. They are on their way to Venice.

We left Milan at 9:45 this morning for Florence. During our journey we saw much badly flooded country owing to the unusual amount of rain and warm weather this time of year. Bridges were washed out in many instances, and railroad tracks were made unsafe. We arrived in Florence after dark, but a nice, fat little porter at the station kindly bundled us off to the Pension Jennings-Riccioli. Madame Riccioli met us at the door, and we are now nicely situated with bright and clean rooms.

Florence, Italy, November 12, 1907

The street in back of our rooms is the Lungarno Della Zecca Vecchia along the river Arno, and we found many attractive shops all along the way. Many beggars and flowers to be found on the streets. Mrs. Coulter purchased a guidebook and I, a Baedeker, so that tomorrow we can go out intelligently.

This afternoon we all settled down to either reading or writing, as it was rainy. Baedeker proved interesting for an hour or more, then I got out my linen, started the centerpiece and worked till suppertime. We discovered floods are delaying all trains, and we may not see them for months. We're now looking out for a wash lady, and a quick one.

I have my friend with me again.

Florence, Italy, November 14, 1907

We started out again this morning to sightsee. At the market it was flower day, and I bought a big bunch of roses for fifty centimes and got back a bad two-franc piece, so I did not get a bargain.

Lucy and I walked across the Ponte Vecchio, an old, interesting affair with shops on either side all the way across. We went to Berchielli's to get pendants we'd seen. I found mine gone, but Lucy got hers.

On reaching home we found that instead of a stranger buying my pendant, Mother had bought it for me for Christmas, and one for Lucy, too. A great surprise, and I went to bed well content after my first disappointment.

Florence, Italy, November 16, 1907

Before leaving the house this morning we bought some waists and a table cover from a woman who came to the house. We then went out and hunted for dressmakers and were partly successful; we found Grossenbacher and Polgini but not Campolini. We have appointments next week.

This afternoon we took the streetcar and went up to Fiesole, an attractive old suburb of Florence. The inhabitants do wonderful straw work. In the museum we saw many interesting excavated pieces from Roman and Tuscan times and some gruesome ones as well. We met Edith Hungate and her husband on our way home.

Florence, Italy, Sunday, November 17, 1907

This morning we went to the Pitti Palace across the Ponte Vecchio to see its gallery. The pictures were much more beautiful than the Uffizi's. Behind the palace we wandered in the Boboli gardens, which are lovely with wonderful walks of arched trees, terraces, an open amphitheatre, statuary and fountains. The garden was on the side of a hill, and the stone walls with hanging vines made me wonder if Babylon's hanging gardens were not like them.

Florence, Italy, November 18, 1907

After lunch, Mother and I went out to get a hat (about the sixth time since we left London), but we could not find one the color of Mother's suit. We visited feather and flower stores, too; everything was very expensive. We also went into some fine art stores and looked for porcelain paintings of our favorite Madonnas and pictures. Mother got a lovely one. I find she still has the cameo craze, left over from Cuba.

I spent the evening reading and learning a lace stitch. Everyone is making lace.

Florence, Italy, November 19, 1907

We went to the Duomo again, going into the various chapels and sacristies with a guide who showed us several famous frescoes by Luca Della Robbia and other members of the Robbia family. I feel the cathedral is not as impressive as that in Milan, either outside or in.

From the church we went to the market and got some lovely Florentine hats and some lace insertions. I'm getting to be quite an expert at Jewing down.

Florence, Italy, November 21, 1907

We had a most interesting morning at the monastery of San Marco. I had just finished reading a sketch of Savonarola's life, so I found everything there as I had pictured it in my mind.

The cell of Savonarola was small and quite dark, furnished as it was in the days when he occupied it. The monastery was suppressed after Savonarola's time on account of the bad reputation of Dominican priests.

The afternoon was spent at the American Express office reading the New York papers. I heard of Mr. Perkin's death in a letter and felt quite homesick for a while.

The Wardells were to have come to dinner, but they didn't show up.

Florence, Italy, November 22, 1907

This morning we received a long letter from the Wardells.

Florence, Italy, November 23, 1907

Lucy, Mother and I spent the morning in the National Museum, a famous old Florentine palace now filled with interesting collections of old bells, carved wood and ivory, tapestries, bronzes, terracottas, china, armor, old jewelry and sculpture.

In the afternoon Lucy and I took a walk over the Ponte Vecchio. Florence certainly grows on one, and in spite of the dirt, smells and cheats, you find you can't help liking it.

Florence, Italy, Sunday, November 24, 1907

This was our second morning at the Uffizi gallery, and much more satisfactory than the first. I marked my favorite pictures so I can get postal cards.

I spent this afternoon reading Vasari's *Lives of the Italian Artists* and writing letters. We are as comfortable as can be in our little sitting room and hope Mrs. Coulter is faring as well in her chilly single room. We spent the evening listening to ghost stories well known in England.

Florence, Italy, November 25, 1907

First thing this morning we went down to the Battistero to see Ghiberti's famous bronze doors and the one by Andrea Pisano. Those facing the cathedral and designed and executed entirely by Ghiberti are the most wonderful and beautiful and took him forty years to make. The Battistero is the place where nearly all Florentine children are baptized.

From there we went to the Church of San Lorenzo. We were then taken by a guide to the Medici chapel, wonderful for its marble and Florentine mosaic work and still unfinished. Semiprecious stones were used freely.

Had tea at the Floreal with music and officers.

Florence, Italy, November 26, 1907

I spent a sensible morning getting a waist fixed, paying my bills and reading the news at the American Express office and nosing around in lace and jewelry stores with Mother. I bought my lovely luncheon set.

Mrs. Coulter came down about four o'clock and she, Mother and I had a long discussion on Christian Science and other religions. I was glad to be interrupted by Miss Shepard and Miss Hinds breaking in on us and changing the subject of our conversation.

I'm still reading Vasari's *Lives of the Italian Painters*. They were certainly jolly boys, most of them, and it's a pleasure to know that they were fond of this mundane life even if they painted nothing but Madonnas and saints.

Florence, Italy, November 28, 1907

This Thanksgiving Day in the morning, I celebrated by washing my hair and was much elated over a few waves which appeared after the washing. I dried it before a little fire in our sitting room.

After lunch Lucy and I went out corset-hunting but had little success. At four o'clock all Americans were invited to a little Thanksgiving tea upstairs where champagne water was furnished with the tea, and "healths" were drunk. Antonio, who has been here in the pension over twenty years, distinguished himself by spilling the sparkling beverage all over the ladies' dresses. There are a nice lot of Americans in the house, and all seemed to be in first-rate spirits.

Florence, Italy, November 29, 1907

Went out in the morning for a short walk, but the mud and smells seemed worse than usual. After lunch Miss Hinds, Mrs. Coulter, Mother and I went to Elizabeth Barrett Browning's house to call. She was not at home (a joke on the bandmaster). Mrs. Browning must have been an idealist indeed to have written poetry in such surroundings as those, with nothing but ugly buildings for an outlook.

Florence, Italy, November 30, 1907

The weather still continues to be quite warm, and it makes me smile as I read of the snow at home and in Northern Europe. We spent the morning at Palagi's Via Por Santa Maria gallery looking at pearls and garnets with Mrs. Coulter and Mother. I fell in love with a mighty pretty sapphire, my birthstone, too.

After lunch we all went our separate ways. On the street I met a poor little artist girl who lost her fiancé a week before her wedding and is the most pathetic creature with her short hair and queer clothes. We came home together, arriving a little after four.

Florence, Italy, Sunday, December 1, 1907

A gorgeous, warm, sunny day today, more like June than December. We had a late breakfast and then hurried off to the Galleria dell' Accademia. We saw Michelangelo's famous statue of David carved from one piece of marble, as well as copies of his other famous statues.

Florence, Italy, December 2, 1907

We all went down to Palagi and Sons this morning to see about some rings, pins, etc. I decided on a sapphire ring, Lucy, a pearl one. Everyone around here seems to think this is the place above all others in Europe to get jewelry, and I don't believe we are being taken in.

After lunch Lucy and I went to Madame Campolini's. Lucy's gown is going to be a beauty, my waist, neat but pretty. From the dressmakers we went hat-hunting again for Mother but again with indifferent success. The only hats that seem to please Mother are those on other people's heads.

Florence, Italy, December 3, 1907

We spent the afternoon at home, the first time in weeks, and I for one enjoyed the rest. I sewed on my Florentine centerpiece and read. Outdoors it rained and lightninged and thundered like a spring storm at home. A great change has occurred in the weather, and I have felt really cold for the first time since we arrived in Florence.

In the evening Mrs. Shepard came down, and the methods of raising children were discussed. I'm afraid Mother got a little of the worse of the argument.

Florence, Italy, December 4, 1907

We were to have gone to Pisa this morning, but we took Madame Riccoli's advice and stayed home. We have put the trip off until Friday, as Mother is determined to see one of the wonders of the world.

At least I got my Christmas presents off at the American Express office and read there for awhile. At 4:30 after a fuss, Lucy and I went to meet Miss Shepard and Miss Hinds at the Floreal to have ices. Many gorgeous Italian officers appeared at the fashionable hour, and we had a good time watching flirtations.

Florence, Italy, December 5, 1907

Immediately after lunch we went out to the Foundling or Children's Hospital where Luca Della Robbia's bambino medallions are to be seen on the kids. We saw all kinds of little ones: legitimate, illegitimate, red, white, big and little, and four or six in the incubator room. The babies were distinguished as legitimate or illegitimate by gold and silver medals around their necks. Almost all of them set up a yell when we appeared on the scene. Poor kiddies; they were sweet but pathetic.

Florence, Italy, December 6, 1907

It was raining when we left for Pisa this morning, and it didn't stop all day. The tower, though smaller than I expected, leaned more than I thought: fourteen feet. We climbed two hundred steps to the top where seven large bells hung.

The cathedral is lovely, too. In the *battistero* we saw the gorgeous Pisan pulpit, and the guard sang for us so that we might hear the echo, which was exquisite; it sounded like a great organ.

At the *camposanto*, a fascinating place where sixty-three shiploads of earth from Jerusalem were dumped, we saw many wonderful old frescoes of Heaven and Hell, etc. and monuments of great antiquity.

Florence, Italy, Sunday, December 8, 1907

All the galleries were closed this morning, it being the day of The Immaculate Conception in the Catholic churches. Almost everyone went to high mass at the Duomo or Santa Croce, but we took a long walk in the sun on the Lungarno and kept warm. Mother "birded" a little, and we had a fine morning.

After lunch I sent off a lot of Christmas cards and wrote four letters. In our little sitting room I found a novel by Orinda lying around and read a little. It was awful, and my last.

Florence, Italy, December 9, 1907

After lunch we sewed and gossiped until 4:30 when we took Miss Hinde and Miss Shepard to tea at the Floreal. The tea rooms were all crowded, but it was a nice change with the music and lights after the dismal day.

At dinner we got into a lively discussion with "Lady Fair Feather" on the question of boarding schools for young ladies.

Florence, Italy, December 10, 1907

After breakfast this morning we almost ran to the dressmakers but didn't get back in time to give Mrs. Coulter a fond farewell when she left for Rome. Mrs. Coulter had several bad breaks before she left. She is to be pitied.

We met a young girl named Miss Blaine who wants to take the Mediterranean trip with us. She seems nice. Owing to financial trouble, a friend who came over with her finds herself too hard up to take the trip.

In the evening we played bridge and ate boiled chestnuts cooked by Dr. Woodhouse, a queer specimen staying here.

Florence, Italy, December 11, 1907

This morning Mother and I went off to hunt up a trunk. I found what I wanted and got it for two dollars less than I had planned for. Each time I started out the door, the store man took a dollar off.

Dr. Woodhouse has taken to coming to our little sitting room in the evenings. Tonight he boiled chestnuts again for Miss Shepard and Miss Hinds. We had some ourselves.

Florence, Italy, December 12, 1907

We have arranged to go to Egypt with one of Cook's parties, and Miss Blaine of Ithaca, New York, is going with us.

I spent the afternoon sewing and reading a thrilling tale by Anne Catherine Greer, *Behind Closed Doors*. I didn't go up to dinner but read instead.

In the evening Misses Graham and Blaine came in, and we talked lace and pictures. Lucy made the discovery that Miss Graham smokes cigarettes, so we must keep this from Mother.

Tonight the wind is howling furiously. Peter came today, and I was rather glad to have him.

Florence, Italy, December 14, 1907

I sewed awhile in the afternoon and then went over to meet Miss Graham and go to the Floreal for tea. I climbed her eighty-seven steps at 2 Lungarno and found Mrs. Dock with her. Both had been smoking cigarettes (the box was on the mantelpiece). A sporty lot they are.

We had a nice time at the tea rooms and raced around some afterwards hunting for lemons for Lucy's foot. Mrs. Sherman and Miss Blaine spent the evening with us, and Dr. Woodhouse brought down his picture gallery.

Florence, Italy, Sunday, December 15, 1907

In the afternoon I desecrated the Sabbath by sewing some. Miss Howland called; we thought it mighty sweet of her. In the evening we all tried to make ourselves agreeable in the drawing room.

Florence, Italy, December 16, 1907

This is our last day in Florence, as we leave for Rome tomorrow. I hunted unsuccessfully for some shoes, as my patent leather ones can't be worn anymore. They affect my game leg.

After lunch, Mother, Lucy and I went out to visit Dante's dismal abode. I believe I could write an *Inferno* if I were forced to live in such a hole for very long. The room in which he was born was without any windows.

After rushing around some with Mother, we came home and packed. My new trunk is a peach. It's heavenly to have plenty of room.

Callers came down and spent the evening. Limericks and verses were the order of the evening. The maid was in hysterics, and there was great excitement on our floor.

Diaries of Holly, Katie and Elizabeth Pierce, 2008

Florence, Italy, Sunday, June 8, 2008

PASSING INTO ITALY, we see the first of Mr. Sun. It has been overcast, really cloudy, misty, lightly raining, truly raining, or pouring down buckets this whole trip so far. It will be good to feel some warmth—in the middle of June!—for the first time.

Okay, I was premature to say Mr. Sun has joined us in Italy. We disembark from the train to an increasingly steady downpour—and in the middle of this, Elizabeth melts into one of her panic attacks. Overwhelmed, she is practically frozen in the street, crying. It is a relay among the rest of us to keep an eye on her, find the hotel, then go back, rescue her and get her upstairs to where she curls up in a ball on her bed, snot running from her nose onto the gold and rust bedspread.

Liz

I hadn't even made it out of the train station before my anxiety became overwhelming. I thought I would be fine, but it became progressively worse on the very short walk to the hotel. It was raining, and I had to dodge people on the narrow sidewalks and my bag kept falling apart, so I practically gave up just around the corner from the hotel. The family came back to collect me and took me to our room. In a state of semi-delirium I was kindly led by my family to a traditional restaurant nearby. I began to feel better.

A XANAX LATER, we are able to get her in an upright position and out the door to Mama Toscana's (recommended by the woman concierge) where a rather indifferent staff serves us good Italian food for what by now seems a ridiculously low price—seven euros for a plate of scampi. Afterwards we indulge in our first cups of gelato—ahh, as good as I remember it!

This evening the shower curtain bar collapses under the weight of wet towels and my carefully laundered white shirt. Katie performs her mitzvah of the day by rescuing it from the wet shower floor and rehanging it from the showerhead. There's not enough room in here to swing a cat, providing you could find one.

Katie

Tomorrow, shopping and the fake David statue since the real one is in the museum that isn't open on Mondays.

Florence, Italy, Monday, June 9, 2008

Katie

Woke up to a street-tiler truck revving its engines and the sound of a circular saw whining through stone tiles. At least there's sun instead of yesterday's rain. Terrible dreams from reading Ruth's comments about women losing their fiancées.

WE AWAKE THIS morning to the sound of chisel against stone: they're replacing the street tile right below our window. A large truck stacked solidly with square gray cement street tiles barely fits into the cross street about one address away. Steel stanchions crudely cordon off the area, and there are cones and other warning items around. Two men in fluorescent vests and hardhats are being industrious—ahhhhh, the wonderful squeal of a high-speed blade cutting tile. Oh, there they go again; it sounds like tree saws on metal. Katie declares weird noises to be the theme of the trip. In Vevey we were serenaded by the crowd swarming back into the square after the finish of the big-screen soccer game a block over—car horns honking, people screaming and yelling, all in chaos.

The Hotel Nuova Italia is worth staying in for its color. I picked it because it was close to the train station, not knowing they were going at the street hammer and tongs. Still, the hotel is full of framed art along the hallways and down the stairs with curlicue'd wrought-iron railings. Much of the art is original. Our room for four is tight and seems eternally damp, but then both days late in the afternoon it rains heavily with spectacular thunder and lightning despite the prior sunny warmth. The dining room is filled with art but has a TV on silently in a corner playing MTV videos, and the women servers hanging out are young and hip. Breakfast is the usual rolls and croissants, orange juice, plus your choice of beverage (coffee, espresso, tea, hot chocolate and more). I feel helpless in Italy now that my French is gone.

Having been to Florence ten years ago, though, I feel pretty confident about finding our way around, and we start early enough so that the crowds have not built to critical mass. Katie comes right along, I believe if for no other reason than to escape the whine of the tile cutters. It being so near our hotel and the train station, the first stop is Santa Maria Novella and its darling and relatively simple black and white façade of squares, circles and arches. I think I rather prefer it because of its modesty in the face of what lies ahead and for its plaza's great shopping stalls.

Shortly after starting out, Katie decides she just wants to go shopping, stretch leopard pants her goal, and skip the sights, but Liz is entranced with the idea of filming everything in sight and so tags along with us. No time to lose. Next stop will have to be the Duomo and its Baptistry, big ones on anyone's list of must-sees. We set off to the south, passing a huge Tommy Hilfiger billboard showing a seductive young couple leaning into each other around the belt buckle region, the billboard situated right next to a centuries' old classic Renaissance building. The clash of new with old—at least the Blockbuster I'd seen ten years ago seems to be gone.

Jarring enough, but no match for our first sight of the massive Duomo. Set off in its vast piazza, the detailing of its black and white exterior stands out against the mousy light brown stone of the buildings around the piazza's perimeter. It's as if the surrounding buildings, a little intimidated, have backed themselves off from this phantasmagoric structure. I know that the red dome is an amazing architectural feat, but it is hard to get past all that contrasting repetitive detail echoed in the Baptistery's eight sides.

Liz

We walked to the Duomo and the practically attached Baptistery and Campanile. The intricate detail of the façade is just astounding. I was almost upset because I knew I just couldn't capture all the intricacy with my video camera, and I wanted to.

The Baptistry was mainly interesting for the famous bronze doors on one side of the hexagon-shaped structure that took the artist nearly his whole life to complete. Exquisite detail incorporated history and biblical stories. Someone was clearly obsessed with his work.

GHIBERTI'S BRONZE DOORS are the Baptistery's big attraction, even though you have to take them in through a fearsome piked iron railing. Even with this, the Italian government has taken no chances, and these doors are only replicas of the ones that have been removed to the safety of a nearby museum.

It's still relatively early, but the crowds and heat are definitely building. A stocky, domineering older female guide dressed in a bright red suit with beige track shoes holds a wand topped by fake iris aloft to help her clientele keep her in sight. Two mounted police ignore the tourists who creep up to have their pictures taken by the police's matched, patient pair of bays. Along the south side of the piazza, their rears to the curb, a row of ambulances labeled "Misericordia di Firenze" wait for the first tourist to drop to the cobblestones from heat exhaustion. In the meantime, Liz with her Handycam is in the crazed grip of having to film everyone and everything—an understandable reaction.

Florence in a day? What next? Obviously the Uffizi Gallery and the Palazzo Vecchio next to it. Stepping right along through lanes filled with ritzy stores full of goods far beyond the reach of our dollars (even if they had been strong), we pass a high-end shop with two windows tastefully displaying leather goods—boots, shoes and purses. A black man is washing its windows, and in the space between the windows someone has spray-painted "KOSOVO È SERBIA! FUCK THE USA!" It's going to take a little more than Windex to remove this sentiment.

Ahh, the Uffizi and Palazzo Veccio, Florence's town hall—but what's this? It's Monday, and the Uffizi is closed. I remember seeing Botticelli's "Birth of Venus" and "Primavera" my first visit, and I remember waiting for what seemed like hours to get in. To be truthful, I knew the Uffizi was going to be closed; there was no way around it. But now I don't have to make anyone whose good nature may be waning stand in line, and I don't have to feel guilty about them missing it. It's a good day after all.

Liz

Outside the Uffizi gallery, there were numerous statues of famous people, but my favorite was Machiavelli because he had been sculpted in such a crafty and devilish-looking way, holding his chin and with a look like he was planning something nasty.

ON TO THE PONTE Vecchio. We walk west through a long, arched passageway that prettily flanks the Arno, passing an iron post encrusted with dozens of padlocks. Some have writing on them, dates or initials. I hear someone say that the locks are put there by lovers who want their romance to last forever—so romantic! We also pass graffiti on one column that declares, "ILLUMINATI—NEW WORLD ORDER" along with the symbol of the eye within the triangle. I know this Illuminati thing is supposed to make me uneasy, but when I find cheap ceramic tiles featuring the eye-and-triangle symbol for sale, I just feel there's not a lot of reason to get worked up about it. Richard and I buy one to take home to Ryan, Liz's partner, who takes this conspiracy theory much more seriously than we. Once at the Ponte Vecchio we find Katie, who has been window shopping all this time (alas, no leopard pants) and is now checking out the bridge's tiny shops with windows chock full of gold and gems.

Today's tour of Florence on foot is fruitful and good. We find many of the postcard sites, although it is obvious that some renderings are a little skewed so as to get all the items of interest into the space of a postcard. One we cannot not find: the atelier of Vasari. I ask a postwoman, a little old lady, and two policemen and their buddy, and all have their ideas as to where it is, but the policeman's friend explains that certain areas of Florence were flattened during the war (all bridges were bombed, save for the Ponte Vecchio), and so it is possible Vasari's atelier was destroyed as well.

Then and Now
L'Or San Michele

Both girls, however, eventually narrow our wandering, what with Katie's rigid eating demands and Liz's potential panic attacks (as Katie puts it, her "pop-up blockers" gradually fade). Both insist suddenly that they want to eat at a certain place ("We don't want pizza anymore," as if two times were too many), and I for once said I would not leave the place of my choice—quiet and cheap. So off they go, and Richard and I eat our crispy pizza slices and large cup of fresh strawberries and kiwis under a canopy in a cool and shady spot off the street.

Later in the afternoon, after Liz sees the one thing she wants to see, Santa Croce for some inexplicable reason, the two take a taxi back to the hotel, and Richard and I continue on. I am determined to find the Pension Jennings-Riccioli (via dei Tintori, 7) where Ruth et. al. stayed and where E.M. Forster penned his *Room With A View*. A very nice young Indian gentleman with impeccable English in the Hotel Silla takes the time to search the Internet and finds the exact spot. At the address I discover that the hotel has been converted into flats, but fortunately one belongs to Fairfield College's Semester Abroad program, and so I press the brass buzzer and am immediately buzzed in.

Its marble interior is cool, quiet and dim, and a nice young lady directs me to the Fairfield office where I suddenly find myself choking on my words, unable to speak. I am flooded with an emotion that expresses itself in tears, startling the young woman at the desk. She brings me a cup of water, and after collecting myself explain why this is such an emotional moment for me. My *nona* stayed here one hundred years ago! Beyond the curly wrought-iron window grate, there is the view of the eternal Arno over which Ruth and both Lucys (Lucy, her sister, and Lucy in *Room With A View*) gazed to the banks beyond.

Liz

Oh yes, I tried the bidet this morning for the first time (first opportunity as well). A brilliant machine, honest. Europeans certainly have some stuff straight. Toilets either have two settings (one for each kind of "deposit" so as to conserve water), or they have flushes with a little stop button so you can stop the water as soon as it has completed its purpose. The flushers are big squares or ovals or even sometimes foot pedals—really smart!

Italy: Rome

Diary of Ruth K. Crapo, 1907-1908

Florence—Rome, Italy, December 17, 1907

We really hated to say good-bye to many in the Rissioli. We left in two cabs piled high with baggage and had no trouble whatsoever with our trunks. We had our lunch on the train, and a good one it was, too—chicken.

On reaching Rome we found the Flora's man on the lookout for us, and we were soon settled in nice, comfortable rooms at the hotel. From our windows we look out upon a Roman wall built many centuries ago and the very beautiful Borghese gardens.

We found Mrs. Coulter sweet and smiling and well satisfied with Rome, the hotel and herself. Miss Blaine has a room nearby.

Rome, Italy, December 18, 1907

With Elizabeth and Mrs. Coulter as guides, we took our first walk in Rome. I purchased a pair of hideous slippers to take the place of my patent leathers. They were purchased in Italian, and they look it.

As it was a peach of a day, we climbed the Palantine Hill to see the panorama of the city and sunset and hear the band play (the sunset was lovely, but the band didn't turn up). Gardens cover the top of the hill where society drives and visits in carriages every afternoon. We saw orange trees loaded with fruit and many other varieties of trees we were not familiar with.

Rome, Italy, December 19, 1907

We started out good and early this morning for the Forum. Postcard boys constantly buzzed around us while we paid our franc and were in the historic enclosure. It took us some time to get ourselves located with our books, but we finally managed it, and it was great fun coming onto things unexpectedly. I never expected to be familiar with the old Forum, but I feel quite so now.

Excavations there are quite recent and still going on. I tasted green olives from the trees there; awful.

Rome, Italy, December 20, 1907

This morning we hunted up the Cappuccini church. We went down into the crypt and saw the skulls and bones of four thousand Capuchin monks displayed on the walls and columns in the most artistic designs. We also saw whole skeletons occupying niches and robed in black. In the crypt there is a lot of earth from Jerusalem in which bodies are buried for ten years, then taken up and their bones used as decorations. It certainly took an artist to arrange those bones into hanging lamps, baskets, vases, etc.! Rather gruesome, but mighty interesting.

Rome, Italy, December 21, 1907

We got a fairly early start this morning and went over to St. Peter's Basilica, the Vatican and Raphael's Loggia and Stanze with the most wonderful mural paintings by that painter and his pupils. At eleven o'clock sharp we were all chased out of the Vatican and went over to St. Peter's. I liked it from the very first minute. Michelangelo's "Pieta," the statue of the Madonna with the body of Christ on her knees, was perfectly beautiful.

Rome, Italy, December 22, 1907

This morning it was off to the Coliseum, the most gorgeous ruin one can imagine. We took a guide and were shown where Christians were imprisoned before being tortured, the Emperor's private passage from the Palatine Hill and his box, also those of the Vestal Virgins, senators, aristocracy, etc. In circumference it is a third of a mile. Seats are twenty inches wide, allowing about fifty thousand people inside. During celebrations five thousand animals were killed there in a hundred days. I know I shall like the Coliseum better than anything else in Rome.

Rome, Italy, Sunday, December 23, 1907

It was the Capitoline Museum this morning, and an immense affair it is, too.

After lunch we all took a little rest, then went out to visit the fountain of Trevi, and all drank from the waters except Mrs. Coulter. It's sure to bring us back to Rome.

In the evening we watched the Christmas tree being trimmed in the hotel parlor. I got to bed at twelve o'clock exactly.

Rome, Italy, December 24, 1907

It's the day before Christmas, and as warm and sunshiny as a day in June. We got a fairly early start for the Palatine Hill. The ruins of Caligula's palace were colossal and truly wonderful, also those of Septimius Serverus, seven stories high and covering an immense area of land. It had heating apparatuses and baths. There was nothing small about those old Roman boys.

In the evening we had our Christmas tree in the hotel, and all numbers of the party drew prizes. Upstairs afterwards, we had our own little Christmas.

Rome, Italy, December 25, 1907

On Christmas day in the morning, Lucy and I were dissipated to the extent of having our breakfasts in bed, while Mother, Miss Blaine and Mrs. Coulter went off to see a dozen or two churches.

The "lazy one" and I were up and ready for business at eleven A.M. when we went to St. Peter's to high mass with Elizabeth Johnstone and Miss Huiskamp. Big doings going on there, with cardinals and all the paraphernalia. No wonder St. Peter's toe is wearing away. Streams of people waited to leave their kisses on his foot. The singing was pretty good.

We have decided to postpone our trip to Egypt until February 1. Miss Blaine is a strenuous traveler with ideas enough to keep you always unsettled. She and Mother are well suited to one another.

Rome, Italy, December 27, 1907

Having heard from a shopkeeper that this was St. John's fête day, we all went to San Giovanni in Laterno this morning. We saw the great relics of the church—the skulls of St. Peter and St. Paul—exhibited above the high altar. It may be easy to fool the Catholics, but I don't believe all I see.

We saw the Scala Santa and hundreds (with little exaggeration) of peasants going up the stairs on their knees and kissing the steps. Each time up the Scala lessens their stay in purgatory by nine years.

Rome, Italy, December 28, 1907

All hands were on deck early this morning and hie'd to the Vatican to see the Sistine Chapel and other sights. The chapel disappointed me some, not Michelangelo's paintings as much as the rest of the chapel. My expectations were too great for once; Raphael's chapel impressed me more. Michelangelo had a marvelous mind to conceive and carry out that ceiling, though. It is wonderful.

We drove home in pouring rain and spent the afternoon writing and sewing. Lucy has lost her pearl ring, I, a pair of gloves and Mother, her umbrella. I'm afraid we can't recommend the Flora Hotel.

Rome, Italy, Sunday, December 29, 1907

It was the Castel Sant'Angelo this morning, or Hadrian's tomb. It was a most interesting and historic old pile. The dungeons are dark and fiendish-looking.

On top is a statue of St. Michael by Bernini, really a peach. It was put there by some pope after a vision. in the courtyard we saw hundreds of catapults made of stone which were used to hurl missiles onto the enemy from above. In Hadrian's time the building was covered with marble, statues and trees, but now it's a mess, but an interesting and imposing one.

Rome, Italy, Sunday, December 30, 1907

We drove out to the catacombs of San Callisto this morning. A fine English monk was our escort in the catacombs; very witty. The catacombs cover thirty acres, and one million people are buried there, two hundred thousand of them martyrs, whose graves were marked by arches. Twelve square miles have been excavated four stories deep. When Christians were being persecuted, they worshipped in the catacombs, and many signs of the fish and anchor were to be seen. We all carried tapers.

Rome, Italy, December 31, 1907

The four of us left early this morning for the Porta Lorenzo train station where we met Professor Reynaud who was to be our guide to Tivoli and Hadrian's Villa. A fascinating gent he was, too.

Hadrian's Villa covers thirty-eight acres of land and is a monumental ruin. Owing to its having been looted so many times, there is absolutely nothing left of its one-time opulence.

However, Professor Reynaud "rebuilt" it for us, and it was fascinating. All of it was built in ten years with covered walks, libraries, a temple and fish pond, baths, bedrooms, fountains, art galleries, gymnasium, running track and every other thing that could help the old Roman boys have a good time. The gods sent them to earth, and they lived high to propitiate the gods.

Rome, Italy, January 1, 1908

It was New Year's Day, and it was actually bright and sunny. Lucy and I started off to do the churches the others visited on Christmas.

At the Church of Santa Maria in Aracoeli they have the Sacred Bambino, or Christ Child, which has the wonderful power of healing and is taken to people when they are ill. It is an ugly doll made of wood, and when we saw it, it was literally covered with jewels which were presents from those whom it had healed. Today there was a manger fitted up with God and all his angels, shepherds, animals, etc.

In the evening at the Grand Opera we heard "La Tosca," a blood and thunder affair but with beautiful singing and a fine orchestra. It was quite an Italian evening.

Rome, Italy, January 2, 1908

In the afternoon we all went out to shop. Mrs. Coulter and Mother went on another cameo fling. The only one I saw that I liked and wanted cost twenty-four dollars. Everything is mighty dear in Rome except brass and flowers. I bought Mother a bunch of violets and left them in an art store where I was too busy driving a bargain to remember them.

Rome, Italy, January 3, 1908

This morning we went off to buy gloves, veils, pins, buttons, ruching and other necessities for our coming trip. Then until four, Lucy and I darned furiously.

At four Elizabeth Johnstone and Miss Hauskamp took us to tea, and we feasted for an hour or more on pâté de fois gras sandwiches and delicious cakes and coffee. One spree of that kind a week I would find sufficient if I were to stay here any time.

Rome, Italy, Sunday, January 5, 1908

All were late getting up this morning. This Crapo was for once the first to breakfast.

We hunted for the Church of St. Cecilia but didn't find it. The dagos couldn't understand our French or Italian.

After lunch we drove off in state for the palace. The carpets were in awful taste throughout, but the tapestries and wall paintings were beautiful. From the palace we went to the stables and saw the hundred and thirty royal horses, and carriages without number. They were well-kept stables, and I was mad about the horses, mostly English- and Italian-bred.

Rome, Italy, January 6, 1908

We went to Cook's this morning, but our tickets for the Egypt trip had not come, and we were furious. There is something always going wrong at Cook's.

We took a car from there for the church called St. Cecilia in Trastevere, a very interesting spot where Saint Cecilia lived and suffered torture and death. Three blows to the neck were administered, yet she lived three days. Long after her death, her body was found wonderfully preserved.

We spent the afternoon sewing, packing and freezing. The weather has taken a turn colder. The people next door are three women, dead broke.

Rome—Naples, Italy, January 7, 1908

The ride to Naples was a beautiful one, almost equal to that from Florence to Rome, with gorgeous mountain scenery, snowcaps and rugged hills close at hand.

On our arrival at Naples it was dark, and such a time as we had getting away from the station. We were surrounded by mobs of men all expecting and demanding tips for merely being there. The noise and gesticulating were awful.

We finally pulled out, all baggage accounted for, and breathed once again. On the way to the convent the horse fell down, the harness broke, and so there was much delay. It was indeed a relief to finally get inside the convent walls where the sisters gave us a very friendly greeting, a good dinner, good beds and candles.

Diaries of Holly, Katie and Elizabeth Pierce, 2008

Florence—Rome, Italy, Tuesday, June 10, 2008

Katie

A scuffle when my sister found us seats in a less-crowded part of the train, but Mom insisted on sitting in her correct seat. There was fighting again with Dad as the intermediary. We sat separate from Mom and Dad. Pretty views of vineyards out the window streamed by. Unfortunately, I kept getting whiffs of shit down the aisle. From the bathroom? I hoped so.

WE START OUT with the usual arguments as to where we are to sit on the train. Never mind that we have reserved seats; the girls are bent on sitting in those they've discovered when getting on the wrong car. Never mind; Katie in particular seems in a nasty mood, and so sharing seats with Richard alone may be the most peaceful solution.

As we speed along from Florence to Rome, the countryside becomes hillier with vineyards set in intermittent plains. Increasingly we see classic rectangular, red-roofed Italian estates astride the rugged green hilltops.

The train line approaches Rome through the grubbier end of town, as such tracks are wont to do. But finally we find ourselves thrust out on the streets in front of the station.

Liz

We took a short train from Florence to Rome. Katie was angry as hell that the train smelled like poop, only to find as we walked out of the train station, strong, nasty scents of urine.

I was struck by this statue of a woman that was on a simple street corner a little ways from the hotel. She was just so casually lounging with one breast hanging out and water spilling out of her tilted urn.

AMAZINGLY, THE Hotel Welrome is just where it's supposed to be. We are booked for four in a room, potentially an explosive situation, but the room is tidy, comfortable and spacious enough. Even the bathroom is acceptably roomy.

A word about Marie, our landlady: we find we know when she is about, as there is a pervasive and cloying scent of lady's face powder permeating the stairwell. Maybe a little over five feet tall, she is round with delicate white hair flying about. Her face is heavily made up, although where the face powder comes in I'm not sure, as her face is quite shiny and pale, a contrast to her bright red lipstick. But she is kind, helpful, has a soft, little voice and speaks admirable English which she uses to tell us everything we could possibly want to know about the city. I suspect she has tutored herself through CNN, as she has the TV (with earphones) on all the time.

Since plenty of the day is left, Liz, Richard and I decide to hit some of the sights. Katie chooses to stay behind, in a mood matching the train's stinky bathroom. Unpleasant odors seem to be her nemesis.

Katie

When they talked about hurrying to see the Sistine Chapel today before it closed, I started to feel overwhelmed and tired of being with the family. I'm tired of my sister's overwhelming anxiety and constant singing, tired of my Dad's always having to go somewhere way ahead of time, the hurrying, and Mom's inflexible, controlling nature. I am tired of the family, period. I love each one so much I would give my life for theirs, but right now I need time to myself.

I went out to buy my *O.K.!* magazine with the article about Angelina and Brad's new twins. When I got back to the hotel, the lady at the front desk asked why I wasn't going with the others. It was at that point the water works started again, and I trudged up to the room with tears in my eyes. I cried and cried for about twenty minutes before deciding to finally take a Xanax. I want to feel my feelings, but I am feeling exhausted by everything. I am ready to go home! I'm not going to meet the family anywhere either. I have this time to myself as the Xanax kicks in. Going to read *O.K.!* magazine and forget my upset.

Read, washed some clothes, took a shower and felt so much better. I just have to remember what *I* want to do, which is what I'm doing today: resting.

WE WILL HAVE TO take the underground to get to St. Peter's, so we start off, but nearby we are caught up short in the Piazza della Repubblica. Wow, our first Roman fountain, the Fontana delle Naiadi! The center statue grouping is a scramble of limbs and fins, hard to make out, but three pretty maidens perch around the edge of the fountain continually bathed by showers of water. After a day of herculean statues, this one will be remembered as pretty humdrum, but right now it looks pretty darned important. Snap! Snap! We take our requisite photos.

Liz on the metro

The metro with its orange plastic seats is clean and debris-free and is unique for its small TVs suspended overhead warning passengers of pickpockets and other potential dangers. "POF!" says a cartoon message balloon, there goes your wallet, over and over until we reach our stop.

As it is, the exit is around to the side of the piazza, and so we walk, noticing as we do the long line of people waiting for entrance to the Vatican museums and the Sistine Chapel; we'll have to get here early tomorrow if we're going to be admitted at a decent hour.

The vast sweep of the piazza finally comes into view, and I find it hard to imagine it packed wall to wall with Catholic devotees. So much space, so many pillars and statues, lintels and porticos! I can't think of many other spaces that wouldn't be humbled in size by this one. Maybe Red Square? or certainly Tiananmen Square?

Liz

Katie stayed in to recuperate while Mom, Dad and I went out. We took the metro to the Vatican and St. Peter's Church. I did think the endless lines of statues atop the columned walkways to be kick-ass. Exquisite detail; I was delighted by that.

THERE MUST BE some kind of zoning laws, as no trinket stands are on the piazza's sacred grounds; instead, they line the sidewalks alongside the plaza and across the street. Oh dear, Catholic trinkets—but wait: what's this? A 2009 *Calendario Romano* with a photo portrait of a cute priest on the front. Well, nothing wrong with getting your calendar well ahead of time. It's a pretty nice one, too; a full page of "Notes About The Vatican" is translated into different languages in five more pages. But shoot, it's one of those with the numbers running along the bottom, allowing the page to be taken up by portraits of . . . portraits of . . . twelve attractive, young priests—in fact, twelve attractive, young, *gay*-looking priests.

Oh my. I have to have one of these, plus one for my friend Connie who I know will appreciate the campiness of this spoof. Fortunately, there are two left, and I snap them up. What a find! Little do I know that I'm not the only one who has made a find.

Katie

I actually found a couple staying here who had a business card for Tango Core Tattoo Shop literally right around the corner from the hotel. They gave it a good, clean rating. I talked to the tattoo artist, but he didn't speak English, so I came back and drew an elaborate diagram showing what I wanted done to my tattoo.

ON TO THE PANTHEON, as it's in the general direction of our hotel. It's impossible to keep track of what we are seeing as we walk along; there is so much, and it is all so elaborate. The Romans seem to be obsessed with fountains full of stuff: gods, of course, and naked maidens and rearing horses and wrestling men and there's one with guys blowing horns. The *Rough Guide* does its best to locate and describe these, but its map of Central Rome is of capillaries overlaid with regular- and bold-fonted names and abbreviations, dots denoting hotels and restaurants and adobe-colored chunks of important buildings. It's a valiant effort, but at this point we probably use the sun just as much to sense the correct direction.

Along the Tiber we trudge past the Castel Sant' Angelo, originally built by Hadrian for use as his eventual mausoleum but later converted by the Vatican into its own fortress in times of siege. On the map it looks square, but that's just its base; above that it looks like a huge and impressive round layer cake decorated with scalloped pipings of frosting.

Still following our noses, we skirt along the river until we cross at the Pont Umberto I and dive into an ochre maze of undistinguished streets and alleys. We happen across an obelisk that is perched on the back of a dear little elephant, the solemn meaning of which escapes us, but the elephant itself is a delight.

Right beyond the little pachyderm, buildings back off, opening a large space for the Pantheon. We know we've found it because of its magnificent dome and the crowds of gawkers. Nearby, a sandwich-board sign declares, *"Attenzione! Set Cinematografico"* accompanied by a bunch of little yellow warning triangles and slashed circles showing the various ways one may be electrocuted, hit on the head by falling or moving equipment, or blown up by inadvertently flicking a cigarette in the wrong direction. They're trying to film here? Amidst this mess of tourists? It would be interesting to hang out and watch how exactly they plan to do this, but we move on to the Pantheon.

The interior of this monument is spectacular, with multiple Corinthian-capitaled columns and the floor a geometrical design of multi-colored marbles. Raphael's tomb is here, although which it is among the number of richly designed chapels is hard to tell.

Liz

Although the outside of the Pantheon didn't exactly sweep me off my feet, the inside was the best thing I'd seen all day—truly stunning. The building had an extremely difficult dome roofing, which the artist designed so that the Pantheon could hold a perfect sphere inside. What a feat! The ceiling was lovely with a circular hole right in the center which allowed an orb of light to travel around the inside of the roof as the sun moved. Lush, richly-colored paintings and carefully constructed sculptures adorned the walls and porticos above a lovely, intricately-designed marble floor. I thoroughly enjoyed myself.

IT'S BEEN A LONG day, and once we leave the Pantheon and begin the search for our hotel, we are hot and exhausted. The rest of the day is a blur, with each doing his or her own thing. I take a walk after dinner and end up getting lost.

Liz

I went back to the hotel to find it was ten o'clock, and Mother had not yet returned. Dad was in his underwear and already in bed but was frightened and got up and dressed to go search for her. Of course just as he was leaving, Mom walked in and all the family was upset with her. As usual, Mom didn't see what was wrong and claimed we were calling her stupid for getting lost—well, she was only just around the corner after all, she maintained. Everything is always unfair to her; she can't see and doesn't think about how worried we are about her. Instead she only sees our fear and upset as an attack on her.

Rome, Italy, Wednesday, June 11, 2008

Katie

More jack-hammering.

TODAY OUR LANDLADY is kind enough to call the Vatican to see if it would even be open, as the Pope and Bush plan to meet somewhere along the line. Perhaps a little tennis match on the Pope's private court which we saw out the window?

Rome: more drama and *sturm und drang*. While Richard and I leave to see the Vatican at 8:30 A.M., the girls go to have Katie's star tattoo on her wrist altered. It was a blotchy job from the start and is a regrettable reminder of her episode with a hideous ex-boyfriend in Oregon. She wants to make the outlines crisper and the center purple, the idea of which she makes clear with a little graphical note for the tattoo artist.

What she doesn't anticipate is that the artist is much more of a perfectionist than the previous person, and the repeated retracing of the outlines makes Katie feel faint, and she has to be refreshed with a backrub and water before continuing. The rest of the day her wrist is purple-y and painful and wrapped in Saran wrap for a reason I'm not quite sure of, except that it keeps the dye from smearing on the sheets and the patch from crusting over.

Katie

Today ended up being the tattoo day. My sister and I got up at nine to get breakfast and be at the Tango Core tattoo place by ten A.M. We waited until the skinny Italian guy came on his motorbike to open the shop. We admired the piercing adornments in the window (I later bought a leopard-patterned plastic tongue stud) until he was ready for me and my detailed Italian diagram. He said it was really good and clear.

At the start of the tattooing I was fine, but soon I felt faint, and I had to stop. A nice man who spoke a little English rubbed my shoulders and put water on my face and throat while I laid down. Then I took a Xanax so I wouldn't care so much. The artist whose name I didn't catch—he only spoke Italian—I could tell was a perfectionist. He carefully went over the black outline.

Once the initial faint feeling was over, helped by a gulp of water with sugar, I was able to go on and finish with the sound of heavy metal in the background. "Wipe these tears from my eyes!" he screamed. Finally it was done, and I was so happy! It was worth the sixty euros cash! The ex is removed forever!

Liz

Katie almost wanted to stop, but I convinced her to see it through, and she later thanked me profusely for it. Now the ex-boyfriend is erased forever. I can't wait to show the videotape to Mom and Dad and shock their pants off because they've never seen a tattoo being inked before.

MEANWHILE, WITH NO breakfast or Richard's necessary coffee hit, he and I make it to the Vatican in good time and don't have to wait in line. We squeeze in before the masses of tours get started and make a beeline for the Sistine Chapel, not stopping to check out the bounty of loot lining the endless corridors. The chapel is full but not shoulder to shoulder with an Italian guard who periodically yells out for everyone to shut up— *"Silenzio!"* He is a tough customer. One is not supposed to take pictures in the chapel, but people are doing it none the less when the guards seem to have their backs turned. A guard caught me once but simply told me to turn my camera off. Strangely, the one terrific photo of the ceiling seems to have vanished from my card.

The Etruscan museum is really the section I want to see. If I were an archaeologist, I'd be out there researching the Etruscans. Their black pottery with its delicately inscribed figures in a terracotta red touch me in a way I can't explain. Horses with stick-slender legs, birds, a parade of tiny hedgehogs marching around the diameter of a bowl—they seem to display much of a sense of both the commonplace and universal that I feel is lacking in the heroic sculptures and friezes of the Greeks and Romans. It is hard for Richard to drag me out. Naturally, the museum bookshop has no little volume on the Etruscans but truckloads on the Pope, plus all sorts of Christian paraphernalia.

Richard is so worried about meeting the girls at the Spanish Steps that we take a taxi, then cool our heels until they arrive.

Then and Now
Scala della Trinita dei Monti, **or the Spanish Steps**

Liz

We walked on to the Trevi Fountain, which I particularly enjoyed. It was quite massive and stunning, yet I found the water soothing despite the hoards of people around. The statues were of men reining in graceful horses which had mermaid tails and wings. I liked that a lot. Underneath them were great craggy juts of raw, white stone. We all made a wish and threw a coin into the fountain.

Katie

We took a taxi to the Forum and the Coliseum. The Forum had some beautiful pink poppies, ruins and such. Dad and I moved on to the Coliseum and walked up so many steps to get to the top and see over the large arena. When we were done, we went across the street to have a too-expensive Schweppes lemonade and double espresso.

SO WE MOVE ON to the Forum. Here is where the trouble begins.

Katie

At the Forum, Mom wandered off again in search of her postcard pictures and left us in the lurch. Dad bought tickets to get inside, but we couldn't give her hers. There was more anger from all of us at her selfish behavior.

I THINK THERE is growing resentment on the girls' part with my determination to find these postcards sites, but they have to realize that this is the basic reason for the journey itself; they wouldn't be here if it weren't for Ruth and her diary. More and more, though, they seem to be appreciating her as a person, reading aloud bits that amuse them as we travel along.

I can see that to get one particular postcard shot I am going to have to walk all the way around to the other side of the site. With the Coliseum right down the avenue, I tell everyone to go on ahead and that I'll catch them there, but Richard insists on the girls and himself waiting.

Bad choice. The walk is long, and once I find my vantage point, I manage to drop the sheaf of Ruth pictures through the iron grating and down into the archaeological site! Much too far away to reach—oh dear. This means backtracking until I find some young archaeologists digging near the fence, and after much pantomiming to a cute young guy in a hardhat, he follows me along the fence until we come upon the papers blown up against a chunk of marble column. He kindly hands me my pics and listens indulgently to my broken explanation until he politely informs me that he has to get back to work.

But by the time I get back to where everyone is supposedly waiting, only Liz is there, livid that I have taken so much time and that she has been sent back to give me my ticket, which she does, shoving it in my direction and yelling at me that we were to meet here at 4:30. Oops—where was "here?" Apparently she meant literally right there, and not in the Coliseum as I had supposed, being handed a ticket to that latter spot. She then stomps off to the Forum, leaving me alone.

Oh well, off to the Coliseum, where I spend the next hour or so looking for Richard and straining to hear his signature whistle. No luck. I look and look while trying to appreciate the glories of this giant stone bowl.

Liz

I went into the ruins of the Forum myself and had an absolutely lovely time, one of the best to date. It was a calm, slightly breezy day, and the ruins were stretched out across much space, and all varieties of wild flowers grew in between them. I felt utterly relaxed and allowed myself to be drawn towards whatever moved me. I ended up spending almost all of my time there, exploring old pillars and moldings on columns, and ancient porticos and arches. I wandered into the Palatine where lovely trees grew, and stumps and brick outlines of old houses and old lives remained. You could see the dome of the Vatican from one vantage point.

In the end, I could have been happy spending the whole day there. I enjoyed being by myself as well.

Katie

We came back to the Forum to wait for my sister and Mom, and that's when things got hairy. My sister got back fifteen minutes late with her sweatshirt over her face. I had to guide her to sit down and then led her like a blind person for twenty minutes until we found a taxi that wasn't full.

Liz

After a while Mom was still a no-show, and Dad told us to take a taxi back to the hotel. It took forever to find one, but finally I was safe in a taxi and trundled home. All was well—until we arrived at the hotel and were alarmed to find Mom already there! But how? And why would she leave without us? Again?

STILL NOT FINDING anyone, I finally decide the only thing to do is to follow the Boy Scout rule: if lost, stay in one spot, and for me that is the hotel. Back I go via the wonderful metro and only getting a little lost on my way back to the hotel. I finally discover that our street is L-shaped, which would have been helpful visually to know when I was lost the night before.

Sitting alone in the hotel, I hear the skies filled with the chatter of copter blades as our area, close to the ambassadorial district, is being "covered" for the arrival of—George Bush. Damn! I call Lyn Terry, Nancy's friend here in Rome where her husband is working in some nonprofit capacity for the Catholic church, and she said all public transportation in the area is shut down. Trust Bush to make life for his captive citizenry difficult to the end.

Eventually everyone arrives back with my husband last.

Katie

We were very upset she had come home without us. She told us she had lost her pictures and then that she didn't understand where we had to meet. My sister was upset enough for the both of us, and while we were waiting Dad and I had a nice conversation about Zen, so I felt able to let go of my anger since I was most concerned about Dad's feelings since he always gets worried when Mom disappears. Figured it was between Mom and Dad to talk out.

The Zen talk helped a lot. It's either "yes" or "no yes," not bad and good. Thoughts aren't "bad." Helped me allow my sister to be angry for us both.

Liz

Mom said the first time she was late, I gave her no chance to explain how she had dropped her postcard pictures into the Forum and had to get someone inside to blah blah blah. She was right that I gave her no chance to explain, but next time I'll either pin the instructions to her shirt or tattoo them onto her damn forehead. Really, it's remarkable how she manages to separate herself from the rest of us so often.

Anyway, I was still upset and waiting for Dad. Finally, thank God, he came back, and, as usual, was Zen and ready to forgive. I was not, and remained silent and sullen at her uncaring. Even if she couldn't find us, I couldn't understand how she could bring herself to leave without us; I couldn't imagine I ever would.

It is interesting that after my explanation regarding the lost postcard papers and the fact that I missed the Forum altogether, Liz is the only one to still hold my disappearance against me.

Liz

She was unsympathetic to our anger, and unwilling to take any blame; she said when I said "Here," she thought I meant the Coliseum. Bizarre, and as a result I was enraged, absolutely spitting fire to know Dad was still there waiting for her. But she was talking casually and all chipper about her day; meanwhile I am smashing doors and such at her nonchalance.

Later on I felt very bad because she didn't understand that she could go into the Forum, as the ticket only had a picture of the Coliseum on it.

Katie

Forgot to mention the U.S. president is in Rome, and the local restaurant owner shakes his fist at Bush and his squadron of loud helicopters flying overhead.

Liz

All evening the sound of helicopters thumping overhead struck the air; it turned out it was Bush's brigade on their farewell tour. Seems as if I can't get rid of the bastard even when I'm out of the country.

Tomorrow we are leaving for Naples, which I am dreading because apparently the trash men are on strike and there are piles of trash everywhere.

Unfortunately, my eyes are too weary to continue writing, though there is plenty more to say. I probably will have plenty of time to finish tomorrow when I'm secluded in my room after several mental breakdowns in Naples. Har-har.

Italy: Naples

Diary of Ruth K. Crapo, 1907-1908

Naples, Italy, January 8, 1908

There's one American inside the convent besides ourselves: from Boston, a regular buzzer, but nice, or means to be. Besides us there are foreign nobility: several Italian countesses, marquises and a nice little baroness. All have the best rooms and think but little of Americans. We like the Portuguese better.

After breakfast we went out and got our bearings here and are really quite fascinated with Naples except for its dirt and noise, which is even worse than dear old Florence.

Naples, Italy, January 9, 1908

It poured all last night, and we were afraid we'd not be able to go on our drive today, but after being assured of a fine day by Sister Marie Angela and our eager driver, we started out. In the mountains, though, we were in a pouring rain. We were game, however, and kept on.

I didn't get out at the grotto where they formerly threw in dogs and then hauled them out to show tourists the effects of sulphur. Stopped at Solfatara and saw the crater of the volcano, still busy in spots. We walked on a formation that resounded with our footsteps and was springy under our feet—quite alarming.

Naples, Italy, January 10, 1908

In the afternoon the sun came out, and the family all left me at home to take care of my game leg while they spooked around in the shops again (Mother brought back five cameos). We had mail from home and a newspaper to read, so I passed a pleasant afternoon except for trouble with my leg. It keeps me awake nights.

Naples, Italy, January 11, 1908

We had an early start for Pompeii this morning. On arriving, we got a guide to show us the sights. Pompeii was founded in 600 B.C. It was destroyed twice, once by earthquake, then by eruption in 65 A.D, and remained buried in ash for eighteen hundred years. We saw temples, baths, private houses, shops, beautiful frescoes, streets still with ruts from chariot wheels, wells, ovens, etc. as well as a museum with the bodies of victims found in the ruins and other interesting things like bread found in ovens, a pig in a stew pan, skeletons of dogs, cats, mice, etc.—a really wonderful time.

After our interesting stay of two and a half hours we took a carriage drive to a town nearby where the last eruption by Vesuvius twenty months ago worked its destruction, killing two hundred people and destroying much property. Two distinct streams came down, and the lava beds were still hot and smoking. It was a wonderful and terrible sight.

Naples, Italy, Sunday, January 12, 1908

It was cold as Greenland this morning with severe wind.

In the afternoon we visited the famous aquarium, and it was well worth seeing. We saw many fish and growths of the sea that I had never seen before, monstrous lobsters and crabs, eel and water snakes too hideous to be described. There were marvelous jellyfish in the process of growth, sea anemones, sea horses, octopus, coral formations, and an electric eel that gave me a shock when I pressed him up by the middle. No one else would be shocked.

Diaries of Holly, Katie and Elizabeth Pierce, 2008

Rome—Naples, Italy, Thursday, June 12, 2008

WE ARE PULLING out of the Rome train station in a light rain, and already there is a disagreement. The girls get onto the wrong coach and find four seats together, disregarding the fact that we have reserved seats in this coach.

So now they are back in the next coach, pouting. Liz comes up to get the "bible," our tour itinerary, and refuses to speak. Everyone around us is quiet as she yanks out the folder and flounces out, then the people around us who can speak English burst into laughter. Wearing a plaid sport shirt and shorts, a silver-haired gentleman named Charles from Hyderabad, India, who is now working in Texas, is chatting with Richard. He has a 24-year-old daughter who he says also has a bit of an attitude, but he is beginning to see the light at the end of the tunnel, and he holds up his thumb and finger in a little circle to indicate the tiny exit in the distance.

Liz

On the train I noticed two Italian soldiers sitting across from us. One would look at me, then turn to his buddy and say something in Italian, and they would both laugh. This continued on, and I noticed a lady next to me laughing as well, but trying to contain it. I was convinced they were saying something nasty, but Katie said they were flirting with me. I gave him nasty looks to try and make him stop.

I felt terribly embarrassed and upset, but ultimately found Katie to be right when we got off at the stop, because I saw his buddy going up the stairs and then discovered the flirtatious one was directly behind me on the escalator. He tried to get my number when we got off, but he only spoke Italian, and I flipped him off. So strange, all of it!

UNFORTUNATELY, ALL of the warnings about the trash strike in Naples are right. As we pull our suitcases along the cracked sidewalks on the way to the Hotel Rebecchino, we pass dumpsters on corners overflowing with trash, some bagged, some just heaped. At least it is *tidy* trash in a way; aside from the hills of garbage surrounding the dumpsters, the streets themselves seem relatively clean. I know it is making the girls nervous, but we make it to the hotel without any breakdowns.

The hotel room is lovely, smartly wallpapered in blues and beige and furnished with pieces that don't look as if they are ready for the thrift shop.

Katie

I think Mom did a good job of picking the *cleanest* hotel in the city.

Liz

Napoli is nothing but a mess to me. The city is dirty everywhere and causes nothing but trouble. It has very few redeeming qualities in my opinion.

Finally, upon reaching the hotel I was slightly calmed by the cool, clean marble interior, but then even more disturbed by seeing the room itself held only two twin beds. They said they would drag two more in! It would not have been so bad if they were already there, but I felt suddenly claustrophobic and as if I had no space to call my own and became quite frantic. Mom seriously asked if I wanted to fly home, and I told her I just wanted my own space!

Finally, after a little time as I began to calm down and start planning space for the other beds, Dad returned to say he'd gotten another room, but quite an expensive one. Now I was really upset and felt I had caused endless trouble. I was feeling very overwhelmed. Katie said she was glad I made a fuss and said she desperately needed her own space as well.

BY THE TIME WE are settled in, it is well into the afternoon. Pompeii is for tomorrow, so we set off for the Naples Aquarium today. Here is where Ruth famously proved her pluck by grabbing hold of the electric eel when no one else would, so it's a definite landmark on this trip. But when we reach its supposed location, while there is a huge, scaffold-encrusted, two-story stone building, the place seems surprisingly deserted.

Well, too bad; this is the aquarium, and it is closed for renovations. Embedded in the pavement in front of the entrance is a metal marker with the date 1905. So if Ruth visited in 1907, it must have been brand-spanking new. I guess a hundred years puts it in line for sprucing up.

We find a little entrance that leads into a foyer papered with photos and diagrams illustrating renovation plans. Beyond that is a small gallery with some rather nice paintings of sea creatures. But the eel! That's what we're here for.

Luck is on our side here: we find a gentleman who directs us into a small section still open. Inside it looks dank and moldering. Deep green tanks hold barely-lit denizens of the sea, including some rather repellant giant eels (not the kind Ruth handled, I hope), sea turtles and sea horses. But over in one corner is a well-lit, waist-high pool open for visitors to touch the starfish, sea anemones and other tidal creatures. We ask the

English-speaking gentleman about the electric eel, explaining the story to him, and he tells us the eel was indeed in this tank up until three years ago. I'm not clear whether it would have been the same eel—I doubt eels live to a hundred years—but rats! A hundred years of eels, and we miss it by three.

Liz

The only good part of the day came next when we went to the old aquarium that Ruth and Lucy went to. It was really just a single rectangular room with another rectangle within, but ultimately I quite enjoyed it. It was cool and dark, and it had all the old brick moldings and columns still there from Ruth's time. Some interesting creatures kept there, indeed: barnacles, sea urchins and big, spiny lobsters with huge antenna branching out. So many crammed together it looked quite queer.

I felt sorry for the two old sea turtles. One of them had maybe only a ten foot by ten foot space to swim around in, and it had probably been there its whole life. Both of them must have been nearly a hundred years old. I had to wonder if they were around when Ruth came. Beautiful majestic creatures, the way they swam and floated. The aquarium personnel wouldn't let the two together and instead had them separated by a wire mesh screen. They would both spend time just staring at each other through the wire. One was eating a little bit of red moss off the wall.

The next tank had hoards of giant eels in them, just like the nasty ones in "The Little Mermaid." They were very large, I mean probably four or five feet long at least, and so many were crammed into this tiny space they curled and twirled around one another. I'm not easily put off, but they really were quite frightful and terrible, although they did have the most striking and colorful patterns on them. But they would bite and fight with one another and were really quite vicious! They had little hooked mouths that made them nasty-looking.

The aquarium had a rather sick and queer side "museo" where they had quite a collection of sea creatures preserved in formaldehyde. Rather disturbing really; some I preferred not to look at. There were dead slimy eels, small dead sharks and gross baby shark embryos literally coming out of a cut-open womb, also a middle-sized dolphin and a baby dolphin with the umbilical cord still on. All were in foul-looking jars and a bit unnerving and frightening.

As we walked back to the metro station it started to rain, and we took cover under a little store's overhang. There was the sweetest old black and white dog lying out front, and Katie and I spent much time sitting and giving him attention. The shopkeeper was quite friendly but didn't speak any English, so we were bound to gestures and smiles. Time with the dog really relaxed us and was so pleasant. Not knowing his name, we simply referred to him/her as "Ultimo," as we found it a fitting description.

When the rain let up we had to step off, so I gave him our family card, and the shopkeeper seemed surprised and pleased. Turning around, we found his sweet old dog had started to trundle after Katie, but he calmly returned as the man called to him. How darn sweet; it completely warmed my heart to the brim.

IN NAPLES WE go to dinner at the Prince Umberto, close by our hotel and recommended by the hotel as a good place to eat. It certainly is full of people, all crammed into a teeny space. There is the table of eight men who you would swear were right out of "The Sopranos." And then there is the very beautiful young waiter who can speak broken English, but apparently not quite as well as we think and as he presents himself. The first offense is when Liz complimented him on his earring and told Katie to show him her tongue stud. He replied, "I don't like it." Good job, guy; isn't the customer always supposed to be right?

Then Katie orders a noodle dish which is supposed to be with shrimp and artichokes. Well, as the waiter put it, artichokes are "finished," but she can have asparagus with it instead of the 'chokes. So she decides on this.

Time drifts on, and we have our shared shrimp cocktail appetizer, the shrimp of medium size in mayonnaise and ketchup—hardly to write home about. Then comes the dinner, and here is Katie's dish: a bed of noodles with two six-inch-plus prawns with all their feelers and legs and little beaks, and instead of asparagus, the noodles have teeny circles of miserable-looking zucchini sprinkled about.

Katie

We went to get dinner finally, and I almost cried when the crustaceans came out in whole form. The giant shrimp still had eyes, and there was no asparagus, and I couldn't just order one glass of wine, I had to order the equivalent of three-plus glasses.

The waiter lied to me about everything. He didn't like my tongue-piercing either. The entirety of it all was overwhelming. Even seeing the guy collecting the fresh clams out of the tank for someone's dinner made me want to cry.

THE LOOK ON Katie's face: aghast, then flushed and tearing up. This was not at all what she expected, much less ordered. So that sets the tenor of the dinner. Suddenly Liz is in her element, sending the offensive plate back to a puzzled waiter. Richard and I eat our undistinguished pizza while Liz shares her pasta with tomatoes with Katie. Meanwhile, Katie is getting more and more upset about the rejected dinner while Liz plans her revenge on the waiter. Asparagus indeed!

Liz
Her jaw just dropped; she looked absolutely terrified and quite at her wits' end. I wanted to laugh at the absurdity, but felt too bad for her, as her eyes were already watering up. Crisis control! We sent the dish back, and she split my tasty pasta with me, and we were both full.

YEARS LATER WE finally get the check, and sure enough, the rejected plate of food is on it. I have meanwhile not been discouraging Katie from letting a few tears drop if necessary, as I know a pretty young woman crying can settle things pretty quickly. Liz, however, is acting the vengeful master of the situation, calling the waiter over and telling him we would not pay for the uneaten dish—we did not order this! The waiter snatches back the bill, then returns with the offending charge removed.

Liz
We found that they had charged us for the shrimp plate! It took me about two seconds to grab someone and tell them to take it off, which they did. The family seemed quite impressed by my directness.

PERSONALLY, I THINK this was the highlight of the trip for Liz so far.

Naples and Pompeii, Italy, Friday, June 13, 2008

Katie
More jack-hammering, I think.

Only thing I care to see is Pompeii, if that. I don't care much for dead people.

OUR VISIT TODAY to Pompeii is wonderful. We take the Circumventia train, about a half-hour from Naples. The day can't be more beautiful, with a cool ocean breeze and a warm, gentle sun. I am most surprised by the greenery and the density of the dead city; somehow I have imagined Pompeii as being flat, hot and an ashy white with no growing thing. I should have realized that time has passed, and life springs back. It is interesting to see how much of the site is under active excavation and reconstruction, with areas cordoned off with scaffolds and netting. Still, there is more than enough to see, and we certainly don't see it all.

It turns out the most valuable and delicate of treasures have been taken to the National Archaeological Museum back in Naples.

Liz

Inside the gates I was disappointed to find all the artifacts had been removed to a museum and only the ruins of the walls remained. Where were the bodies? I whined. We spent all day in the sun trekking these ancient streets and seeing bits of paintings on the walls and some leftover mosaics, but overall, it wasn't terribly exciting. I wanted to see the human remains! Nonetheless, the weather was very fine, and the little bits of delicate artwork you did stumble upon were like little mysteries waiting to be found.

There *were* some archeological trays with bones peeking out of the solidified dirt in which they were ensconced. This was by far the most interesting part to me. Thanks to my osteology class, I could tell a number of things just by looking at the few remains I could see.

What surprised me most was that the people were quite small in stature. It looked as if they averaged around five feet, but other signs indicated this was not due to ill health. Of the three crania I saw with teeth in them, they had all of their teeth! I found this surprising and quite impressive. You could tell their diet was heavy in grit as the teeth were uniformly worn down to a smooth, plain surface. The ridges on the long bones also suggested that they were very muscular. Overall, it was really quite fascinating.

As I left the remains, several workers in a pit below me called out and blew me kisses. Funny how forward the men are here!

Katie

We went to Pompeii where we were disappointed to find only a few bodies curled in the throes of agony. Not as many ruined remains as we had hoped to find.

One of the tour guides saw me eating a focaccia, mushroom and pepperoni lunch and told me that if I ate like that I would get fat. I told him to shut up. I'm not sure if he wanted me fatter or if he was just being rude.

I saw many stray dogs which were very sweet, but I felt sad for them. The ruins also evoked a sad feeling, especially in the moments when there was no one around, and it was peaceful. I loved the fluffy white clouds and the weeds growing tall on the walls.

AFTER A COUPLE OF hours, Katie has had enough. I find she has no interest in archaeological digs. So we ride back to Naples, and Katie goes back to the hotel.

Katie

The hotel guys brought in a TV to the sitting room for the soccer game where I watched the game with F. and the front desk/bar man. Watching the pre-game with F., he attempted to tell me what was going on. They appreciated my cheers and boos: cheer for Italia and boo Romania.

BRAVELY ENOUGH, Liz is determined to see the museum despite the difficulties raised by her potential anxiety attacks, and so we take the metro to the stop closest to the museum. It still entails passage through a narrow little park over to the other metro station, which only is a problem for her on the way back.

What do we see in the museum? I must have photographed half the stuff in there: delicate blue- and green-tinted glasswork, mosaics created with stones the size of pinheads, black, foreboding-looking statues with staring white glass or ivory eyes, huge terracotta and black pottery incised with delicately drawn images of warriors and goddesses, fish and shells.

Liz

There were some originals of famous artwork even I recognized. They had the famous mosaic of a man and his wife from Pompeii. It was much smaller than I expected, but I guess it's always been blown up when I've seen it.

BUT WE SEE NO human Pompeian remains; the two in dusty cases back at the site were the only ones we saw. An American student tells me she thought the figures had been shipped off to somewhere else, but has no idea where. Oh well, the teeth-clenched agony on the face of the one body at the site was enough for me.

Despite her initial bravery, getting Liz back to the hotel is dicey. She takes a Xanax, and we wait for it to kick in as we sit on the museum steps being deafened by the Napoli rush-hour traffic. We have finally persuaded her that going back by metro would get us to our hotel faster than by taxi, as the traffic with its fruitless, angry horn-honking and scooters roaring along the sidewalks was in gridlock. So after I have kicked all visible trash off the museum platform, we start on our way, with me holding her by the elbow and encouraging her to *keep looking up*. She takes matters into her own hands once we reach the little park, as she takes off running, head in the air, arms waving. I won't say what she looked like, but it did cause some head-turning by others in her path.

Once we hit the pavement again, I take her by the arm and we talk about what there is to see above ground-level. And she makes it past the tables and stalls of belts and converters and cell phones, hats and T-shirts and people of all colors hawking their wares (there are more black Africans here in Naples than farther north, even mothers with babies wrapped on their backs). I am proud of her. And then, after a wait, we go to the Hotel Cavour for the fixed price dinner.

Another ruined meal. We enter the restaurant where the owner ushers us in with a flourish as the first customers of the evening (naturally). He is very elegant in his gray silk suit, gold tie, bald head and an unfortunate wen right on the tip of his nose. We are in a convivial mood, which means that Liz's voice is booming in its usual fashion. At one point the owner comes over to tell her to quiet down, and then later, when the restaurant is filled with customers, he comes over and, leaning over Katie's shoulder, tells Liz to "shut up her face."

Liz

We had the "meal de jour," which included several courses. I was talking a bit and was greatly offended when the restaurant head honcho came up to me and put a finger to his lips and told me to "shut up my face." I don't think he really knew how offensive what he was saying was, he just knew I was loud (earlier he had told me to stop talking and start eating), but it put me in a foul mood nonetheless. Why would he have the nerve to tell a paying customer what to do in this way?

OUCH. IT IS downhill from here. I know he was just trying to be funny, as he calls Richard "Omar Sharif" and Katie "Julia" as in "Roberts," but this is no consolation to Liz with her face righteously squinched into a terrible pout, and after picking at her meatloaf, she leaves to walk back to the hotel. "Where is Sharon?" (as in Sharon Stone) the owner queries dramatically when he sees that her seat is empty. Nice try.

Italy: Sicily

Diary of Ruth K. Crapo, 1907-1908

Naples—Sorrento, Italy, January 13, 1908

We started off bright and early this morning for Cava, but when we arrived at the railway station, we found we were an hour and a half too early for our train. That shows how one can depend on Cook's.

At Cava we had lunch and then started by carriage for Sorrento. I never dreamed of such scenery as we passed through: high, towering mountains on one side and the water sparkling on the other, adorable little villages straight up the mountainsides and in the deep ravines, great rocks projecting into the water.

Our drive ended in the most gorgeous moonlight, stars overhead fairly alive with delight at the adumbration they were receiving and inspiring. At Sorrento we went to the Hotel Tramontano and have rooms overleaning the sea, a gorgeous outlook, fine beds and a little heat—or is it my imagination?

Sorrento, Italy, January 14, 1908

After a walk through the orange groves around the hotel where I picked my first orange from the trees, we took the boat for Cápri and the Blue Grotto. We had lunch at Cápri in a little restaurant over the water where we sat out on the balcony.

In the evening some Italian peasants danced the tarantella for us and sang Italian songs. They were most picturesque in their gay costumes playing their inlaid mandolins and castanets. I bought "O Sole Mio" on the boat today but lost it in the excitement of getting off the boat. Two more francs gone, a mere drop in the bucket.

Sorrento, Italy, January 15, 1908

We all loved our beds pretty much this morning and slept late. After breakfast we took a carriage and drove to Castellammare, a most attractive fishing village where we took the train for Naples. We certainly saw the real life of the Italian peasants en route. They sure do love the macaroni, and we saw any quantity of it drying in the sun in the most unattractive spots. However, I can still eat and relish it. My leg has been off on another bat, and I'm feeling anything but spry tonight. I wonder if I'll ever get rid of the pain and bandages again.

Sorrento—Naples, Italy, January 16, 1908

It was packing and Cook's this morning, and we are about ready to set sail for Sicily, the land of mythology. The boats are said to be bad, and we are all prepared to be seasick. After supper we sallied to the dreaded steamer, a long drive. At the wharf we had much fuss with the *facchini* [porters] and our bags. They are regular land pirates. The boat is a new one and seemingly comfortable. Mother, Lucy and I have state rooms together with two port holes, so we ought to have plenty of fresh air. The stewardess assures us that we will have smooth sailing. Miss Blaine is in a room by herself.

Palermo, Sicily, January 17, 1908

No one was seasick at all. We enjoyed the sunrise as we came into the bay at Palermo. We went to the Pension Swiss on Miss Blaine's friend's say-so, but found it rather dismal and very cold. Cheer up, Ruthie.

After breakfast we sauntered forth to see the town. Along the shore Palermo is very pretty; otherwise, we find it pretty unattractive. The fancy Sicilian carts were very picturesque with wonderful biblical and historical scenes depicted on their sides in vivid colors. The harnesses were also very elaborate and the donkeys, mere atoms.

Palermo, Sicily, January 18, 1908

Went "churching" this morning. We then visited the ruins of the church of San Giovanni, an old Moorish edifice with its rounded cupolas and old cloisters entirely overrun with vines and flowers. The custodian was an old veteran who had fought with Garibaldi and was wounded. He liked all Americans: it was *"Vivo l'Americans!" "Vivo Italia!"* and *"Vivo Garibaldi!"* all the time we were with him. He wore a little locket containing a picture of Garibaldi which he repeatedly kissed for our benefit.

We met Miss Daisy Hugh Pryce this evening, the author who lived two years in a Turkish harem as a governess.

Palermo—Girgenta, Sicily, Sunday, January 19, 1908

We left Palermo this morning for Girgenta. The countryside in spots was very rugged and craggy, while in others, rolling and fertile. Pink and red geraniums grow wild and to enormous size. Wild purple flags and narcissus, not to speak of the sweet alyssum and daisies and many other wild flowers, are all in bloom this nineteenth day of January.

Girgenta is the quaintest and crudest place one can imagine. Sicilian men all look like pirates and brigands and wear long capes and queer headdresses.

Our pension was awful even though recommended by friends. Mother doesn't like the town and only hopes to get out with her life. Our only consolation: good food.

Girgenta—Syracuse, Sicily, January 20, 1908

We were up with the birds again, this time to Syracuse. We were not told we had to change trains, and at the little station Mother had an exciting experience while we were out foraging for food. The train got in between us, and we lost each other for a short time.

We got into Syracuse after dark and had a great confab at the station with the hotel porters. We finally decided on the Bellevue. It's a dear little country house, pink in color and overlooking the sea. Our host is the essence of hospitality, and tonight we have a nice little oil stove buzzing away as we write in our diaries.

The good red wine has rather gone to my head, and bed is the place for me. A grand old moon promises much for tomorrow.

Syracuse, Sicily, January 21, 1908

We all had queer experiences in the night: Mother's water bottle leaked, and she slept in a puddle; an insect bit Miss Blaine in the eye and almost shut it up; Lucy's top mattress slipped off, and she had to hang on for dear life, while the fleas and unmanageable bed clothes kept me busy.

In the afternoon we drove up into the old Greek fortifications of Epipolae, the highest spot in Syracuse, spooked around inside and enjoyed fine views. We had much trouble with our horrid little driver who whipped his horses.

Syracuse—Taormina, Sicily, January 22, 1908

I never saw such fertile country as around Taormina. Crops grow in the very rocks. Situated on the side of a mountain, the rugged coast below and still higher mountains above, it is perfect. In the distance Mt. Etna, immense, smoking and covered with snow, is beyond description.

The town itself is most picturesque and clean for Sicily. No beggars; all of the poor are put to work, an institution supported by the English. We are much pleased with our hotel and love Sicily after all.

Taormina, Sicily, January 23, 1908

After breakfasting by our open window overlooking the sea (we have been having fresh dates from Tunis as refreshments), we took a walk around the town. We stumbled onto the Greek theatre, a lovely, lovely ruin overhanging the sea. Inside were numerous artists, men and women under gay-colored sunshades in straw hats and no coats. It's hard to believe it is January. The ground was carpeted entirely with little flowers blooming and nodding in the sunshine.

In the afternoon we had a jolly donkey ride up to Mt. Venere. Georgie was my little animal, and a surefooted and hungry beast he was.

Taormina, Sicily, January 24, 1908

The weather seems to be made to order for us here in Taormina.

After lunch, we all went out for a walk. We went to the Greek theatre again and met several Sicilian carts filled with peasants and women with water jugs, baskets and bundles of grain on their heads.

Our donkey boys of yesterday tried to get more money out of us this morning, but Miss Blaine pulled out her book, showed them the tariff, and they fled.

Taormina, Sicily, January 25, 1908

This morning Mother and I started off on a jaunt up the mountains. We climbed up high enough to see Mt. Etna, a glorious sight this morning in the sunshine.

On our way down I tore my skirt badly scrambling over some brambles. We met a huge flock of goats and sheep coming up the mountain accompanied by two barefooted shepherds and dogs. One of the boys was playing on a reed or bamboo pipe, and it was too foreign and quaint a sight for words.

This afternoon we visited several of the schools where the girls are taught embroidery and the boys, manual training. Two warships came into the harbor last night. We could hear the music up here then saw them steam out this morning.

Taormina—Messina, Sicily, Sunday, January 26, 1908

This Sabbath morning we were up with the birds again, catching another train. Will the time ever come when I won't have to catch a boat or train? The proprietor of the Navarralina sent each of us off with a bouquet of carnations and violets.

We arrived in Messina with six hours to kill before the boat left at six o'clock. We hired two cabs and took the much-talked-of drive along the marina. It was anything but lovely; even the mountains looked dirty and threatening, while the streets all along the way were crowded with horrid little kids squirming in the dirt and filth. I never saw such sights before and pray I may never see them again.

Diaries of Holly, Katie and Elizabeth Pierce, 2008

Naples—Taormina, Sicily, Saturday, June 14, 2008

WE LEAVE THE LOVELY Hotel Nuovo Rebecchino this morning, dragging our suitcases bumpety-bump along the square, black cobblestones, bags tipping over now and again, and that forty-pound purple backpack weighing me down. We get to the station to find the train delayed and us with no idea which platform to go to. When the train finally comes in, we discover that the platform is one of the ones underground, so in a total panic we all surge to the stairs, Richard grabbing my bag; thus I earn the anger and scorn from the girls for letting Dad do so.

So we get to the platform and as usual our coach is about a half a mile away. About halfway down Richard starts yelling, "Get on the train! Just get on!" which they all do but me, who now with my backpack sprints down the track to Coach 4, our first-class coach. Working my way down the aisle, I find a scrawny little old lady wearing embroidered jeans sitting crunched into my seat. By now I have lost my compassion regarding train seats, and waving my reservation ticket at her, make it clear she should clear out.

So she moves over to the seat opposite—*another* one of our reserved seats. Richard and the girls eventually arrive, and I indicate that *all* these four seats are ours, all ours. At that point the crone's husband shows up, takes her bags, and she painfully stands up and moves along on what I realize is a gimpy leg. Her husband probably told her to sit for the moment while he found their seats. I feel chastened.

The train lurches out of the station, and we're not five minutes out before Liz suddenly discovers that her necklace is not around her neck. Catastrophe! Sobbing, she bends over into a semi-fetal position. I know that necklace is important to her, as she has had it on for months past. Oh dear, once again, the trip is on the verge of dissolving into chaos.

Liz

I touched my neck to find my necklace missing! It was my favorite one in the shape of a teardrop with a black and gold bird inside. I burst into tears, convinced it was unrecoverable and lost forever. I was certain that I lost it while sleeping, and it was my fault for not checking the room well enough before we left.

So I DECIDE to walk back through the coaches with the hope that it fell off in the train. At the last between-train platform, just beyond the metal steps down, I spy what I think is a string of gum, but no: it's the necklace. Catastrophe averted! I carry it aloft triumphantly back to our seats.

Katie spots me first: "Mom found it!" Liz jumps out of her seat and gives me a crushing, damp embrace—"Thanks, Mom, really." So at least for the next fifteen minutes I am the heroine of the hour, if that's possible. Effusively, everyone tells me that the next time I'm in trouble with them, all I have to say is "necklace," and all will be forgiven. Let's see how long that will last.

WE ARE AT A standstill on the rails outside the town of Angri and have been so for maybe half an hour. The word is that a man has killed himself by stopping his car on the tracks to await death via train wreck. Meanwhile we sit, entertaining Marco, a young, handsome Sicilian, with the details of our trip. He is coming back to Taormina from Rome, where he is studying film, for a little visit with family. When Richard says Liz films as well, he calls her "camera girl."

Now the train man has come to sit in the seat opposite the Sicilian student and is excited to tell us he is from a town near Pompeii. He seems a jolly sort, big smile, crinkly face, no worries, chewing gum, in his green jacket and brimmed cap. Oops, a stone-faced woman in a jeans jacket and carrying a fake Gucci bag ousts him from his seat.

Meanwhile, an American couple comes crashing through the coach, looking for their seats, even more lost-acting than we. Their English is so clear; they sound like us. In fact, it turns out they are from Santa Rosa. Crazy! They have been on a seven-day Italian tour and have decided to hit Taormina before returning to the States. As they say, it's a small world, but is this any weirder than how Ruth et. al. constantly ran across people they knew? I think it is; we're not on a Grand Tour, and few people do that anymore anyway.

We're off again after an hour's wait.

Liz

On the train down the west coast of Italy towards the town where we will take a ferry to Sicily, most of the scenery was quite lovely, with tall, green mountains dotted with red terracotta roofs. Every now and again we got a quick glimpse of the remains of the old, arching aqueducts made of red brick. Perhaps the best sight of all was the pure, aqua-blue sea which periodically showed itself at one window. Near the shore it was a clear, crystal blue, while farther out it faded into a deep, dreamy, cobalt blue. Sometimes steep, green, rocky mountain shores wrapped around it, and with the ocean lapping along its edges it looked absolutely unreal.

After an exhaustingly long train ride to Villa San Giovanni on the southern tip of Italy we hopped off the train thinking to catch the ferry, and I almost forgot my backpack—a first for me! Shameful. We came up to the conductor and asked how to get across. He pointed to the train. But how will we get across? Train. Under the water? Train.

So it was "train" for us, and we promptly got back on. We soon found out that the train itself was literally loaded onto the big ferry! Our jaws dropped at this. They separated the cars of the train and pushed each one into the yawning black back of the boat. As we crossed the water we were able to go up onto the deck and see the deep, blue seawater passing by. It was charming to see little clusters of fishermen out on the water in brightly-colored wooden rowboats harvesting the day's reward. Some things never change. The image of all these tiny rocking crafts spotting the deep, glassy sea with the bright coastal hills rising in the background remains floating in my memory like a dream.

Finally reaching the Sicilian shore, we were greeted in the harbor by a lovely golden statue blessing the city, and the train was loaded off again directly onto the tracks.

Katie

We finally made it to Taormina around seven P.M. We took a taxi up a very steep hill to the top to the Condor Hotel. Despite its two-star rating it is actually lovely with a living room and kitchen, bath and *two* bedrooms! Seems princely after most times being crammed into one room.

Liz

We took an old diesel Mercedes converted into a taxi to our hotel. Up and up it went on narrow, winding roads curving around the mountainside, passing through little cobblestone arches and by old villas covered in bougainvillea. The farther up we went, the more spectacular the views became of the beaches and towns below. I couldn't wait to get in the water!

Finally we reached the Hotel Condor and were pleasantly surprised by the charming little living quarters we were given. We were all squawking with pleasure at the separate rooms and the combined living room and kitchen area; we weren't used to such luxury! Out my window you could see a grassy hillside, rich in shades of adobe and covered in sprawling cacti.

At the restaurant the family insisted on dining inside due to the fumes from passing cars, but I sat outside and watched the town's stories unfold around me. I observed a young girl pushing her baby in a stroller to see her baby's daddy who worked at the restaurant across the street. She wore tall pink heels, little short shorts and had straightened blond hair. She put on a big show of being exasperated and annoyed, throwing up her hands when his cigarette lighter didn't work. But she warmed up as they smoked and joked and threw passing glances at their baby.

After she left, I saw him looking every passing woman under forty up and down thoroughly, and I was no exception. If, I thought, she could only see him now! So it seemed she had reason to be insecure and put on quite a show; the man didn't look as if he would hesitate, given the chance!

ON OUR LITTLE BALCONY at the Hotel Condor looking out over the strait of Messina, the hotel has considerately provided a clothesline extending beyond and along the length of the balcony railing plus a little basket of multicolored clothespins. In the twilight a gentle evening breeze moves down the mountainside. I decide to wash my red "Where's Mom?" dress and some undies in the sink. It's so tranquil out that even washing clothes is a treat. I pin my underwear to the line with conscientious care. After gently wringing out my dress, I put it on one of my wire hangers and hang it out on the line, pinning the hook in place. It dances softly in the twilight, swinging back and forth to the domestic sounds echoing across the mountainside. I am enchanted.

Katie

Lovely Mediterranean weather, lots of local cats and dogs and sweet-smelling flowers. It's to bed early and the beach tomorrow. I love the smell of the bleached towels and sheets.

Taormina, Sicily, Sunday, June 15, 2008

WHEN I AWAKEN this morning, I make an alarming discovery: my dress is gone. It must have flown away on the nighttime wind. In fact it has; below our balcony it rests in the top branches of a glossy-leaved lemon tree. I can see that the tree is tall enough that trying to rescue it from the ground would be impossible. What to do?

Go fishing, of course. I hook two long bungee cords together, then kneel down and lower my line to the treetop. How convenient; the bungees even have hooks on their ends.

The line reaches my dress, but in the course of the night the dress has become well entangled in the branches. The plastic-tipped bungee hooks are useless when I discover they can only lift a corner of the dress, then let it fruitlessly slip away. I finally realize that hooking the dress itself will not be successful; it's the wire hanger I want. I push the fabric around with my line, all the while checking to see if anyone is watching this embarrassing performance. And someone is.

"What are you *doing*?" It's Liz, stepping out onto the balcony in her nightclothes to find out what her insane mother is up to now.

"My dress. It blew away. I'm trying to hook it out of the tree down there," I explain.

She looks over the edge. "Oh God."

Now she's into it. She squinches down next to me, offering strategic advice: "Get it over there. The hanger's over on that side. Let it down more."

Finally the bungee hook snags the hanger, and I slowly, slowly reel in my catch, all the time praying none of the fabric will catch on a lemon thorn and rip, much less drag the whole dress off the hanger. But we're successful; the dress is finally hauled up over the railing. It isn't even wrinkled.

At least in the United States, today is Father's Day, and Richard only wants to relax by the water. You can just imagine how the girls feel about the prospect of "postcard hunting" with me, so Richard and the girls spend the whole day down on the pebbly shore, just lazing.

Liz

Katie and I took Dad to the beach to hang out by the water. We walked through the town to the "Funtera," which was basically an enclosed gondola that took you down the steep hill to the beach. We were all crammed into one with this adorable little boy and his mother. He had a big, happy grin on his face and was squeezing two fluffy stuffed animals.

When we inquired, his mother said, "They're Pogo and Bertie, aren't they, love?" It was so sweet it put a smile on our faces for the rest of the day.

Katie

Dad, my sister and I took the funicular to the beach, and we got an Italian cigar for him. The man in the store was so distracted by our bathing suits that he almost forgot to charge us. We sunned on loungers for eight euros each, but that didn't include a towel, so we went without. Dad enjoyed his cigar even if it wasn't a Cuban. I felt confident in my attractiveness.

Liz

The beach itself was lovely, with clear, blue water, rocky outcroppings, and a messload of burnt people on the beach. We quickly rented three sun chairs and an umbrella and were set for the day.

After a dip in the water I went back to my sun chair and said that I had been stung by a jellyfish. Katie felt thoroughly vindicated in her refusal to stick a toe in any water not completely enclosed in cement. After a few minutes an enormous red and white welt appeared in the middle of my right calf.

Katie

My sister actually did get stung by something like a jellyfish in the deeper water. She told me after I had waded only a few feet in, so I could jump out fast. My sister was in the water pointing to a jellyfish stranded on the sand. Poor jellyfish. Even after getting stung, my sister was splashing water on it to help it live.

Liz

Despite our pleadings and warnings of translucent jellyfish, Dad swam all the way out to a small rock island just off the shore and made a magnificent dive back into the water. All in all, it was a lovely, relaxing afternoon.

So I AM ON my own. Sheer bliss! The weather is sunny and warm, but cooled by the sea below. I climb all around Taormina's environs with a tourist map as my guide, hunting down each card while dawdling along checking out shop windows.

The first place I hit is a Catholic church where the most beautiful and haunting singing can be heard, it being a Sunday. Despite my bare shoulders, I remove my sunhat and step just a few feet into the rear next to an old gentleman seated on a folding chair who simply gives me a welcoming smile. He was belting out whatever hymn the congregation was singing while communion was being bestowed on the locals. All the white satin, flowers, gleaming brown wood, and embroidered linens made for a sacred richness which I couldn't help being drawn to, despite my annoyance with the Catholic church and the way it plunders its followers of their meager riches.

Following the Condor's walking tour, I pass under a Roman gateway arch into the city and come upon St. Catherine's church, another holy edifice in the pantheon of Taormina's wealth of old buildings. I don't think it has any active congregation, but it does have a little one-room museum full of Christian relics in its gloomy interior. Strange: women get in for a reduced rate if they are over fifty-five, while men have to be sixty.

Anyway, lots of Baby Jesuses and a collection of old lace ensconced in dimly-lit, dusty old cases and an interesting depiction of a rather plump Jesus descending from the Cross are among the more mundane holy objects. Better are the examples of crèches described in the *Italy Rough Guide*: miniature 3-D scenes of Jesus and Joseph and Mary, but they are usually secondary to all the action going on around them. There is stuff connecting them to the local scene like giant cacti with cactus apples, oleander and craggy rockery like that along the Sicilian coast. Teeny white doves dangle from threads and scrawny sheep wander through the panoramas.

These crèches are created of different materials: paper maché, clay, some even carved out of seashells. There is a ghastly Jesus head plopped down and listing backward in a box, eyes closed in death, which looks as if it could have been made of wax, but it is difficult to tell since I can't read Italian, and it is in a particularly dark spot. Next to it in a shadow box is a baby Jesus dangerously drooping forward, deliberately placed or not, smashed into a bed of faded fake flowers.

Miraculous escape from death by merry-go-round

But the oddest is what I call the "Wall of Miracles" in a little side gallery. This consists of Italian versions of Mexico's *retablos*, license-plate-sized paintings commissioned by those who have escaped or survived some sort of grisly accident of one kind or another: death by merry-go-round or by the birth of twins, blindness by tennis ball or arrow to the eye, survival of an attack by a rabid pack of dogs in a pizza parlor or a crazed bunch of cats biting a woman in shredded garments. At the end of the little hallway is a large but simply executed painting of St. Stephen with four or five crude darts stuck in his pale, doughy, naked flesh, little threads of blood trailing from each puncture. His bemused expression suggests not so much pain as curiosity—"Hmm, I think this might hurt"—or perhaps that of a person first experiencing acupuncture.

A certain measure of success: tonight we all have a pleasant supper in a downtown square in Taormina, with nobody mad or pouting.

Katie
We ate dinner at the Trattoria Ristoro, something like that. I had the capricciosa salad as did Mom with hard-boiled eggs, olives, cucumbers, tomatoes, onions and corn. Dad and my sister shared their spaghetti a la carbonara and the artichoke, olive and cheese pizza. I paid the bill! (My sister wanted to help but didn't have the funds.) Dinner was to honor Dad.

Liz
After dinner, Mom took us to see the "wall of miracles" on display at a local church, and we found it to be quite engaging. There were painted wooden plaques showing the variety of miracles Mary had bestowed upon individuals in saving them from certain demise: attacking dogs, tennis balls to the eye, arrows in the chest, people falling through roofs or getting thrown off horses, etc. We found it all endlessly entertaining.

To Greece

Diary of Ruth K. Crapo, 1907-1908

Naples, Italy, January 27, 1908

After the usual scrabble at the station with *facchini* and hotel men, we arrived finally at the convent. We almost didn't get rooms, but by the three Crapos bunking together, it was possible.

In spite of angry feelings in my bum leg, I ventured out in the afternoon to tend to some business. I met Mrs. Hodges, whom an aged snail could beat walking, and we trailed around some together.

I bought *A Thousand Miles Up The Nile* by A.B. Edwards and read that until dinnertime, only to be interrupted by a heated discussion with Mrs. Hodges on how the present king of Italy's grandfather came to rule the United Kingdom. Both of us were pretty stubborn.

Naples, Italy, January 28, 1908

I had no sleep last night on account of my leg and am beginning to get scared about it. Mother and I went out for a short time to see about some canes and a pair of shoes for me.

We decided to have a doctor come in. He was Italian, young and spoke very poor French. We had a hard time making the *medecin* understand my case. He took my temperature by putting the thermometer under my arm for ten minutes. I prefer taking it in the mouth like a lady.

At last he had a glimmer of light after asking many fool questions such as if my family had gout or rheumatism, etc. He wrote out a prescription that Lucy had filled, and I expect it to work wonders tonight.

Mother went shopping by herself in the afternoon and actually got back without getting lost. It was a record-breaker for sure.

Naples, Italy, January 29, 1908

This morning Lucy and I bought an immense bouquet of mignonette and violets for one of the sisters for one franc. The flower vendor tried to make me take a lead and plugged two-franc piece, a fifty-centime piece no longer good here, and a few bad pennies in change. I raised a row, and finally a man in a store nearby came out and rescued me from the irate salesman.

We also all had hair washes, Lucy and I being the extravagant ones going down to the Gallery Victoria to have ours done. I washed Ma's before going downtown, so was both shampooer and shampooed.

Naples, Italy, January 30, 1908

Downtown again this morning in the rain. I bought silk for a ruffle and sped home in a hurry to put it on an old petticoat. I sewed like mad until noon, had lunch, then went at it harder than ever. At four P.M. the petticoat looked like a new one with two handsome ruffles decorating it. I started to finish up, then discovered that some new waists of Sorrento silk I'd brought home in the morning didn't fit, and I had to hurry downtown again with them.

Naples, Italy, January 31, 1908

We started for the archaeological museum at an early hour this morning. We then went out to finish up shopping in Naples (belt buckles, shoes, etc.).

Lucy got the mail that brought a very agitating letter from Shelby about taxes, and this evening we are all much upset. Mother is sitting up late writing business letters in a furious manner to Shelby, Edith, Cliff and others. I have just written a corker myself. Taxes pursue us wherever we go, even into southernmost Italy.

On board the *Senegal*, February 1, 1908

We left the convent this morning for the *Senegal*, which was to take us to Piraeus and round to Jaffa. The longshoremen were on strike at the pier, and the Cook's man got us out to the boat in a very roundabout way. We were not impressed by the looks of our steamer.

Almost at once we met all the first cabin passengers and found some to be very nice. The afternoon was spent on deck and not getting unpacked.

This evening the sea is chopping up a bit. We sat up until eleven o'clock in the saloon joking with some of our new acquaintances and playing the piano, singing, etc. I dread bed.

On board the *Senegal*, Sunday, February 2, 1908

Last night was a perfect nightmare for everyone on board. There was a terrific storm, and the steamer bounced around like a cockle shell. Three times the machinery broke down, and the downfall of ship crockery was something awful.

Even in our room the water basins rolled helter-skelter around the room, and tumblers and toilet articles were smashed. Mother had a hard time keeping in bed, and as for me I was first on my head and then on my toes, then shaken like a rat and left exhausted. At one point when the machinery broke down, we were buffeted around more than ever and finally became frightened. We were assured it was nothing but couldn't sleep the rest of the night.

We spent Sunday in bed and had nothing to eat. Dr. Smith popped his head in several times to inquire after us. Even he had been "half seas" over, and the only two who were not ill were Mr. and Mrs. Fitzsimmons of Dublin. They didn't miss a meal.

On board the *Senegal*—Piraeus, Greece, February 3, 1908

It was noon before the haggard crowd appeared on deck this morning. All looked a bit seedy but game. The sea was still high, but we all managed to hold ourselves together. I didn't see the dining room all day. We got into Piraeus at five o'clock, and if we could have landed, we would have seen Athens by daylight.

However, a nervy little Cook's man with a boat met us, bundled us into a train, and off we went to see Athens by starlight. We got but a vague idea of it and went back to the ship a pretty disappointed crowd.

On board the *Senegal*—Athens, Greece, February 4, 1908

Such a day as this has been, and such a night as last! I woke up once and noticed a queer motion to the boat but had dozed off again when I reawakened, becoming curious as to many loud noises and poundings.

Jumping from my berth, I opened the inside door and found Lucy white and shaking, hustling into her clothes. In loud tones she informed me that the boat had sprung a leak, and all hands were ordered up on deck. At the other door Miss Blaine was screaming that the ship was on fire. It didn't take Mother and I long to jump into something, and grabbing our valuables, made for the upper deck. We passed the men working on the pumps, and I tell you, it was exciting!

We found a motley crowd on deck in every state of dress and undress, and baggage heaped around. One woman was in hysterics and fainted. Once up, no woman would go downstairs again, but Dr. Smith rescued our belongings for us, even to my back hair.

It was quarter to three. We were told that land was in sight and that we were making for Piraeus, but we couldn't see anything. After a long, cold wait, and reassuring ourselves by the fact that the boats were lowered and the sea calmer, we saw a faint glow in the distance and were told it was Piraeus.

By and by, word came up that the leak was under control, and there was no cause for alarm, as only ten feet of water was in the hold. We sat on deck in the cold and damp until daylight when divers came out and hunted out the leak. The water was within two feet of the machinery when it was finally gotten under control.

At about ten o'clock we left the ship and went to Athens to await developments and to see what Cook's would do for us. Almost all have decided not to resail on the *Senegal*.

Items from the wreck:

Watch and my crepon, rescued by Dr. Smith.

My bed-slippers, found on deck by man in nightshirt.

Miss Coe's corsets, on deck.

Mrs. Smith's corsets, in dining room.

Nightgowns, flannel skirts, etc.

Diaries of Holly, Katie and Elizabeth Pierce, 2008

Taormina—Bari, Italy, Monday, June 16, 2008

ANOTHER HELLISH TRAVEL day. To get to Bari, we discover that we can either take the train to Messina at three A.M. or take a taxi for ninety euros at 4:45. So taxi it is. It is barely getting light when we haul ourselves into the waiting cab in front of the Condor, and yes, winding our way down the steep and craggy Taormina mountainside is lovely in the breaking dawn with the silver-blue water of the straits of Messina, but my blood pressure is low and I'm feeling nauseated.

The highway is empty, and we arrive in plenty of time for the hydrofoil to the other side. First mistake: we have no idea there are two ferry landings across the strait, one next to the train station and one about a mile east. We unwittingly take the wrong ferry and have to take that mile-long walk along the waterfront. It could have been a pleasant stroll, so early in the cool morning air; the seaward walkway wall is of an elaborate iron scrollwork, palms line the broad walkway and Grecian excavations with explanations in English periodically enliven the way. Two men in a sulky driving the most elegant black trotter pass by, the horse's shoes striking a smart rhythm on the concrete.

Liz

We took a taxi to Messina in the wee hours of the morning while even the sun was still asleep and then rode on a little hovercraft from Messina to the mainland. No breakfast and no sleep, but I was holding up all right. Then it turned out we had nearly an hour's walk from the landing to the train station, dragging our overflowing luggage behind us and not a taxi in sight. I was distraught, and my anxiety began to skyrocket as the rest of the family took the walk briskly and I straggled behind.

ELIZABETH HAS gone into meltdown, crying and picking up bits of trash. What could we do with her, folded up on the sidewalk? We finally decide we must continue walking and trust that she will eventually follow suit. What choice does she have? Get left behind?

Well, maybe. We finally get to Reggio di Calabria Centrale, Liz eventually straggling in, only to find that the train to Bari has been cancelled.

Liz

I was terribly upset upon arriving and just sat down and cried, letting all the pent-up emotions of the trip pour out. Wrong idea! Within minutes several female Italian train officials descended upon me, concerned I had a medical problem that needed to be solved. How to explain? It would have been difficult enough in English, but with the language barrier it was impossible. Their attentions just made it all worse; I so wanted them to leave me alone, but I did not know how to say this without being rude.

Worst of all was the attention they attracted. With the family in the background, I looked up to see other Italians staring at me as if I was some oddity to be taken in. It was completely mortifying, making it the worst experience I had had in quite some time.

HERE IS LIZ, crouched against the wall with her face buried in her pink-flowered hankie, sobbing. As we are dealing with the no-train situation, two women watch her with increasing concern. I finally step forward and explain to a competent-looking woman with reddish shoulder-length hair and a white linen blouse that my daughter is "mal." Incredibly, the woman understands what I mean when I say Liz is suffering a panic attack.

Immediately Liz is surrounded by women train officials crouching around her, giving her a paper bag to breathe in to cure her hyperventilation, offering her StarBursts, stroking her. I am amazed and touched by their true care and concern. Does she need an ambulance? a trip to the hospital? to go home? They are ready to facilitate anything we decide. By then Liz has taken her meds, and both these and the women's care have started to calm her down, although she is still dazed.

Meanwhile, what about the train? The expensive train to Bari has just pulled out, and we are down to piecing together some patchwork path across southern Italy. Everyone seems to have an idea as to what kind of schedule to follow. The auburn-haired woman takes me over to what looks like a glorified ATM and starts punching in alternate routes and sighing in frustration. A few moments later a stout, green-jacketed train woman interrupts us with a little piece of paper outlining what trains we should take. Some pretty tight connections, but we would go as far as we could.

On the first train, this one to Naples, a young, fresh-faced conductor checks our little scrap of paper, and after much hand-gesturing and pocket phrasebook consultation he gets the idea across to us that he will personally lead us to the next train. By this time Liz is pretty much her regular self after a fitful nap on two seats. Everyone is captivated by this charming young guy and plenty grateful once he leads us to our next train in which we are installed in a second-class, six-seat compartment; while there is no first class on this local, he assures us that this compartment will be ours alone.

Liz

Mother once again suggested I return home, but I was adamant about staying; I've just got to see the pyramids. I've begun to wonder if she suggested my return because of concern for my well-being or merely because I've become a bother and am impinging on her pleasure.

Katie

At the train station we discovered that there was no train to Bari after we made my sister walk way too far for her anxiety levels to handle. She freaked. She had a panic attack when we finally got to the station, and all the ladies were crowding around her wondering what was wrong. She was huddled in the corner crying because it was too much, and she hadn't taken her medication yet; she refused to until nine A.M., and it was only seven A.M. when we started walking. After some sleep and a lot of help from the train's omsbudswoman, my sister seemed to be feeling better and we were on our way.

Of course my sister had to examine the map so she could know exactly what was happening. I had my headphones on so I didn't have to hear her complaining about the time and the train changes. Mom and Dad were seriously considering sending her home on the next direct flight from Athens to SFO. What she didn't get was that she might not have a choice, even though she said, "I'm not going home!" Mom and Dad aren't having fun with her constant breakdowns.

LATER, ANOTHER UGLY scene. Four Americans in a six-seater, and at one stop a bunch of soccer-aged young men in tight shirts and short haircuts get on with their gigantic, hard-sided suitcases. On the way to Naples we have been okay, as we were installed in the compartment next to the conductor, but on this leg our new conductor has no idea about our situation. So here are the young bucks with their huge suitcases attempting to elbow their way into our compartment.

Now, since we are in second class, in theory they have every right to take two of our seats. But there is no way I am going to let them intrude. Grabbing the two-month-old reservations from Rich, I stand in the doorway, blocking their way, waving our now-defunct reservations and declaring that they could *not* enter. They are babbling at me and gesturing to the decal on the sliding glass door indicating six seats—yes, yes—but I keep babbling back in my most belligerent, unintelligible (to them) voice that I want "to speak to the conductor! Where is the conductor? Does anyone speak English? Where is he? This compartment is *ours!*"

Eventually the one drags his red doghouse-sized suitcase out of our partially-opened door, deciding it is just too much trouble arguing with a het-up female foreigner. I slam our compartment door, and that is that. Later we agreed that I was the only one of us who could have done this, seeing that if Richard had tried the same gambit, they might have slugged him to make their point, and the girls were admittedly not brave enough. Mama Bear triumphs.

Now we are finally on the correct (I think) train to Bari; at least it is a EuroStar, and we are riding in air-conditioned first class seats with the numbers of our original reservations. The girls have their ten-dollar bottles of wine and are back to discussing the same damn rag of a gossip magazine, I have my bottle of San Benedetto Limone thé, and Rich has just finished *No Country for Old Men*. The coach is nearly empty as we rock through the fertile Italian countryside covered in blankets of vineyards, rolled bales of hay and groves of grey-green olive trees. Let's pray there are no more crises today; it's 5:20, so at least there isn't much time left to have a crisis.

No MORE CRISES? Think again. We finally get into Bari and into our Hotel Costa, hard by the train station. Honestly, it is like something out of a Mel Brooks movie, and yet inexplicably it is a three-star hotel. What is this rating system all about? Off a dirty, narrow sidewalk, the hotel's reception area is marked by a giant, canary-yellow sign with an arrow in the foyer pointing to the front desk to the left. The man who signed us in is pleasant enough, but there is an Igor-like helper lurking about, rubbing his hands and smiling cravenly.

Our room for four is right off the foyer on the ground level. I would guess that it was originally used as a storage room or some such thing, but has been converted for foursomes like our little band. The bathroom is pink and white tile and actually not bad, but the bedroom has four beds side by side in a row alongside one wall of the room, with three small overhead down lights by the wall opposite the beds. Other than that, and any light from the bathroom, the room is so dark you can't read a thing on the bed side of the room. The windows have no bars, and the louvers are painted shut, so that precludes any window opening.

There is a standing lamp with an olive green fabric up-cone plugged in over by the three down lights, and that we drag over to the other side of the room, but surprise: there aren't any outlets, only a crudely cut-out square through which random wires erupt. I get the bright idea to use the adapter and plug it into the outlet intended for shavers in the bathroom. I really feel this might work, as when the cord is draped through the doorway, the light turns on.

Alas. The lamp casts such a feeble glow that it is less than useless and is partially blocking the bathroom doorway as it is. And after a few moments, we detect a slight but suspicious burning electrical smell. So much for the lamp. Liz then discovers two bedside lamps, the cousins to the olive cone, hidden away in a cabinet, but as we have already discovered that electricity is not this room's commodity, we just hide them back.

By now Katie is in a foul, ravenous mood, so food is next on the agenda. According to the *Rough Guide* pages I'd ripped out, there is a fabulous (and the nearest) restaurant about six blocks away, which then presents the problem of getting Liz there without her melting down. Six blocks is a distance, and I am willing to stop should we find some place along the way, but surprise, the southern half of Bari (and we are at the very southern end by the railway) is completely, and I mean *completely*, commercial enterprises with high-end pastry shops, elegant and ridiculously-priced clothing stores, bars and bistros, but nowhere offering just food. So I'm glad when we reach the *Rough Guide* address—only to find that it's closed because it's Monday. Another glitch we hadn't counted on.

I ask a girl in a gelato shop where there might be a place to eat, and she makes a mark on my map, but we can't find it once there. Down a close-by street there is a café with huge umbrellas staking out territory in the street, but the waiters seem to have their noses in the air and the clientele seem equally icy and just too cool for us.

At this point I enter a corner coffee bar (no food again) with Katie to ask the two men there as to where anyone eats in this city. Again no English, but Franco turns out to speak Spanish. Ahh: this is Katie's forté, and soon she is chatting away with Franco who agrees to walk us to several possible eateries.

Liz and Richard have promised to stay by the "Ice Palace" while we go to inquire, but little do they know we will be gone quite so long. Off Franco goes into Old Bari, ever more farther north. With silver hair brushed back, a deep tan, and tiny, jeans-clad hips, Franco turns out to be a fifty-ish hairdresser who has done some magazine work, so Katie is in her element. But even Franco can't make it be any day other than Monday, so we wander to several spots before we finally come upon Il Pescadero, situated on the far north end of town by the harbor. No one is there, as it is only we gauche Americans who eat so early, but *"Grazie! Grazie!"* to Franco, and we give him enough lead time so I can hustle south again on my own to collect Rich and Liz, leaving Katie with a full bottle of wine (which we later give the partial remains of to a very grateful, scrawny student foursome when we leave, as only Katie has wanted any; another menu mistake).

Katie

After we got to the hotel we decided to eat on my urging, but Mom had to look at what her guidebook recommended first. We finally found a place noted in the book, but when we walked the nine blocks that my sister kept bitching about, it was closed. We wandered until my sister started screaming at us to slow down, saying she couldn't take it anymore. The problem was an abundance of tiny specialty cafés and plenty of shopping, but no open regular restaurants because it was Monday.

Mom and I left my sister and Dad stationed somewhere so she wouldn't complain about walking and her anxiety while we searched for food. Finally, Mom asked this nice man, Franco, a hairdresser slash journalist, where to find food, and he and I chatted in broken Spanish mixed with broken Italian (he informed me I was speaking both) while he guided us all through twisted old cobblestoned streets trying to find an open place to sit down and eat. We gave him our card.

Finally got the family to an acceptable, mostly-fish place.

ONCE WE ARE finally gathered together, we have a good dinner. I have "Fisherman's Noodles": fresh-rolled noodles with *les fruites de la mer*: calamari, clams, shrimp, and some white slices of something I can't identify but seem to taste like everything else. By the time we finish, the place is packed with patrons choosing to eat at a more civilized hour. Richard makes the executive decision (there seems to be more and more of those) to take a taxi back to our creepy hotel.

By now everything seems to be so bad after such a very long day that anything is now laughable. Igor greets us at the door, and we hustle into the bat cave to get to bed as fast as possible. Last into her camp bed, Liz flops down, resulting in the bed producing a most angry and tragic screech. She turns over; more screeches of protest. Katie's isn't quite so bad, but she has discovered something else even more eerie: when she presses her hand slowly against the wall, it produces a slow groan as it caves in and out.

Katie

The hotel really should be called the Creaky Hotel because Mom, my sister and I stayed up for half an hour laughing at the ridiculous noises coming through the dark. I took a Xanax to fall asleep right away, but couldn't resist pushing on the wall some more to make it creak slowly and steadily, causing more laughing. The floor, door, our beds and my wall squeaked in a cacophony of ways accompanied by the humming of the turning fan overhead. Dad didn't wake up because he had his earplugs in.

Liz

I lay down on my wire frame bed to find it so loud! Every time I moved it made a new creaking or squeaking sound; additionally, our fan made the funniest "thub-thub" noise, and the floor shouted in protest any time you stepped on it.

But what really set us off into hysterics was that the wall next to Katie made the loudest groaning noise when she pushed on it with her hand! Oh, by the time we got over that, our bellies hurt from laughing, and we had lost another half hour of sleep. It was so funny, though, all of us cracking up in the dark at this ridiculous wall. I hadn't had a really good laugh like that in a while!

Bari, Italy—Athens, Greece, Tuesday, June 17, 2008

Liz

Thank God we left Italy. There are some beautiful things there, but Christ, it drove me crazy! It will be awhile before I will be able to convince myself to set foot in that country again.

WE LEAVE BEFORE 6:30 A.M. (and miss the Hotel Costa's undoubtedly fabulous and free breakfast), as we will be taking an international flight. Another taxi, but worth it. It's only a little warm, and the rising sun slants in the rear window in a lovely way as the radio plays some bouncy new-to-us tunes like "Big Girl, You Are Beautiful" and "To Sara With

Love." We can't help it, we just have to sing along, and the cute cab driver grins at our warbling harmonies.

Expecting the usual debacle, we dutifully arrive at the airport a little more than two hours before our nine o'clock scheduled departure. Surprise: the place is deserted, except for the woman by the entrance who sternly gestures for me to put my camera away. We try to find the check-in counter for MyAir, our carrier to Athens, but we see no sign of it. Oh dear.

Having never heard of MyAir, I was initially a little dubious about booking one of these cheap-ticket airlines that hops around Europe on a wing and a prayer. Once airlines really began to suffer from high fuel prices, I was afraid we would arrive at the airport only to discover it was no longer in operation. But in February I had actually Googled MyAir to check its viability before booking and discovered that their golden CEO Edgardo Badiali was already being wooed to head India's GoAir, a reassuring fact.

Finally, at the stroke of seven o'clock a woman snaps up the MyAir shingle at an empty counter, and we and maybe three others check in, leaving us two hours to hang out. The airport is surprisingly very modern and spacious, with lots of glass and exciting and tasteful murals painted in the upper reaches. I really want a photo of these works of public art, so after I station myself with a round white pillar between me and the finger-wagging no-photos woman, Liz tells me when she is not watching and I take my shot.

After that bit of high intrigue, what next? We wander down the way to where a couple of food counters are open. One advertises freshly-squeezed orange juice, and so that and a pastry are breakfast. The orange juice is fabulous.

Strolling around, I notice a large sign near the entrance that includes lit numbers along its right side. It's mostly in Italian, but after a little study I figure out the airport identifies itself as a "photovoltaic plant," which I suspect has to do with solar energy. The six phrases ending with digital numbers have to do with how "green" the Bari airport is. I really only understand the last two lines, which enumerate how much fuel oil is saved and units of CO_2 that are not being emitted into the atmosphere. These Italians! How did they get so far ahead of us? I am truly impressed and drag Richard over to see this wonder.

Our flight is what can be expected from a economy airline: cramped quarters, no snacks. A couple with their little baby is sitting behind me, and the baby is squalling away, ack, ack, ack, and someone has some electronic device going and making a racket. Meanwhile, the girls have already ominously reverted to their bicker mode with each other, snippity-snap, so pleasant to hear.

Despite all my misgivings, our orange and white plane makes the short flight over the Mediterranean without crashing or going out of business. We arrive in Athens, and here's the thing: the Olympics were held here in 2004, and so all the infrastructure and public transportation is top-notch.

Katie

In the airport we were arguing about whether to take a taxi or the metro, and I asked Mom, "Don't you want us to be pampered?" and Mom said "No." It's all about the diary, and we are secondary to the goal of the trip which apparently isn't to enjoy ourselves to the highest. "Vacation" then becomes a misnomer, a quote from my sister's mouth, but I agree.

I can't get what Mom said out of my head. She said the money was *hers,* and not hers and Dad's. Dad brought home the money and Mom raised us, but that doesn't make us only her children and only his money.

Greece

Diary of Ruth K. Crapo, 1907-1908

Athens, Greece, February 5, 1908

The day in Athens was spent doing the sights and meeting for news from Cook's. Miss Coe and I went out this morning to see if we could see the Royal Palace. The Queen was holding a reception, and it seems we were not expected.

We ran up against soldiers in the most barbaric and fascinating costumes: frilled petticoats, turned-up toe slippers with rosettes and bared, curved sabers.

We took a walk through the residential part of town and found it beautiful and very clean. They tell us there is cholera in Constantinople and the plague in Egypt, so we may have trouble getting in or out of those places.

Athens, Greece—on board the *Ismalia,* February 6, 1908

This morning we spent our time seeing some more of Athens. We had a last walk on the Acropolis, visited Socrates' prison in the rocks and then home by way of the stadium. I have yet to see a city over here that I'd rather live in than Athens. It's clean and beautiful.

After much cussing and discussing, we decided that we should leave Athens at four o'clock this afternoon on the mail steamer *Ismalia* for Alexandria and that it would be unwise to try to go to Constantinople, Smyrna and Beirut. Of course we struck out along with the storm. It was blowing all day, and we went on board prepared for another siege.

Diaries of Holly, Katie and Elizabeth Pierce, 2008

Athens, Greece, Tuesday, June 17, 2008

Katie

We took the airport's express bus to Sýndagma Square in the heart of Athens, speeding past an Ikea (just like ours!) and a modern Holiday Inn with orange, 3D-framed windows (better than ours!).

Liz

Everything is golden! We are in Athens now, and life couldn't be better. As Ruth said, this city is beautiful and clean. But what's more, it has unbeatable food and the friendliest and funniest people I have yet met.

I was simply slack-jawed by the metro as well. I couldn't see a single piece of trash or smudge of dirt anywhere, not even on the railroad tracks! And they also had these glass display cases set up with copies of old artwork in them. I am just overwhelmed by the "goodness" of this city and am sure that I have to come back. It even tops Switzerland for my favorite place so far.

It's BEEN A LONG time since that fresh orange juice, so we are all starving; we need to eat before hunting down the Backpackers Inn. In the Diros Restaurant we are handed menus with a tempting array of authentic Greek food: "Fried squish frozen" (and only eight euros, or twelve dollars!); "Galf liver grilled or fried"; "Staff squash"; and "Staffed wine leaves with rise." We have to give them credit for trying.

Back outside, it's plenty hot. We are looking forward to our newly remodeled, air-conditioned, four-person flat. I show a taxi driver the address for the Backpackers Inn. He's probably ferried plenty of fares there, or he may not have; after all, this is a youth hostel, and penurious traveling youths for the most part don't travel by taxi.

The driver lets us off right at the inn—lovely! Leaving the others out on the sidewalk, at the desk I show the e-mail confirming our reservation to a tall guy behind the counter. He is young, pony-tailed, in charge and loud; he has to be, considering the racket filling the tiny lobby. There are kids everywhere, hanging out on the stairs, lounging in doorways, huddled around the computers. Strange; I feel a little out of place.

The counterman does some back-and-forthing between my e-mail and his computer. When he looks up, I know he has something bad to say.

"I don't seem to have you listed," he yells.

Crap. "But I made this reservation back in *January*! See, here's the reference number on the e-mail," I protest, pointing to 6324-8820839. "We're supposed to have one of your new four-person flats."

He looks some more. Then: "I see the problem. Daniel e-mailed you in May offering you the flat, but you never wrote him back to confirm it."

Well, that's possible. I did reconfirm eighteen hotel reservations in May; perhaps I missed the *re*-reconfirm part. Nevertheless, that e-mail from Daniel did say if we didn't want the flat, he was copasetic with the original hostel reservation for the six-bed shared room with *ensuite* bathroom.

Seeing the dismay (and sweat) on my face, he says, "Hold on. Let me call Kerry over at the flats. I think we may have a three-person that would do." Oh boy, who gets the infamous cot this time?

With his phone plastered against one ear and his forefinger stuck perpendicularly into the other, he converses loudly with Kerry, all the time pacing randomly about behind the tiny counter. Then snap! he shuts his cell phone.

"Okay, the flat's empty, and Kerry can put an extra bed in there for you. Go check it out and let me know." He then gives us directions to the building, a five-minute walk away.

Bumpety-bumping along, we drag our bags over the cracked sidewalk under the iron-fisted Athenian sun until we figure out which building we're looking for. It is wedged between two streets, and it's pretty skuzzy-looking. The lobby runs through the width of the building with smudged glass at both ends, and the pavement is filthy. It's unclear just where the flats are until we spot an unclearly-marked panel of buttons—is this one for the hostel or the hair salon?—dirty with dried stick-um from previous tenants' nametags. Fortunately, we push the correct one. Kerry buzzes us into the glass-sided lobby, and we take the lift up.

Kerry turns out to be a nice young girl, English or Australian we guess (but not a hairdresser), who is also accommodating when we see the flat and realize the "sofa" is just another bed tricked out with large pillows. Without complaint she drags out the extra bed she has just set up. The place is perfect: two sparkling, air-conditioned rooms, one with a double bed, the other with the two twins, Ikea lamps and a private bath to boot.

By this time, however, the last two days have taken their toll. After the grueling and dicey trip yesterday across Italy's "ankle" and this morning's 6:30 A.M. arrival at the Bari airport, I feel like crap. My stomach is queasy from fatigue, but worse is the mental exhaustion from dealing with bogus train reservations, the foodless town, an arcane confirmation system, and cranky and pissed-off children. Everything is my fault. And so it is time for my very own breakdown. At least it's in an air-conditioned room.

Richard and Katie wait outside while Liz soothes a sobbing me.

Liz

We were ready to go to dinner after a while, but Mom woke up from a nap feeling terrible. Just as we were leaving, she broke into tears, so I spent some time with just her and me, holding her and comforting her and making her feel better. She is just as fragile as the rest of us, but I think she has a harder time showing it. I calmed her down, got her propped in bed watching CNN with a bottle of cold water by her side.

"I KNOW, I KNOW," she says, hugging me, stroking my hair. "It's been really a long last couple of days. I bet you're hungry."

"Nuh-nuh nooo," I snuffle out. "My stomach is killing me."

"Would you like something to drink, some more water anyway?"

"Nuh-no," I sob. "I think I just need some alone time. I need to be by myself."

"Okay, I totally understand. How about if we go to dinner and bring you back a little something?" she murmurs.

"Y-y-yeah, that would be nice," I sniffle.

"Okay then, you just rest, and we'll be back in a little while. I love you," she adds. With a squeak she gets up off the bed and after placing a bottle of water by my bed, steps out the door, closing it quietly behind her, leaving me alone to feel sorry for myself and then, finally, to fall off to sleep.

Katie

Mom had her own breakdown tonight. She felt ill and cried with my sister. Dad and I waited outside while my sister soothed and calmed her down.

Everyone at God's Restaurant was very nice and joked and complimented us. It was a lovely dinner—tzaztiki, Greek salad, spaghetti carbonara and baklava with Coke and then a shot of red wine at the owner's insistence. I think the two women behind us were slightly disturbed by our noise, but their baby dropped a plate so they had nothing to stare at. We foraged hot pita bread, fresh-squeezed orange juice and a banana for Mom to bring home to calm her stomach.

Katie
When we got back from our dinner, she was feeling better. She was much more rested, and everyone was nice to each other again. Happy all around. I showed off my Carmen Electra dance moves to Mom who liked and appreciated them. I told her I loved her.

Athens, Greece, Wednesday, June 18, 2008

EIGHT O'CLOCK, AND IT'S going to be a hot one in Athens. The girls are sprawled out in their underwear on their beds, recovering from the day before. I'm dragging as well, but there's a lot to see today. I need to hit the Temple of Olympian Zeus to take a photo matching that of Lucy's postcard, but the temple is in the opposite direction of the Acropolis from our flat. So, trying to disturb them as little as possible, Richard and I tell the girls we'll come back for them around 10:30.

Out on the street, it's only a couple of blocks east before we reach a tangle of converging avenues. Across the way stands Hadrian's Arch, practically flush with the sidewalk. It reminds me of Stonehenge right next to the freeway, except that in this case, Athens has swollen around its wealth of ancient monuments like a rising tide fills in around rocks in a tide pool. Given all the empty space surrounding England's sacred monoliths, I still think the British could have routed their freeway a little farther away.

Since it's early, the traffic isn't thick yet, and we easily trot across the multiple avenues. Beyond the arch and down a gentle slope we can see the temple, or rather what remains of it, in a rectangular space that reminds me of a football field. The site is fenced, however, and the entrance is on the far side of the grounds, so we stroll downhill to the entry, enjoying ourselves in the yet-to-be oppressive heat.

At the entry we discover that we can buy day passes that will allow us onto the Acropolis as well. Furthermore, Richard has cleverly remembered to bring along the girls' student IDs, so we buy four tickets, two at the student rate. This way we can all just walk into the Acropolis grounds together without waiting in line under the broiling sun.

Given where the surviving fifteen columns stand, this temple must have been huge indeed. Plenty of open space surrounds the temple site, and around the borders are scattered chunks of carved marble: big, barrel-shaped pieces of fallen columns, a touching stele of a wrinkled old woman flanked by two robe-draped men, rectangular blocks which once formed the great temple, a huge set of stone toes long missing its owner. Richard helps me figure out from which angle the postcard's image must have been taken, then waits patiently while I tramp over to the far end of the field to take the shot. Hardly anyone else is around.

The other "postcard photo" I'd like to get is one of the Greek soldiers in their elaborate get-ups stationed in front of the Parliament building, something the girls really couldn't care about less. Our map places the building above the National Gardens, a sort of Athenian arboretum. It's uphill, but we don't care; it's still relatively cool in the garden's shade and greenery. Groomed dirt paths twist and turn through the grounds, where we discover modest fountains, a long, leafy hallway of an arbor of vines, acanthus in bloom (the plant upon which the Corinthian-style capital was based), a row of stately palms lining a straight walkway. We find a floor mosaic left in situ, its tiles curving in intertwining circles.

Best of all are the two tortoises we discover plodding along amidst some dry weeds. Tortoises! They bring back childhood memories of camping in the deserts of Southern California where once we found and brought home (illegally) our pet tortoise, Oscar. I remember summer afternoons lying on my belly on the lawn at tortoise-eye level, watching Oscar's prehistoric beak slowly open wide, his pointed pink tongue extending, then his lipless mouth chomping down on a delicious clump of Bermuda grass.

We eventually find our way out of the gardens and into the streets lined with cafés and flower vendors. The Parliament building isn't difficult to find, but when I go to take a photo of this soldier who definitely is no longer decked out in red fez and turned-up slippers, I discover that my camera's second digital chip is full—and we're only to Greece? I use Richard's camera, but this is a serious problem for me, the compulsive picture-taker.

It's pretty steaming by now, so we decide we'll take the metro back down to the hostel's neighborhood. The map shows two metro entrances here in Sýndagma, a major Athenian hub, but where are they? It's pretty chaotic and burning on all this cement. I definitely can't see wandering aimlessly around, so the idea is to find someone likely to speak English—and there they are, two TV people, one the sweating young cameraman and the other, the cool-looking gal reporter in her red suit.

"Excuse me," I ask tentatively, "but do you speak English? We're looking for the entrance to the metro."

Her eyes light up. I suddenly realize she's got a live one here. She signals to her cameraman to move around to a more advantageous angle.

"Tell me, where are you from?" The cameraman's fuzz-covered microphone aims straight at us.

"Um, from the United States, from California?"

"Do you think it's hot today?"

Duh. I look at Rich. I don't want to be the Ugly American, insulting their country. "Yeah, it's pretty hot, but not unbearable."

She presses: "But do you think it's *really* hot today?"

I get it. She's the weather girl, and she needs vacationers to validate how punishingly warm the weather is in Athens today. We need to be impressed by just how hellishly hot it is.

Both Richard and I respond: "Oh, yeah, it's really hot. We're feeling pretty sweaty right now—whew! It's a scorcher!"

The woman signals to the camera guy to cut, then directs us to the nearest metro entrance, where we descend into the cool of the underground.

AT THE FLAT, the girls are ready to go. I've already asked at the main hostel where I might find another chip for my camera. We decide that the girls will head on up to the Acropolis, while Richard and I will make the detour to the camera shop and then meet up with them somewhere on the grounds. He hands over their student tickets.

At the camera shop the salesgirl suggests that in addition to a new chip, I should get the second chip's photos transferred to a disk so that if I fill yet another chip, I can erase the contents of the copied chip. This spooks me some; erasing chips without their contents securely on my computer is something I just don't do. But we decide to go ahead with this plan.

Then and Now
The Parthenon

Finally, it's off to the Acropolis, the really big show. By now it *is* a scorcher, and that march up the south side of the hill in full sun is grim. We come upon an Indian family lined up against the hillside, with Dad in a blue-striped polo shirt arranging them all in his camera's viewfinder. No, no, no; they've come all this way, and Dad's not going to be in the picture? So we take a photo including all of them, something we end up doing a lot of up top, and which others do for us.

As we trudge up the path, we pass others coming down with the most delightful bamboo and fake silk parasols with painted cherry blossom branches. And what colors! Hot pink, grass green, sea blue, canary yellow—seeing these parasols flitting and floating along like delicate butterflies over the Acropolis, you'd almost forget their practicality in this blast furnace. I want one.

A little farther up the path and we come upon the parasol vendors, dark young boys of an indeterminate nationality lugging huge bags of cellophane-wrapped umbrellas, moving among the clusters of tourists. One boy approaches us, his dark, long-lashed eyes looking at us questioningly.

"How much?" Everyone understands these two words.

"Five." Five euros: that's seven and a half U.S. dollars. No way.

"Two," Richard counters.

The boy winces, but he's hip to this game. He looks at us pleadingly. "Four, mister."

It suddenly dawns on Richard that he, too, might want one of these parasols up on the rock. "How about two for six?"

Two for six. The boy takes a moment to think about this. Then: "I must talk to my boss first," and he darts off down the path, bag banging against his skinny legs.

We cool our heels for a moment. The boy returns. "Okay," he says grudgingly. "Two for six."

I quickly pick out two parasols, deep pink and green—green is Richard's favorite color—while Rich fishes the six euros out of his pocket. I rip off the cellophane bag and pop up my umbrella. Awesome! It's so much nicer than wearing a hat, and in my favorite shawl-collared traveling dress I feel a charming sight even if I'm not. I've always been one for costumes, and this cheap Chinese umbrella takes me back to Ruth's era of strolling, stately women bedecked in lace and silk and carrying ruffly-edged parasols.

Avoiding that line of tourists waiting to buy tickets, Richard and I pass through the entrance to the Acropolis and make the climb up to the Parthenon, passing what we later discover to be the deconstructed Temple of Athena Nike. I'm kind of glad not to have a guide; then I can simply enjoy what attracts me rather than standing around in the shimmering waves of heat being inundated with mind-numbing, forgettable facts (not that freelance guides don't try their best to snag us unaccompanied ones).

The walkway up to the top level is paved with geometric chunks of beautiful, multicolored marble, of which I stop to take pictures. Piles of Ionic capitals are stacked like vertebrae. I know, look up! I reprimand myself, what deserves the camera's lens rises in front of us: the Parthenon, for heaven's sake! And it is magnificent, and yes, the columns are ever so slightly curved inward, and curses on Lord Elgin, but it is also covered in scaffolding and you can't go inside or touch it, and it is surrounded by masses of sweating, dehydrated people. The staccato tongues of the guides, the raucous laughter and prattling voices of teenage tour groups and the whine of small, feverish children interfere with any attempt to silently sense the immensity and timelessness of it all.

At least I can try to get some shots similar to those of the postcards, an effort that ends up taking us out to various edges of the rocky hilltop, where we realize that once again artists a hundred years ago took some liberties with the placement of their subject matter. Never mind; I do the best I can, then gaze out over the tightly-packed city and the lightly smog-smudged skyline. I think I've had enough, and Richard agrees.

One thing, though: we have yet to find the girls in this mess of humanity. There may be a lot of bodies up here, but there isn't a vast amount of space. How could we have missed them?

Katie

We got there earlier, but the girl wouldn't let us in, even with our tickets, because we didn't have our student ID cards, thanks to Dad not trusting us with them. We waited for Mom and Dad for an hour in the heat before they finally showed up, already having gone through.

WE WALK BACK down, keeping our eyes out for a mountain goat with a Handycam and checking any bored girls sitting in the shade. No luck. We leave by what we discover is the northern entrance/exit. Surprise: from a bench under some olive trees Katie and Liz come storming at us, their voices shrill with anger and indignation: "Where have you been? We've been waiting for you all this time!"

For once it's Richard who's in trouble: "We couldn't get in because you have our student IDs! They wouldn't let us in without them! So you've been up there all this time? Thanks a lot! We've been just sitting here waiting and waiting!"

A pause in the tirade chorus, and then they demand their IDs. Snatching them from Richard, they rule that we must sit here and wait for them while they go up and see the Parthenon. Okay, then we will. Would they like to take our parasols? Yes. They stomp away indignantly, fuming.

You know, it's really not so bad sitting here sweating quietly in the thin shade, repenting our mistake. Wish we'd known there were two entrances. Wish they could see it was a simple oversight. Wish it weren't quite so hot. Wish we had a little bottle of water to drink. Richard goes and tracks one down, and we sit some more, wishing parents weren't always so stupid and wrong.

Katie

It was very slippery with my flip flops on the steps and the giant ants to watch out for, but I made it up to the big structure covered with wirework. Quite hot and I had to pee, so I only spent about twenty minutes total at the Parthenon before I went down again.

AFTER ABOUT FIFTEEN minutes Katie returns. Not being a lover of "old buildings," she's had quite enough for today and is going back to the flat. Richard gives her some euros to buy something cool to drink at God's Restaurant. God appeasing a mortal? Now there's a switch.

Katie

I bought two scoops of strawberry gelato (spent four euro on payment and tip, although it was probably too much since one scoop was 1.30 euro. Oh well, I can be generous even if it *is* the parent's money!) to carry home where I finally figured out how to operate the fan, and the guys next door had stopped jack-hammering.

Liz

We went to the Acropolis, which was my second time [at thirteen Liz had gone to Greece with her grandmother on an Elderhostel trip], but just as pleasurable as the first. It was scorching hot, and there was no cover to speak of, but I enjoyed the awe-inspiring ruins and spectacular views despite the heat. There was more construction going on since last time, and the whole temple of Nike that had been there was totally gone! Also, the Acropolis museum was closed; I later found this was because a whole new museum was being constructed.

The Parthenon brought a calming feeling to me. It felt special to be returning to such a sacred place that I had walked upon before, with its dim sense of familiarity and yet still new and interesting to my senses. The sun reflecting off all of the white marble nearly blinded me, but it left me with a sense of wonder. Old Greek fables came rushing back to mind: the story of how the olive tree came to Greece and the city was name after Athena.

WHEN ELIZABETH EMERGES with her Handycam, she has cooled down somewhat, and we make amends by giving her euros to buy her own parasol. She returns with a yellow one, having bargained some kid down to two euros. Trust Liz.

One more to see: the Thiseon. Man, Lucy bought a lot of postcards of Greece. We can see it in the distance. We figure a dirt path down the western slope will eventually get us there, and so we start out clumping awkwardly down the steep hillside.

We stop when we come to a little fork in the path. We can see an interesting little church unlike anything else we've seen up through the trees to the left. We think it's worth a look, and we're right. This is the sanctuary of Ayios Dhimetrios, a Byzantine relic, compact and roughly circular in shape. It's cool and deserted inside. Tall, narrow, arched windows with rows of flower-shaped cutouts in place of glass lead the eye up to the dome overhead, adorned with a partially restored mosaic of a Byzantine Christ, the brown-bearded one with the elaborately illuminated halo and right hand pointing upward by the shoulder, thumb lightly touching the ring and pinkie fingers. Small white, rose and gray marble tiles weave circular patterns over the floor.

I like best the frescoes faded with age, especially the one of a red-robed woman with a Mona Lisa smile. The simple use of color and outline remind me of the artist Ben Shahn. There's nothing dated about these works. They make me feel comfortable.

I note the two birds carved in high relief facing the knob in the center of one door as I step outside to rejoin Richard on the tiny but tidy parched lawn. As a few more explorers enter the church, Liz finally emerges after filming every square inch of this little gem. This is the kind of discovery that makes traveling worthwhile.

Back on the path we make ground level and find ourselves in the agora, Athen's ancient marketplace. It's hot but quiet here, too. No heavy restoration is taking place; instead, blocks of stone lying jumbled about are all that remain of what two millennia ago was Athen's bustling center. Dirt paths offer a dozen ways to nowhere. Olive and cypress trees stand motionless in the noonday heat. It's here, alone and undisturbed, that I finally feel the past tapping on my shoulder.

THE THISEON IS another long, pillared temple in the style of the Parthenon, only it has its walled interior intact. It's not as pretty as the Parthenon;

instead, I feel it heavy and dour despite the tidily trimmed rectangular lawn which a woman over in the shade officiously waves us off of. Its eaves are smudged and blackened by its entrance, testament to whom this temple was dedicated, the fiery Hephaistos, god of blacksmiths and metalworkers. Can't get in, of course, but I'm not sure I'd want to. Instead, I try to get that postcard shot, our excuse for tramping out to this distant location.

On our way back through the agora, I hit the jackpot: two women in their early thirties pass me who would be perfect to replicate the postcard of the "Grecque Paysannes," an artist's corny rendition a hundred years ago of two Greek women in native dress, one holding a jug on her shoulder. But will they agree to pose?

"Excuse me," I call as they are walking off down a path among the olive trees. "Do you speak any English?"

They turn and approach: "A little," one says, curious.

"You see," I say as I flip madly through the worn pages of the copied cards—ah, there it is! I show it to them.

"My *nona* was here, in Athens, one hundred years ago," I enunciate slowly, gesturing all the while to get the idea across. "I am taking photographs of all these places"—I circle my hand over the pages—"as they look right now." I look at them anxiously as I show them the Paysannes again. "I want to take your picture, like this."

By now they are laughing; they get it. "But we are from Italy!"

Who cares? They're perfect. "No problem," I say, and back up slightly, camera at the ready.

Then and Now
Paysannes Greques, or Greek Peasants

And so they pose, two Mediterranean goddesses, their skin a deep golden bronze, each with an arm affectionately wrapped around the other's waist. The shorter one wears a gauzy, form-fitting dress with a deep V-neck swimming in purples, oranges and golds, while the other, taller woman with short, golden curls wears what looks like a version of an abbreviated Roman toga, white with a black and orange waistband. Both wear shades and are grinning ear to ear; the shorter woman even lifts her arm as if she is carrying a jug. They're loving it.

Snap—"Got it!"

"One more!" they insist.

Snap! again, and we laugh and I show them their pictures on my camera and thank them so much for modeling. Then the goddesses disappear among the olive trees.

BACK AT OUR FLAT, we are totally exhausted by the heat and the trekking—all but Katie, who, when not napping or writing in her journal or perusing *O.K.!* magazine, has hung out at God's, eating and flirting with the cute waiters. It's close to five o'clock, "Happy Hour" on the rooftop of the Backpackers Inn. This means hauling ourselves out of the comfort of our rooms again and walking the couple blocks back to the hostel, but after today I'm willing to do so for the sake of getting some "happy."

At the hostel we discover there is no lift up to the rooftop for the sake of us oldsters, so we climb the five steep and narrow flights to what they advertise as an exceptional view of Athens. We emerge from a small rectangular hole onto the rooftop and—egad, the entire tiny rooftop is packed wall-to-wall with college-aged kids, leaning against the elbow-high restraining wall or sitting or lolling on the gold futon cushions depending on their state of "happiness." As Richard says in wonderment, "If I were thirty-five years younger, this is definitely where I'd be."

But here the parents are, thirty-five years too late, so we will just pretend while remembering The Summer of Love. Drinks are ridiculously cheap, and the perspiring bar guy with the brown ponytail is churning out the watery mixed drinks as fast as he can.

Liz

The tiny rectangular rooftop was completely packed, and I felt just as awkward as when I arrived at a college party when I was a freshman. But I quickly lost any stiffness and managed to strike up a conversation.

THE GIRLS HAVE already found kids to talk with, while Richard and I make ourselves as inconspicuous as possible wedged into a corner by the sweating bartender. We end up having a conversation with a couple of girls who are actually interested in the details of our odyssey, which gratifyingly shows that we oldsters aren't totally dull.

The sun is closing in on the horizon when we decide it's time to eat. Liz, who has found an audience, is hard to pry away, and I'm sorry for that in that she needs all the fun, stress-free time she can get. But we are off to God's Restaurant, by now the girls' favorite with its adorable waiters and God himself. If the All-Encompassing God were to look as most people picture him, Restaurant God would be his double. Short and sturdy in stature with snow-white beard and overgrown hair flying in all directions, he welcomes us in growly Greek and gestures us in with a sweep of the arm. After a long, broiling day, we are relieved to put ourselves into God's competent hands.

Katie

We went to dinner at God's Restaurant again so we could introduce Mom to it. Greek salad with tzaziki and chicken souvlaki, a coke and red wine, then baklava. They know us by now. It's fun.

We could see the Parthenon in the setting sun. Very nice. We chitchatted and reminisced at dinner until Mom didn't want to hear anymore about us smoking pot in the garage on the Joe and Dee couch that we later Febreeze-d.

Athens, Greece—Jerusalem, Israel via Amman, Jordan, Thursday, June 19, 2008

Katie

Jack-hammering. Got up to an uproar. We had to check out at eleven, so Mom and Dad were frantic about seeing the museum, packing their luggage and getting breakfast.

After they left, my sister and I woke to more jack-hammering and hammering by hand that shook the building and was truly annoying to try to sleep through. So we got my new *O.K.!* magazine and then settled in for another glorious brunch at God's.

ANOTHER BLISTERING hot day in Athens. We saw all the ancient Athenian structures yesterday, all stripped of their statuary and anything on a more human level. Our plane leaves in the afternoon, so leaving the girls lolling in bed, Richard and I head off to the museum tucked in by the Acropolis which holds all the fabulous marbles, gold and bronzes.

That is, we think we are. But just as we're about to reach the corner of the street climbing up to the revered hill (a climb I'm steeling myself and my parasol for in this heat), we come across this gorgeous, very modern building with a sign out front identifying it as the "New Acropolis Museum." Hmm; here's where a guide would come in handy to clarify matters. What is it?

But since we're right here, we decide to go in. Hey, no charge! Now, isn't that a surprise. Even more surprising is that, aside from a beneath-ground-level exhibit of yet more excavated ruins, there's nothing in this museum save for a few fakes and some cardboard cutout statuary. Nevertheless, from the entrance at the top of a wide flight of stairs, the view of the interior is breathtaking: pale marble that seems to run on forever with light filtering into the space from skylights and banks of shaded glass windows. We descend the stairs into the cool. To our left, a man teeters on a ladder trying to hang a modest-sized relief on a wall stories high as two women steady the ladder's base. Nothing much else is going on, just a few other tourists like us wandering the great hall.

We discover that this building will replace the old one we were mistakenly headed to. The protest we skirted yesterday on the way to the Acropolis becomes clear now: some citizens of Athens are angry that this museum will be run by a privately regulated board rather than by a public entity (and aren't I glad we weren't getting caught up in one of those Internet Department of State "I told you so" affairs). I can see their point, but this is going to be one gorgeous setting for Greece's treasures.

Since there isn't much to see—we're about a year too early—we decide to take the metro up to the National Archaeological Museum. Set in a huge swath of grass with a too-long, baking cement avenue leading to its entrance, this is a much more conventional building in appearance, two stories with a central facade of white Ionic columns towering above broad steps, two lengthy wings to either side, and a little Greek flag on a pole stuck up top. We pay our entrance fee, and the minute we're inside, all those images from my old Jansen book required for my college art history class (Part I) come flooding back. I just know that the golden mask must be here, along with the marble statue of the young man carrying a calf.

And they are. Fortunately, the crowds have yet to overwhelm the galleries, and so it is easy for me to see the solid gold death mask of Agamemnon. It's right up front, but in my opinion not displayed to its full advantage. So it's cool, but not totally exciting, and not as large as I'd expected it to be. A little disappointing, in a way.

In the center of another room is a larger-than-life dark bronze statue of Poseidon, his arm drawn back to throw his trident. This one really wows the crowd, who stand four and five people deep around the base upon which the god is poised, raising him majestically above us mere mortals. It's almost as if his body forms an X, legs planted astride, arms lifted and straight, head turned to the side in mid-aim. You can feel the tension in his body, and it is pretty heady stuff.

Then there are tons of marble statues, buckets of gold and gem-encrusted jewelry, and endless rows of varicolored and delicately incised pottery. It would take days to do justice to this museum. I find myself drawn to the smaller, more humble objects like the dear little seated clay badger holding a cup in his paws and the unexpected warm smile on a marble head mounted in a case in one corner of a room. It's harder for me to relate to the stone-faced gods and goddesses.

And then: there's the red room. Here is where I'm captured, helpless, held hostage by the vision of a life-sized, lithe, long horse, stretched to its fullest, leaping into the air as if to take flight. The dark bronze animal, supported in space by a thin, bronze pole and surmounted by a little boy, is striking against the China-red walls within which it has been captured. No other room that I can remember has been painted this red. Ears laid back and teeth bared in the midst of a wild and full-throated cry, this horse must have been someone's favorite. I know it's mine. I could stand here forever, drinking it all in.

Then Richard finds me: hour's up; time to get back to the hostel and shove off for the airport. We find the girls and decide to eat one last time in God's Restaurant. Goodbye, goodbye. We all bid farewell to God—the white-haired, hip oldster owner—and the cute Greek waiters the girls have flirted with. Strangely, Katie and Liz don't object when we take the blue-line metro to the airport rather than a taxi. Thank God (not the one in the restaurant) for the 2004 Olympics; the city has been a clean dream of a place to navigate. I'm only wishing the journey to Israel via Amman, Jordan, could be as easy. This one's going to be tough.

To The Holy Land

Diary of Ruth K. Crapo, 1907-1908

On board the *Ismalia*, February 7, 1908

Today it was rougher than rough, and almost all the party stayed in bed. I crawled up on deck in the afternoon and sat for a while with Mrs. Fitzsimmon, the Irish woman who is never seasick and hasn't missed a meal or a morning plunge since she came on board. Her husband has kept her company, too, and they make us tired.

A lot of queer people are on board. A pretty tough lot of Austrians sat near me at table who used their toothpicks continuously and played for money, as did the ladies. They ate like so many pigs.

On board the *Ismalia*—Alexandria, Egypt, February 8, 1908

We arrived in Alexandria early this morning and expected to get off the steamer, but not at all. It was quarantine for us for thirty-two hours, as our boat had touched at Constantinople before it left for Alexandria. *Maybe* we weren't mad as hornets, but we had to make the best of it like good fellows.

I was dressing this morning in all my clean clothes getting ready to leave the boat when a swashing big wave came in through the porthole and soaked me to the skin. The entire cabin was dripping, too, not a dry spot left. It was the last straw. I was ready to kick the bucket or anything else handy.

Alexandria-Port Said, Egypt, February 9, 1908

Outside the breakwater a fierce storm raged all day, and we were glad to be in the harbor. About noon the quarantine doctors came on board and felt our pulses and decided that we were well enough to go onshore.

The Cook's man appeared finally and helped us through the custom house into carriages. The house inspector spotted my pigskin bag and examined everything carefully. She told me that many natives smuggled in jewelry and firearms and that she was there to catch them. She evidently took me for a native.

Port Said, Egypt, February 10, 1908

Port Said is right on the Suez Canal, and immense steamers come right up to the main street of the city. Sitting on the hotel piazza, one could wave good-bye to friends and hear the bands playing in the steamers going to all parts of the world.

Off the main streets Port Said was very dirty, but around the hotels all was clean. The people are simply fascinating, every race and color, and their costumes almost unbelievable, so foreign and weird. The waiters at the hotel wore white "nighties," red sashes, fezzes and slippers and were genuine blacks. A scary lot.

We all purchased white canvas helmets for our Holy Land trip and sported them all day. We had Turkish Delight and other queer sweets.

Port Said, Egypt-on board the *Lloyd*, February 11, 1908

In the morning we took a long walk up the Suez Canal. The dirt and filth in some parts were simply frightful, and it's hard to understand how people manage to live in it. At one spot we came upon twenty-three camels working along the canal carrying dirt in great boxes. They are queer-looking beasts and were gaily decked out in collars and necklaces of beads.

The different oriental costumes you see in a day are marvelous. We came across some Bedouins in their skins of goat, camel, etc. We also saw many natives carrying goatskin bags and women with water bottles on their heads and babes in their arms.

We sailed at six o'clock, four in a state room. The water is smooth.

Diaries of Holly, Katie and Elizabeth Pierce, 2008

Athens, Greece to Cairo, Egypt via Amman, Jordan— Thursday, June 19, 2008

THE ROYAL JORDANIAN flight is just about perfect. Boy, they know how to treat their customers. No sooner are we seated than they pass out blankets (the cabin is freezing) and then commence to serve an afternoon meal that makes Southwest's pretzels look pretty pathetic. Chicken with rice in some kind of yummy yellow sauce, a little Greek salad with olive oil and vinegar, a bun with Laughing Cow cheese and a pat of butter, water, a square of quite delicious chocolate cake plus complimentary wine. Phew; I'm stuffed.

The crew seems very courteous and open to us, but I suspect that English is not totally their strong suit when a young steward comes by to pick up trash. As I hand him the Happy Cow packet which Liz accidentally squished, I say apologetically, "My daughter sat on her cheese."

"Oh, that's good!" he replies enthusiastically.

Jordan seems to be the neutral hub for Middle Eastern travel. It seems there's no getting around stopping here if you're flying to Israel from just about anywhere but the U.S. No, that's not true. When making our reservations for this leg from Greece to Israel, I could have booked the cheap Olympia Air flight that left at two o'clock A.M. and arrived two hours later. But even as tight-fisted as I am, I just couldn't subject us to such a hellish night, so here we are on Royal Jordanian, the next-cheapest alternative (by hundreds of dollars). It's going to be bad enough as it is to be arriving in Israel at quarter to eleven at night.

Flying over Jordan—what a wasteland, and I mean there is nothing here, just pale brown nothingness. Even the sky is a dusty whitish color. I know it has something to offer, but what, other than Petra, and where is it? No mountains I can see. I can't help thinking: poor, gorgeous Lisa Halaby, now Queen Noor, gave up her American life as a Princeton grad for this?

As we land on this vast plain of nothingness, it is around 5:30 P.M. I know no one (lizards?) is scrutinizing us through our tiny unwashed windows as we roll along, yet I feel as if I'm breaking some law as I furtively snap a quick shot of an Iraqi Air jet, a funky old model painted and logo'd an unimaginative white and green. The Iraqis have an airline? We bypass

Terminal B (the terminal where everyone hates us Americans) and taxi into A, which is Western-friendly. A soldier in camouflage with a green beret and a pistol on his hip surveys the scene alone on the tarmac until a jeep drives up with two others, one with a red beret, probably tagging him as higher in rank. We step down the stairs, then onto a bus that transits us to the terminal.

As I pass through the checkpoint, two grinning Arabs ask if I know any Arabic, and so I trot out my "*Salaam alekum*," the reverse, and "*Shukran*," that just cracks them up. They have to know my name and try to pronounce it, but with little success.

Liz

At first, when we landed, I felt very nervous. Going into the airport I felt as if my heart was in my throat. I felt just like I did when I landed in Africa: quiet and passive, able to be swept away by the slightest breeze.

I went to find the bathroom in the airport. I went upstairs looking lost and immediately several people nicely ushered me into it. As I came out of the stall a friendly woman immediately handed me a towel and regaled me with "Where are you from?" Her genuine friendliness comforted me and made me smile.

As I walked back downstairs my heart sunk back into its proper place. I feel like people here want to do anything but hurt you. Probably just another distortion by the American media. I have yet to see hostile faces and big guns as portrayed in mainstream movies and am beginning to look forward to our stay more than I expected.

WE HAVE A FOUR-HOUR wait in the airport before we can take our ten o'clock flight into Israel. We drop our bags in a square of chairs before passing through the security checkpoint so we can pass the time checking out the almost-deserted duty-free shops—and aren't they the same the world 'round. Next to us is a Cinnabon shop, while down the way is a Popeye's chicken bar. Richard buys some Cuban cigars from a shop that can only be entered by pushing a large button, allowing you into what is essentially a room-sized humidor. Katie and Liz are thrilled to find a new issue of *O.K.!* magazine on the racks; "My Post-Baby Booze Binge" and "Best Butt Awards" (Beyoncé wins "Most Booty-licious") are sure to keep them occupied for a while. I wander around, checking the price on Diorissimo perfume to see if by some miracle I can afford it this trip around (I can't). But there is a little shop of relatively inexpensive imports, and I spend some idle time trying on eight-dollar beaded necklaces which are really quite nice. I decide to go get Katie, as I feel this is something she might be interested in.

Back at our bag-laden chairs I find a family of black-shrouded women with various children sitting across from us. Grandma is confined to a wheelchair, and her daughter is attentive to her. I wonder idly where they are from: Egypt? Lebanon? Saudi Arabia? Their voices are low, but even if I could hear, what would that tell me?

Liz is sitting closest to them, and I realize she is actually conversing with them in some manner. Well, gosh, it turns out they're from Chicago. They're flying to Israel for a wedding in Jerusalem and so have dressed appropriately to meet all their relatives. Boy, do I feel dense; leave it to Liz to discover the truth. She is now busily explaining to them the purpose of our trip and showing the grandmother Lucy's postcards, who loves them because they depict her old homeland.

Liz

Here we are now, waiting for our flight to board with the really nice Israeli-American family that is flying in for their brother's wedding. I don't know what is in store for us, but I feel much more relaxed and excited about the journey. Israel sounds like a warm and colorful place. At the moment, I'm not even that sad about leaving Greece because instead I am excited to see what happens next!

Now THEY ALL want to see the cards, including the young teenage daughter and a little girl about nine years old in beige pants and a lavender sweater who has been munching away on some Popeye's. Liz promises the grandma to send her copies of the Israel and Egypt cards (to Chicago, of course) once she gets home.

Katie

There was terrible jack-hammering in the airport; it seems to follow us everywhere!

MEANWHILE, I PRY Katie loose from "Britney Spears: Happy At Last" and take her to see the necklaces. She is enthralled. After much deliberation she chooses the blue and green one with tiny beads hanging in a V from her neckline. It's really very pretty on her, and when we get back to our seats, the Chicago family gets very excited and must go check out the necklaces themselves—won't they make great gifts for the relatives! As we pass the shop on the way to get something to eat, I see them crowded around the display, happily cleaning out the shopkeeper's necklace supply.

7:45 P.M. The shops are old news by now, I've used the bathroom, and now there is nothing to do but sit. Watching travelers pass by, I estimate that about fifty percent are in traditional dress. Men wear flowing white robes with red and white twisted checkered bands anchoring their headscarves. Women are covered from head to toe in black, flowing, coat-like dresses and head scarves wrapped tightly around their faces. I've seen it all before, but this alien dress never fails to give me a little shiver of excitement.

8:30 P.M., and they've changed the departure gate to number four. We transfer our luggage, the handles of the three parasols—magenta, yellow and green—sticking out of my purple backpack. Announcements continue to flow out of the speakers, first in Arabic and then in English, and so we are being tutored in "*Shukran*." I think I need another walk.

Sometime after ten o'clock we board our aircraft. Finally aloft, it is a beautiful sight outside, with vast spaces of darkness pricked by tiny settlement lights, which Katie likens to jewelry. And the flight is plenty short as well, what with Israel in Jordan's backyard. Before we know it, we're landing at Ben Gurion Airport, which sports a gigantic, blobby gold menorah out front floodlit from every possible angle. It seems a little over the top to me, but for heaven's sake, it *is* Israel.

The Holy Land

Diary of Ruth K. Crapo, 1907-1908

On board the *Lloyd*—Jerusalem, the Holy Land, February 12, 1908

This morning when we arrived at Jaffa, it was blowing a gale. In spite of high waves, we were taken off in big rowboats and actually thrown from the steamer. A woman in the boat after ours fell into the water.

The trip to shore was an awful one, little Ruthie actively ill all the way. Had we been an hour later, we couldn't have landed at all.

Jerusalem, the Holy Land, February 13, 1908

It was hard to realize we were actually in Jerusalem this morning. After breakfast our dragoman [translator] appeared. We went through the narrowest, dirtiest streets, winding and steep with queer little two-for-a-penny shops and arches overhead in which people lived.

We first stopped at The Church of the Holy Sepulchre. A pilgrimage of Russian peasants almost filled the church. They were a typical lot with their long hair, queer dress and shoes. Five different religions simultaneously worship here: Russian, Greek, Latin, Armenian or Copt, and Egyptians or Arabs.

In the afternoon we visited Bethlehem and saw the Church of the Nativity. Latins, Greeks, Russians and Armenians worship there, and much fighting goes on in the church.

Jerusalem—Jericho, the Holy Land, February 14, 1908

We were all up at 5:45 this morning and off for Jericho in cold and showery weather. Had lunch there and then had a fine drive to the River

Jordan. Our driver presented me with a ring. He was a jolly good fellow, always good-natured. We were accompanied by Bedouins as bodyguards, and they were a fierce-looking lot.

We forded the Brook of Cherith twice—most exciting. The country is rolling and rocky, and the hills are covered with flowers.

This afternoon one carriage broke down near the Good Samaritan inn, and one got stuck in the Brook of Cherith. We had a fine race with two Bedouins going to Jordan. Mother filled her bottle with Jordan water, and all got covered with mud on its banks. It was a fine day, all in all.

Jericho—Jerusalem, the Holy Land, February 15, 1908

This morning we started for Jerusalem at six. The roads were bad and rocky, and it was an awful pull for the horses, with one giving out completely and having to be left behind.

We had a fine view of the Dead Sea and the Jordan running into it. We stopped at Bethany and saw Lazarus' tomb.

In the afternoon we saw the Jews' wailing place, a wall of Solomon's old temple taken away from the Jews. They wail because they lost it. Each Jew brings a nail and sticks it in the rocks, a sign of their faith in the time when the temple shall be theirs again. I saw eight or ten at it and also our first lepers.

In the evening we went to the theatre and saw a tragedy, the funniest show I ever attended.

Jerusalem, the Holy Land, Sunday, February 16, 1908

This morning, accompanied by the dragoman and his guards, we went to see the Dome of The Rock, built on the site of the Temple of Solomon, pride of the Jews. It was taken from the Crusaders by the Muhammadans. We had to wear slippers over our shoes.

This afternoon we visited the Mount of Olives and saw the locality in which Christ ascended into heaven. We saw the place where he wept over Jerusalem, the Garden of Gesthemane and the tomb in which He was supposed to have lain for three days. It was a glorious afternoon.

Jerusalem, the Holy Land—on board the *Saidich*, February 17, 1908

It was another rush this morning getting out of Jerusalem and off for Jaffa. We found the sea there quiet as a mill pond. Our steamer wasn't in when we arrived, and we waited a pretty long time. I spent most of it eating oranges and bargaining over dinky little lace doilies.

Lots of passengers—people we met in the Holy Land—are on board, and we spent a pleasant evening on deck in the moonlight. We were much interested in a man from Dakota, plus a rich widow and her daughter. We couldn't make out whether it was the mother or daughter he was after. We left "Mother" singing to him on deck.

Diaries of Holly, Katie and Elizabeth Pierce, 2008

Athens, Greece—Jerusalem, Israel, Thursday, June 19, 2008

Liz

We had a bit of an interesting arrival in Israel. We went to the passport control area, with me more nervous than it turned out was necessary. Mom was about five people ahead, with five or six Indian or Pakistani people in front of us. We looked behind us for a moment at a woman who was making a fuss, then looked back to find about ten more people had cut in front of us to join their fellows, which was why the girl was upset, no doubt. She was telling them to get in the back of the line like everyone else, and we loudly agreed, but they only stared forward and ignored us.

Oh, but they got theirs! When it finally came time for them to go up to the passport booth, every single one of them was sent to the secret investigation room in the back corner. They even took away every single person's passport from them! So as we approached the booth ourselves, we watched person after person in the cutters-in-line group get turned away with a disappointed look on their face. Well, justice was served!

It's ABOUT 25 MILES from the airport into Jerusalem, and I've read of public transportation, but once we step outside, we see a long line of shuttle buses ready to whisk passengers off to the Holy Land, and by this time we are closing in on midnight. Fine; we're exhausted, so we climb into a shuttle ready to be transported.

Well, that's the plan, but we discover that this shuttle has more in common with a Ghanaian *tro-tro* than with what we call a shuttle. The driver is not about to rev up the engine until his van is completely full. Lots of shouting and to-ing and fro-ing go on outside as the shuttle drivers vie to fill their vehicles. Every now and again the tailgate slams open, a bag is tossed in, and another body hauls itself into our van's dark interior.

When we are finally packed in to the driver's satisfaction, off we go, winding over and through Israel's hills and valleys. By now I can just taste my bed at the YMCA 3 Arches. After what seems an eternity we begin to enter Jerusalem's outskirts.

But what's this? Instead of heading straight to the anticipated depot in town, our shuttle is driving through quiet residential streets. It reminds me of the time ages ago when Richard and I took a Greyhound bus that got lost after midnight on a dirt road in the Central Valley's onion fields on its way to Los Angeles. *What is going on?*

The shuttle pulls up to a curb. A man in a short-sleeved dress shirt and a yarmulke atop his head steps out, briefcase in hand, and the driver happily bids him goodnight. Then off we go to the next address on his list! Damn—I realize this guy must have an actual clientele! By the time we arrive at the 3 Arches, it's 1:30 in the morning, and we are frantic with fatigue. But they are still up and chipper at the front desk, and we finally make it to our room that is amazingly commodious for what I'd imagined a quad at the YMCA would be.

Even though it's 1:30 A.M. I call Sandy, our Israeli guide who has instructed me to call her once we're in, no matter the hour. Am I surprised when a booming female voice with an unmistakable Southern accent answers!

"You sound just like Molly Ivins!" I exclaim.

"I'd better not! My mama would be rollin' in her grave to hear that!"

Oops—one strike already. She's conservative and from North Carolina, as it happens. But she easily forgives me, and despite her wanting us to hit the road at eight o'clock tomorrow morning, we agree to meet down in the lobby at nine o'clock, a blessed concession to our late arrival.

Jerusalem, Israel—The West Bank, Palestine, and back, Friday, June 20, 2008

FRIDAY, AND Shabbat begins at sundown tonight, so Sandy has scheduled our visit to Palestine for today so she can get ready for the evening feast. Nine A.M., and you couldn't miss her. There she is, big smile, big body, big energy, wonderful big voice, dressed in a blue cotton camp shirt and wearing a pink raffia cowboy hat over her blond hair. A delicate sheen of sweat crosses her upper lip, attesting to the already-hot day. It's hard to keep myself from humming "Big Girls, You Are Beautiful." She has set us up with George, a favorite Palestinian guide of hers, and with Muhammad, a young man she has been grooming as a driver. She has been working in this business for fifteen years and so has built up a good working staff.

As we wait out front for Muhammad to arrive, Sandy tells me about the King David Hotel directly across the street. It is the hotel where anyone who is anybody stays, and that means heads of state like George Bush. Today, areas of the street are cordoned off because French President Nicolas Sarkosy is arriving, and I wonder if his hottie First Lady, Carla Bruni, will be with him.

While standing in the heat of the front steps, Sandy relates a story to me she was told by the YMCA director about when the British were still in command of the King David, and it was rumored there was a bomb in the laundry room. The British personnel chose to brush off such an absurd idea, with the result being that shortly thereafter, a huge explosion destroyed the south end of the hotel. The blast was so powerful that it shattered windows and tore out chunks of the 3 Arches' facade. Human body parts were found stuck to its exterior. She points out that while most of the destruction was repaired, a small section was left untouched as a reminder of that horrifying day. She points out the capital of one of the hotel's columns, and I can see where it is still damaged.

By now Muhammad has arrived. Sandy has ordered a van for us, as she thought we were all coming, but Katie is not; she has decided to remain back in our room at the hotel. I'm only just now coming to understand that the fears Katie expressed during our pre-departure family meeting must be very real to her. To facilitate this meeting, I had made up a sheet with questions like, "What are your expectations about this trip?" and "What would bum you out the most?" Under "What are you most afraid of?" she had listed "Israel & Egypt" and "terrorists," and to "What don't you want to do?" she had written "Go to the Gaza Strip >> Join up with the terrorist rebels."

Like the British at the King David, I guess I had just brushed off these answers as her being tongue in cheek. Yet I think of her having dyed her naturally light brown hair almost black before leaving, so that, as she said, she would "attract less attention from men." This is a young woman—my daughter—who is truly afraid.

In her second year at college in Oregon, Katie survived a brutal attack that left her suffering from PTSD, or Post-Traumatic Stress Disorder. With determined effort from her family and an excellent and compassionate attorney, however, she received a settlement from the college and the national food service involved directly in the case. Since then, however, she has continued to see a psychologist to deal with issues that have deeply scarred her psyche. Seven years later, and she is still not healed and probably never will be fully. But she has developed ways to cope with her fears and phobias, and I now see that dying her hair black and remaining within the safety of the hotel are two of them.

From this point on, I no longer push her to accompany us on our day trips. Part of me is angry that we brought her all this way just for her to hide out in hotels; after all, she seemed to be so excited about going on the trip and the idea of following the diary (in fact, she didn't read the diary beforehand, instead preferring to read it city by city as we traveled so as to sharply and fully sense the contrast between the times). And there is the matter of our going on this month-long journey at a time when the dollar is worth so little against the euro; we have dug ourselves into a very deep financial pit with this one.

Since she seems unwilling to discuss her difficulties, it is up to me to try to empathize with what she is going through, an effort that takes me almost the whole trip to do—and perhaps I am wrong about this; she has yet to articulate to us what lies at the heart of her contrary and sometimes unpleasant actions. But if she feels the need to hide out, then she should. I am just so sad for all she is missing during this once-in-a-lifetime opportunity to see those things she will probably never return to see.

Katie
I decided to stay back here at the YMCA 3 Arches (right across the street from the place President Bush stays when he visits) because, as Mom was kind enough to remind Dad, I'm afraid of terrorists and Palestinian-controlled territory. I felt as if it weren't worth risking my life, plus I wanted some time alone to just do nothing. It is glorious to lounge about all day in the air-conditioned room without an agenda at all. Not even the swimming pool seems to be able to tempt me out.

RICHARD, LIZ AND I pile into Muhammad's taxi and we're off, winding out of the city, heading east into the blazing sun. The countryside is dull and scrubby, and I think about how much blood has been shed over the possession of this unattractive piece of real estate.

Eventually we come to a checkpoint, the first of several we pass through this day, and I'm surprised: a simple, flat-roofed structure tall enough to accommodate a bus's passage, it looks like nothing so much as someone's carport with tiny booths within its shade. It is nothing like the jammed, noisy and polluted border crossing at Tijuana. We cruise up to a booth, where a soldier speaks with Muhammad. I remember stories of foreigners being arbitrarily delayed at checkpoints for hours; isn't this what the Department of State warned us about? But the soldier simply takes a quick glance at our nervously smiling faces and waves us on. We are officially in the West Bank, the land our country officially insists we enter at our peril.

Liz
After a quick breakfast, Mom, Dad and I met our driver Muhammad in the parking lot and began our drive to Bethlehem. The drive itself was stunning: great, white, rolling rock cliffs dotted with scrawny, olive-green bushes and trees. Not a bit of it flat at all. Alongside the road was a huge concrete wall dividing the two territories.

As WE TRAVEL along the highway in this barren land, we come alongside the wall the Israelis are building to separate themselves from the Palestinians. I'm bad at judging heights, but this monstrous thing must be at least 40 feet high, and it is obvious from its construction who is being kept out. The lower portion looks like huge corrugated concrete, then halfway up, the wall leans in, towering over us at a treacherous angle, its top slimming to a knife's edge. The wall winds sinuously up and over the parched, hilly countryside. Sometimes we hug its ominous side, while at others we see it snaking its way from a distance.

Israel's wall

But the land on this side is so open and non-perilous-looking that we are soon settled back in our seats. In general, it's quiet and there don't seem to be many people out and about. A young man in a turquoise T-shirt mounted bareback trots along the side of the road, the horse's foal skittering along behind its mother. A sign advertises the "Al-Kababji Restaurant and Steak House" at the Olive Tree Tourist Village, while an entrepreneur named Husam has his own yellow and red painted sign:

Shiny Polish for Cars

Polish—Clean Car

Chairs

Clean House Salon

I contemplate what it is that Husam is actually offering when buildings begin to amass, and we are in Bethlehem. Concrete block and a pale, rough granite stone are the building materials of choice, creating a uniformly beige outlook. We pass a shuttered shop, its hinged blue panels adorned with a row of weathered poster portraits of Yasser Arafat in his checkered head cloth. A modest metal sign advertises the "Korean Cultural Center." Muhammad parks and enters a storefront, where he picks up George, our Palestinian guide. A clean-shaven man of medium height, George could best be described as a Middle Eastern version of my retired dentist, also coincidentally named George. He climbs into the car, and we head for the center of town.

The square holds the new and hopeful-looking Bethlehem Peace Center, but we bypass it for the Church of the Nativity. For such a colossal and ornate holy site, its stone doorway is tiny enough to force one to crouch to enter, deliberately built this way for a reason George explains but which promptly escapes me. Israel is so full of potent landmarks that unless I take notes, I can never hope to keep track of every arcane detail. In this heat, damp, sweaty notes are not called for.

Inside, however, it is cool and quiet at the height of the day. It is also dark, with rows of Corinthian columns, dozens of hanging oil lamps and a glass-covered opening carved out of the middle of the marble floor revealing a swirling mosaic of curling waves and a large circle formed from a patchwork of colored triangular tiles—the original church floor during the Byzantine period.

Liz

We stepped through this nondescript rocky hole in the wall into the heaviest atmosphere I have ever experienced. For just a moment everything was still and quiet in this dark, long church with a wooden beam roof letting in soft shafts of light. There were two things I noticed right away: a strong, spicy smell which flooded my senses and the thick, heavy energy which filled the room and engulfed the body.

I sometimes speak of how walls are dense with power, but this was something I had never felt before. The energy in that church was so thick that it filled the entire space, so much that I could feel it heavy and coating my skin. I could feel it fill my nose and lungs. For a moment everything seemed to stop as my whole system was taken aback by this strange, new feeling. It was certainly not bad, but it surprised me, and then I enjoyed it. And then everything else came back, too, and other tourists began emerging from the woodwork.

AT THE ALTAR, George notes that this sacred spot is also a place divided. The Greek Orthodox claim the area to the right, the Armenians, the left, and somehow the Franciscans are in the mix as well. Above all this hang the most ridiculously ornate chandeliers encrusted with chains and gold filigree work, while behind them the wall is covered with layer upon layer of precious metals and gems fashioned into angels, stars and other religious what-nots. It is this sort of rich ostentation that makes me cringe in the face of the starving millions outside this church who obediently give up their last coin to support their faith. As if faith needs support, I think sardonically. Isn't this idea something of an oxymoron?

Liz

The priests there were very nice and friendly, and one of them invited me to go behind the velvet rope to get a closer look with my Handycam. It was then that I noticed it, faint but clearly visible. At the foot of Jesus Christ in the church where he was born, there was a small smooth wooden circle and engraved within it: the eye of the Illuminati!

A chill ran through my body, and for a moment I was in total shock; how could it be there? I had thought that these theories were a bunch of mumbo-jumbo, but it was at that moment I knew there to be some truth to it. What, I wasn't sure, but in a church this old, this sign at the very foot of Christ meant something. I couldn't shake the feeling for a long time. My mind kept turning it over and over, thinking of it all again and again.

Katie

My sister saw the Illuminati sign at Jesus' feet in his church of birth *and* I heard jack-hammering nearby.

WE ARE NOW descending the steps into the true inner sanctum, the supposed spot where Christ was born, which lies behind and beneath the altar. Here only slim, white tapers and dim candles set in colored-glass lamps provide light in this dark and close spot, along with an incongruous eight-pointed fluorescent star in the low ceiling. Heavy woven brocades and holy paintings enclose a small area on the marble floor, in the center of which is a beaten gold star bolted to the stone. If you are a believer, here is Christ's birthplace, long since built up from its humble origin.

Worshippers and visitors alike kneel to touch the holy spot, in the belief, perhaps, that this personal contact will add spiritual dimension to their faith. Well, I've come all this way, and even though I will soon be studying to accept Zen Buddhist precepts, it would be pretty small of me not to honor this holy site. So I, too, kneel and touch the star. I don't feel anything like sacred electricity coursing through me, but then I didn't expect to. I think again of how lucky, in a way, are the believers.

Outside we go into the heat, and we are off to tour other holy spots.

Liz

And it was then that the strangest thing happened. When I was back in Greece, my mother gave me a small turquoise stone, because the tradition there said that if you kept it with you, you would return in three years' time.

Well, as I walked out across the courtyard of that church I saw something colorful and bent to pick it up. My whole mind shuddered in awe and almost fear. There on the ground was another piece of turquoise, exactly the same as the first. I was suddenly and completely spooked by this discovery following my almost unbelievable church experience. My body felt rocked by these dual revelations for a long time, unsure of what to make of either. I remained very quiet and still, turning them over in my heart.

WE SEE THE Milk Grotto where Mary, the new mother, apparently dripped some of her breast milk on the ground, instantly turning the cave's walls chalk-white. According to George, women having lactation difficulties come to touch the dusty grotto walls to alleviate their problems. (I'm careful to keep my hands to myself.)

Liz

We descended the well-worn steps into a small, cool, underground chapel, and as I passed into the room I placed a single drop of holy water on my forehead between my eyes. For a moment it seemed to burn in the cool air. I felt deeply purified and protected.

THERE IS ALSO Lazarus's tomb, the entrance of which opens right onto the street. Just as in Lucy's postcard, an oldster is standing by the entrance, ready to "guide" us down the steps and then collect his pittance. Unlike the woman in robes a hundred years ago, though, this gent is thoroughly modern in his long-sleeved plaid shirt, gray slacks and a baseball cap to keep the sun off his walnut-brown face. Liz has no interest in descending into this steep, damp grotto, so Richard and I climb down into the cool, check out the undistinguished scene, then clamber back out, passing our shekels on to the old guy, who accepts them wordlessly.

Liz

On the way to Jericho we stopped off to see Lazarus' tomb. Mother found this interesting, but really it was just a hole in the ground. The story behind it was much more interesting than the site itself. Besides, everyone knows I get creeped out by going underground. Such a cold and slimy feeling, honestly.

BETHANY, THE Garden of Gethsemane—they all blend together in my heat-addled mind. We are now ready for lunch, but before this we must visit George's brother-in-law's shop. But of course. We trudge past the shuttered "Alleluia—Bethlehem Souvenir Discount Shop" and are escorted into a clean, well-lit, air-conditioned room that is absolutely stuffed with *tchotckes*—olivewood knick-knacks repetitively carved into every conceivable shape, ceramics glazed with holy motifs, prayer beads, Dead Sea cosmetics, coasters and posters—it's all here, my worst nightmare. My guess is that George has phoned ahead to inform his brother-in-law of our coming and, unlike the Alleluia—Bethlehem Souvenir Discount Shop shut up during this worst heat of the day, to stay open. Two women try to coerce me into buying some forty-dollar mud product, while Liz is being herded up to the counter with a sixty-dollar olivewood bird carving. Richard is crafty enough to show interest in the plastic laminated placemats with a photo of the holy birth star on one side and pictures of the church's interior on the flip side. It's unfair; we are the only customers in the shop, so there are two of them on each of us. (In retrospect, I figure I can hardly blame their hard-sell tactics; after all, I don't imagine the West Bank to be hosting much tourism these days.)

It isn't until I ask about a one-of-a-kind, old-looking metal lion over in a dusty corner case that they catch on: antiques! Forget about this tourist stuff; it's time to bring out the drawers of antiquities! By this time I am ready to beat it out of here, but the drawer of old teardrop-shaped pottery oil lamps catches my eye. They look authentic, but . . . ? As I pick out one, George's brother-in-law is busy pulling tiny photos of the drawer's contents out of an envelope. He is searching for the photograph of my oil lamp. This one? No—shuffle, shuffle—perhaps . . . ? No . . .

Do I care? Just get me out of here. We consider ourselves lucky to escape with my oil lamp, a key ring and Richard's set of laminated placemats, leaving the brother-in-law still pawing through his photos. I figure this at least must say something about its authenticity.

Starving, we are led two doors down to George's cousin's cafe. No one is there but we three. The waiter brings us our order, and then some. Did we ask for this purple slaw stuff? and what about this other giant plate of fries? In the end the bill comes, and we are charged what amounts to seventy U.S. dollars. Too late we realize we've been taken in again. But we are too exhausted to argue and pay up.

Later we report this scam to Sandy, and she is furious. It's doubtful any of her customers will be seeing George's relatives anytime soon, and perhaps maybe not even George.

Liz

Our suspicions were confirmed when Sandy told us this was an extortionist price and was outraged on our behalf. Not only was it an upsetting experience overall, but we felt it created an inordinate amount of ill will between our two cultures.

AT THIS POINT we somehow lose George and are left with our driver, Muhammad. It is now deep into the heat of the afternoon, and we drive through the empty and dry scrubby hills.

Liz

On the way I spotted a cluster of dark, moving dots on a sandy hill: a small herd of sheep accompanied by a single man, miles from anywhere. These we later found were Bedouins, nomads for thousands of years but forced into settlements by modernity. My heart ached to see more of these people and to film their lives and dreams, the stunning beauty of such vibrant life against these empty hills.

JERICHO IS FINALLY in sight: just another dusty, undistinguished city set up against a barren hillside. The postcard is much more fun, depicting a small number of low-lying hovels labeled "Modern Jericho." I can see in the distance where the hillside slopes down from the west behind the town, and I have Muhammad stop the car at the point I feel most duplicates the card's landscape. I snap my pic, then climb back into the car's feebly air-conditioned interior. Okay, check that one off; we're ready for the 3 Arches.

But instead of making at U-turn and heading back, Muhammad continues on into Jericho so we can see its true splendor, scrawny chickens, cruelly-overloaded donkeys and all. Broken sidewalks with crumbling curbs line the streets. Skinned sheep carcasses hang in the broad doorway of an open-air butcher shop. The town seems hardly a hive of activity, but

I chalk this up to the suspension of activity during the warmest part of the day; only we ignorant tourists are crazy enough to be traveling around in this furnace.

Liz

Eventually we reached Jericho, after passing through several army checkpoints surrounded by broken concrete blocks where the most important question asked was if we were Jewish. Driving through town we saw buildings riddled with the holes of past bombshells, rebar sticking out like sun-bleached skeletons. It is a dry town far from anything but the Dead Sea, which stretches low and blue in the valley below.

Not much to see, really, and we soon turned off into a small parking lot containing a store with bathrooms. Stepping out of the car, I felt intense waves of heat blowing over me in heavy sheets. After briefly using the bathroom and purchasing a wicked pair of sky-blue sunglasses to replace the ones I'd crushed, I wandered into the corner of the parking lot where a large tour bus was parked. A group of overweight white tourists with Southern accents were taking turns heaving themselves onto an old, worn-out camel. They shrieked as the camel stood up suddenly, nearly toppling them off. The poor beast repeated this routine over and over.

I waited until they had returned to their big buses, their chatter fading away with the trailing exhaust. I approached the camel and introduced myself to the owner and his small son who seemed intent on marrying me, immediately demanding to kiss me on the cheek. The camel's name was Sunny, he was ten years old and would live to be about sixteen. I chatted briefly with them and took a quiet photo before we all took off again. A sweet and patient beast was he. Yet I still wasn't sure what to think of it all.

Then and Now
Modern Jericho

WE FINALLY PERSUADE Muhammad it's time to turn around, but I make him back up at one corner so I can catch a shot of a red and green carefully-lettered banner suspended between two light poles on which the Eizarieh Local Council has declared, "WE SHALL NEVER KNEEL OR SURRENDER—THE WALL SHALL FALL." We continue on out of town and then head south along the way we came, ostensibly heading back to Jerusalem.

But no; Muhammad has decided that since we are so close to the Dead Sea, why, we must see it! It is difficult to get him to understand that we are the dead ones here now, and at this point the dark body of water in the barren distance holds no fascination for us.

"But you have come all this way! It is only a little bit more!" He drives on resolutely. Oh well; we give up. It's harder to argue now than to just go along for the ride, and so the dark water gradually draws nearer.

Finally, we're here—in a parking lot. Wait a minute; I had envisioned us pulling off at the side of the road along the shoreline, wading around a bit, then heading back. But this is a full-fledged bathing/picnicking/bathhouse-ing establishment where we discover it's going to cost us thirty American dollars *each* to buy access to this grubby lakeshore.

"Sorry, Muhammad, but ninety dollars is just too much."

"But you are here only once! You must see it now!" he says, a tone of both reverence and desperation in his voice.

"But we didn't bring our bathing suits." A logical point. This either doesn't sink in or he doesn't understand or—

"But you have come this far! It is right there!"

"No bathing suits! We didn't bring them!"

"You can swim in your clothes!"

I have this absurd image of us splashing about in the brackish water fully dressed, then driving all the way back to Jerusalem, damp, tired, salty and miserable. I also have this uncharitable idea that perhaps if he can get us Americans into the water at this insane price, he'll get some sort of kickback.

"You know, Muhammad, in America you do not have to pay to swim in the sea"—well, in most cases. "You swim for free. We just won't pay to do this. Isn't there a place along the shore where you can swim without paying?"

Maybe he is sincere about us making contact with the holy water, for he gets on his cell phone, calls Sandy and asks her where we might swim for no shekels. Apparently there is such a place, but it is a good distance farther south, much farther than we're willing to go this late in the day.

Liz

We intended to stop briefly at the Dead Sea simply to dip our feet in, but found it would cost each of us thirty dollars to walk onto the beach, so we simply looked through the chain link fence at the water nearby instead. Perhaps it was different when you actually experienced it, but from my viewpoint its trash-lined banks looked like any old stupid pond.

WITH GREAT REGRET and many heavy sighs, Muhammad realizes he is defeated, and we trudge back across the baking parking lot to the car. There's a lot of tension in the air, and we are all silent as we drive west into the sun. I ask myself why I should feel guilty about disappointing this young man. He's our driver, and he should be taking us where we want to go, not the other way around.

But I do feel bad. I know this has to do with what Sandy told me earlier about him. An unruly young child in a large and impoverished Muslim family, Muhammad was relinquished to an orphanage. He was later adopted by a Christian family for a reason I can't fathom—certainly not to educate him. Given his mixed religious background set against such an explosive part of the world, we are curious what he believes.

He has no particular belief system, relying instead on his own ethical standards built on principles of compassion and peaceful coexistence.

"When I am in bad traffic," he explains, "I just wait instead of being angry. I am quiet. Why should I honk my horn? There is nothing anyone can do."

Hmm—this is beginning to sound familiar. When we mention Buddhism to him, he has no idea what that is—understandable, seeing as he doesn't know where Asia is. But when we say that we practice these same precepts, he wants to know more about this "Buddhism." We explain as well as we can how Buddhists believe that everything is one, that there is no duality of being. People always want something—cars, a new house, a beautiful new look, even health, happiness and to somehow escape death. In fact, it is that concept of duality that gives rise to unhappiness and suffering in life.

"Yes!" he says. "This is what I believe!"

The discussion gets a little dicey when Muhammad wants to know about Buddha: is he God?

"Well, in Buddhism we don't really believe there is a God."

"You do not believe in God?"

"Not really."

"Oh, so do you pray to Buddha?"

"No, he was just a man who discovered the truths that make up Buddhism." I try to give him the short version of the prince and the bodhi tree.

"Then who do you pray to?"

"We don't. Everything is one, right? So whom would we pray to?"

"I see," he says doubtfully. Then another thought strikes him. "But what about heaven? Do you go to heaven when you die?"

"Well, no, we don't believe in heaven—or hell. If we did, it means we would think there was a god who could like you and send you to heaven, or be angry and send you to hell. That would make God no better than a man, with a man's feelings. What kind of god would that be?"

He mulls this over, and he seems to be satisfied with our answers. In fact, he sounds positively excited. He wants to know more about this Buddhism. Maybe he is a Buddhist and doesn't know it!

By now we've reached the 3 Arches, and it's time to say goodbye for now. But we promise to talk to him more about Buddhism when he drives us tomorrow, okay? Yes! He would like that very much. My heart goes out to this young man so excited to have discovered the beginnings of some meaning in his fragile life.

It's now evening and time to usher in the Sabbath, and for us that means walking over to the Western Wall to see what that entails. Sandy has promised us it's quite the sight to see. So Richard, Liz and I set off walking across to Old Jerusalem.

Liz

Mom, Dad and I began to walk to the Wailing or Western Wall, to witness the beginning of Sabbath. Katie once again preferred to stay within walking distance of an air conditioner.

Katie

Today is the start of the Sabbath—Friday night, I guess. I took off my old nail polish and can't wait to coat my toes anew.

Down, then up through a little valley we walk, not sure if something specific happens at sundown or not, so we hurry not to miss it, if there is an "it." It's not hard to determine where the western entrance is, as more and more people are flowing in that direction. All we have to do is follow any tall man dressed in a black, long-tailed coat and wearing a dark fur, tire-shaped hat. If a boy child accompanies him, he is dressed in dark slacks, a long-sleeved dress shirt and with curls down his cheeks (*payots*, that, with no disrespect meant, are like single dreadlocked sideburns) matching his father's. But I mostly seem to see these fur-hatted men in clusters, hurrying up the hill by this main avenue through town.

There are some families dressed more familiarly, men in sport shirts and slacks with tidy yarmulkes on their heads and women dressed modestly while children dance around them in excitement. Others who are dressed according to their sect (where's Sandy to decipher these?) join the flow through the gate.

The way to the Wall is not as obvious as I think. Old Jerusalem is divided into four sections: Armenian, Christian, Jewish and Palestinian, and we are now scrambling our way up and down through the narrow alleyways of the Armenian section.

Liz

I enjoyed walking along this narrow cobbled path the most, as it was lined on both sides with small, warmly-lit shops containing beautiful and mysterious things. Bowls filled with spices of every color carefully shaped into tall peaks, metal basins filled with shiny rocks, wide trays of every kind of exotic candy, long chains of metal medallions or bejeweled cloth camels hanging down from doorways. Each new discovery tempted my senses, and I indulged them, feeding on it all.

LIT BY GLARING bare bulbs and fluorescent lights, shops here remain open, and shopkeepers call out to us obvious tourists with promises of fabulous and unbelievably rare treasures which naturally look just like the guy's olivewood camels and chess sets next door.

Then and Now
Holy Land warriors

167

And at every twist in the alleyways there are the soldiers in their camouflage and berets, submachine guns slung over their shoulders. I see mostly young men; they look to be in their early twenties. Military duty is mandatory here in Israel, and for women as well. I see a *sabra*, a young woman soldier, in an archway playfully adjusting another guy's beret, and by their proximity it's obvious their relationship is more than military.

Up one more long stretch of alley, around a bend to the left, and we are at the top of a long flight of stairs which opens out and down into a broad square. Above, the sky is an exquisitely delicate shade of pale blue, fading into a violet twilight. The Western Wall makes up its far side, a vast slab of pale blocks of stone. As we descend the steps, a woman official approaches us quickly to warn us it is prohibited to take pictures and so to put our cameras away. Mine is so small, it slides easily into my pocket, ready to snap illicit photos when the "photo police" have their backs momentarily turned.

While I've heard of this being called the Wailing Wall, there is no wailing going on here. Instead, it is a madhouse of gay festivity. The devout drop down into an area directly in front of the Wall, which is separated by a sturdy stone and iron retaining fence from the rest of the square. This area is then divided by a six-foot wall which segregates the men from the women. It is hard to tell which side is having more fun.

Liz
I noted that the space was divided unequally, so that the men's section took up two-thirds of the space.

RICHARD AND I wedge ourselves into a little opening in the crowd right next to the ramp leading down into the women's side where we can watch the activity in the more sacred space. Here, high school and college-aged girls are holding hands, dancing mad horas, their multicolored dresses awhirl, their teeth flashing in faces filled with joy. They are laughing and yelling and having way too much fun. I discover that many of these girls have come during their summer vacations as part of youth groups organized to experience the sacred sites and renew their Jewish identity. Some are even so bold as to peer over into the men's section, where a young man in a black suit and red tie is waving his arms, leading a crowd of men in boisterous singing.

Not all are so outwardly joyous. A lone girl of about fifteen wearing a long-sleeved turquoise T-shirt with a matching kerchief stands right below us, rocking back and forth ever so slightly, her head bent as her lips silently recite the holy text she holds in both hands. Far to our left in the men's section, the fur-hat contingent is solemnly huddled together. Ahead, against the Wall itself, we can barely see figures of men and women who we guess are reverently inserting their written prayers into vacant cracks between the stones. To our right up against the women's side of the enclosure is what looks like a large bookcase from which women are pulling down and examining texts—perhaps a two-hour lending library for those who come empty-handed?

There's no one around to answer our questions except a young photo policeman who catches me in the act and sternly asks me to put away my camera. I know he's going to be keeping an eye on me, but I don't want him to think we're just heathen gawkers, so we ask him earnest questions, such as why some women walk backwards up the ramp when leaving (they consider it unholy to turn their backs to the Wall). By the time he walks away, he's smiling and okay with us—as long as we don't take any more pictures (thank heavens he doesn't know about Liz, who has climbed a steep, rocky embankment far to the rear of the square and is tucked away behind a low wall having a field day with her Handycam).

Liz

I crept up onto a white, sandy hill at the back of the enclosure and quietly filmed the scene. Mom took guerilla close-ups with her camera and was scolded more than once.

BY NOW THE SQUARE'S incandescent floodlights have overcome the cool blue of the fading twilight. People are starting to leave. We decide nobody's going to blow a ram's horn or look at a thread or anything like that, so we'll go, too. On our way toward the steps I try to find an abandoned copy of "Shabbat Live!" as a souvenir but am out of luck. Reaching the top of the stairs, I turn one last time to take a quick, panoramic shot, a photo that catches the stern photo policewoman in mid-stride, lurching up the stairs toward me, mouth wide in a yell, arm outstretched (I later discover the photo to be pretty badly blurred—serves me right). We quickly beat it around the corner into the maze of alleyways.

Some of the shops are still open, though the clang of steel shutters hitting the pavement indicates that most are calling it a night. We emerge from the Western Gate into a soft and balmy evening. Cars slow down for families crossing the boulevard. Liz is in an ecstatic mood after all the excitement, but thanks to the busy Sabbath chaos, her anxiety is kicking in.

I want to help her with this, and she lets me. I take her by the elbow and in an effort to simplify her vision and calm her mind, I urge her to look up and savor the beauty of the emerging stars. We make a game of it, striding along: "Chin up! Keep that chin up!" At stairs (of which there are many) I tell her when to step up or down, and after a distance we eventually pass the King David's tall rear walls thickly coiled with concertina wire. We find the front of this venerable hotel, host to so many heads of state, an elegant sight, but the rear is strictly business. I feel content to be going back to the 3 Arches instead. It may be a YMCA, but as the architect who drew up the plans for the Empire State Building designed it, I can tell you it's one heck of a YMCA.

Jerusalem, Israel, Saturday, June 21, 2008

IT'S SATURDAY, the Shabbat festivities are over, and today is our day with Sandy at the helm. She and I were in e-mail contact long before we left on this journey. I met her through TripAdvisor; I'd had a question, and she seemed to be the person most in the know about the area. Once I found out she was a guide, I thankfully put us into her capable hands.

Our order was a tall one. After telling her about my grandmother's diary as the force behind this trip, I sent her a list of those places and sights Ruth had seen. Not knowing which should be high on the list of must-sees, I made no attempt to winnow down this rather extensive list. Despite its length, she was fascinated by our story and was eager to explore with us.

Well, darned if she didn't make a plan covering everything, plus a few extras thrown in. I am certainly impressed and almost overwhelmed by her two-page, nine-point-type itinerary with Ruth's list highlighted in red, explanations and extras in black, and dinner suggestions in blue.

Breakfast is at 8:30 in the 3 Arches patio out front, where Sandy rallies the troops and briefs us on what lies ahead. She is also carrying an orange backpack into which she has stuffed her notes, a Bible and probably the kitchen sink; she is very prepared. Katie is staying behind.

Katie

I believe my one-glass-plus of red wine a day has kept me healthy throughout this trip. Plus the probiotics in the tzaziki has helped. As I heard Mom say this morning, I'm very protective of my sleep. Yes I am. Top two beauty tips: sleep and water. I think I've got both down pat.

AFTER OUR EPIC trip into the West Bank, Liz has decided to keep Katie company at the Y and try out the swimming pool. Unfortunately for both, we awoke this morning to discover our room distinctly smelled of stale urine. The source was tracked to a clogged floor drain in the bathroom, over which we placed a wastebasket as a stopgap measure and opened the window wide.

We wave goodbye to Liz, who has stuck her head out of the little window of the Y's tower.

Liz

I had been excited by the prospect of the hotel pool noted in our guidebook, so we donned our bathing suits and went down to the promised swimming pool for a nice dip—but nooo! First we had to go through the dressing room where we were accosted by fully nude eighty-year-old women, a true fright fest I'm sorry to say, and then, as we entered the indoor pool area, we found the chlorine smell that permeated the air so strong we could barely breathe, and the pool was filled with clusters of old ladies exercising.

Okay, so we could deal with that, but then we found they expected us to wear a swim cap in the pool, which we had to buy for ten shekels! That was the last straw, so we promptly left and went back to our room.

Katie

Liz sorted her trash and I painted my toenails—or was that earlier? Now I'm working on my fingernails, letting the left hand dry before I do the right. It is the palest pink color that Mom picked out in the airport. The housekeeper knocked on the door despite our "Do Not Disturb" sign and looked so sad when I told him not to make our beds, almost as if I had denied him his pleasure.

I just assisted my sister with a terrible leg cramp. Only thing I could figure: imbalanced ions. Needs to eat a banana? That's about all I know.

To ORIENT US, Sandy begins with a taxi ride that takes us around the perimeter of the old, walled and most contentious piece of Israeli real estate, Jerusalem's Old City. I recognize the Jaffa Gate from the evening before, but the others we pass are something of a blur. I only remember the Lions Gate because, well, there are lions carved in the wall. We walk from here, passing through the gate's archway and soon come upon St. Anne's Church, a memorable structure because of its extraordinary acoustics.

Sandy tells us she's going to sing for us, and I think she's kidding, but after putting down her pack, moving farther down the aisle and clearing her throat, she lets go with something by Bach. I am astounded and moved. Her clear, sweet voice reverberates throughout the church's modest and unadorned interior, surrounding and filling us with wonder. After she falls silent and we leave the hush of the church, she confides in us that she majored in music in college. This obviously must be one of her favorite places to take visitors.

Just outside the church, Sandy steers us around a corner to a site where intensive excavation is going on. This is the Pool of Bethesda, Jerusalem's ancient water supply, though precious little water runs through it now. I usually think of pools as being round little ponds where you might go swimming, but instead this pool is an excavation with some pretty dark and deep holes in the ground. I know I should be able to perceive the various ground levels representing stages in the history of Old Jerusalem, but not having taken archaeology in school, I only find it incumbent upon me to back away from those scary pits.

Liz

At twelve-thirty Sandy called to try to convince me to come out for the afternoon. I was disoriented from sleeping. I talked to Mom and asked, will they be walking or driving? and it was all walking, of course. So I hear Sandy in the background going, "Oh please oh please oh please," but thankfully Mom understood and said she would call later at the restaurant for lunch but conveniently never did! Whew! Sometime she can be quite the angel, I swear.

TIME TO HEAD back to the taxi and on to the Mount of Olives, separated from the heights of Jerusalem by the Kidron Valley. Nicely enough, Sandy has planned it so that the driver lets us off at the top of the Mount, so our walking tour will be all downhill from here. Even though it's hot, it's blessedly quiet away from the noisy and crowded city. We enter the grounds of the Church of the Pater Noster, planted with sharp arrow points of Italian cypress, the requisite olive trees and tidy beds of roses lining swept walkways. What we've come to see is outside the church: wall after wall of the Lord's Prayer translated into languages from every corner of the earth. Multiple tiled rectangles bear the beautifully lettered prayer, plus the nation that has paid for the placement of the sacred text. Indonesia, Estonia, Burma, Bulgaria, Serbia, China, Sudan—we're moving along too fast for me to write down every one. Even languages such as Alsatian and Zulu have their own translations.

It's so serene and hopeful in its way. Every corner we turn has a new row of prayers, except for one small corner I peer around where I find a wall topped with coiled concertina wire. Yes, even here.

Sandy's plan is to walk down the Mount of Olives to the main drag, where we'll pick up our taxi outside the Old City. We clump downhill in the heat and dust past an ancient Jewish cemetery, where we see graves that have been vandalized, leaving only gaping, stone-framed rectangles, much like the raw holes left by teeth pulled from their sockets.

Stepping off the main path we climb uphill to what looks like a fairly new, small-sized building—the Sanctuary of Dominus Flevit. Sandy tells us it's supposed to resemble the shape of a teardrop, because "Dominus Flevit" translates as "Jesus wept," the verse every Sunday schooler can recite when put on the spot. The Franciscans built this over the place where Jesus was thought to have cried over a prophetic vision of Jerusalem destroyed. At least now I know why He was upset.

A service is in progress, so we wait until it's over to take a look inside. There are beautiful views of Old Jerusalem from the church's windows, but I think I like best the circular mosaic of a hen (with a halo?), wings spread protectively over her chicks. What this has to do with anything I don't know, but it's very nice.

I keep thinking we're going to go to the Russian Church of Mary Magdalene; after all, its seven gold onion domes flash against this pale, rocky hillside, a shining beacon of interest. Sandy gives some history on it, but we don't stop. Too bad; I later learn it entombs the body of a Russian grand duchess who, after dying in the Revolution, had her body smuggled through *Peking* to be buried here, an amazing example of faith, sheer determination and adept skullduggery.

At the bottom of the hill we finally reach the Church of All Nations, so named because a bunch of European countries pitched in to build it. It resembles a little Parthenon in shape, complete with rows of Ionic columns and a pediment bearing a colorful mosaic frieze of Jesus bestowing peace on all nations.

Inside, things are not so gay. I'm mostly attracted to the striking and unusual deep purple-, dark amber- and ivory-colored stained glass windows, but their rich, deep color accounts for the somber interior. Up by the altar is the real attraction, the "Rock of the Agony," a large, flat slab of smooth stone about fifteen feet wide where Jesus is supposed to have sweated blood. The stone is surrounded by a foot-high wrought-ironwork design of intertwining thorny branches with the occasional little perched bird lending a less-severe touch to the scene. A down light highlights the rock surrounded by kneeling women leaning over the treacherous ironwork to kiss the holy relic (ick; I'm glad Sandy doesn't press us to do this). With most kneelers, it's not like a little peck and we're up and away, but a lingering, impassioned and highly personal communion. There are lots of mostly women's bums sticking up in the air. Terrible to say, but the sight brings to mind ants packed in around a little drop of syrup. It is deathly quiet, warm, stuffy and pretty darned creepy. I'm glad to leave.

Outside it is hot and bright, a relief. We learn this is the Garden of Gethsemane where Jesus is said to have spent His last night before His crucifixion. Bright pink hollyhocks are blooming, but the garden seems otherwise undistinguished, and we don't take the time to stroll reverently around. Instead, we continue downhill past neatly planted olive groves to the spot where we will pick up our taxi.

Sandy gives our driver a ring on her cell, while Richard and I stand in what little shade there is, which happens to be right next to two *tchotchke* cars. Their hoods are draped in blankets that in turn are buried under mounds of Holy Land trinkets: wooden beads and crosses, gaudy plastic necklaces, fake gold menorahs, stuffed animals for the kiddies, commemorative coin collections, fanned displays of faded books, baseball caps, olivewood everythings, and other assorted bric-a-brac. I brace myself for the hard sell, but it doesn't come; parked under some thin shade the two young merchants lean against a low wall, chatting desultorily in the stultifying heat.

Our driver arrives, and we are let off at the Zion Gate in the southern wall, where Sandy points out how the wall is densely pockmarked by bullets. We finger one ragged hole where a bullet is still wedged in the stonework. I don't want to think about how recently this bullet might have been fired.

Once inside the gate, we are in the Armenian quarter (Armenia was the first country to adopt Christianity, so they have always had this little stake in the southwest corner of the Old City). Sandy leads us into a shop. Ah-hah, I knew we couldn't escape this ploy, even with Sandy. But no, despite the fact that there are pieces for sale, she really just wants to stop by to say hello and introduce us to the talented calligrapher who painted all of those Lord's Prayers we saw. Open pots of different-colored glazes sit on his workbench. He is busy painting a plate, but he is glad to see and chat with his old friend Sandy. His flowing white hair and bushy mustache stand out against his smiling brown face as a little fan hums, stirring the warm air.

Back out on the sidewalk (no bag in hand), we pass the Armenian Genocide Museum, which is closed for renovations. The back of a street sign bears a red-lettered sticker reading "RETURN NOW" in both English and what I assume is Hebrew. We enter a quiet courtyard that belongs to St. James Cathedral. The church itself is closed, but the wrought-iron gates enthrall me (these people really have a way with iron). The iron is worked in patterns of repeating circles adorned with tiny, painted gray-green leaves and faded red-orange pomegranates. I know this scrollwork was created centuries ago, but William Morris and the Arts and Crafts movement come strongly to mind. I can hardly leave for all the pictures I want to take.

Passing by the Citadel (the erstwhile Tower of David), we start to walk down a narrow alleyway, me trailing as usual, where a man is spiffing up a hotel entrance with red paint. A sign catches my eye: the "Grand Imperial Hotel." Wait a minute: that sounds familiar. Wasn't the hotel Ruth stayed in called something like the "Grand New Hotel?" I remember thinking it was a rather strange, self-evident name. I had given up trying to locate it, as nothing by that name came up in my Internet search months ago. But now—"Grand Imperial Hotel?" "Grand New Hotel?"

"Rich, stop!" I call excitedly. "I think this might've been Ruth's hotel!"

Richard and Sandy start walking back to me. I'm almost positive the name was the "Grand New Hotel." I have to see.

The surroundings don't look like much. If it is the hotel, its bottom floor has been broken up into shops. A cloth banner advertising an Internet cafe is strung across the alley. A tacky plastic purple and blue sign signals a beauty salon to non-Hebrew speakers with its picture of a rather butch-looking blonde-haired woman. Out on the street side are the Cafe Ido, the St. Michel Cafeteria and the Samara Restaurant and Coffee Shop. And then there is the entrance to this hotel's lobby in the alley.

"Is the hotel open?" I ask the young painter.

"Yes, yes, you can go in," he responds.

Heart pounding, I climb the steps and enter the lobby. There on the wall is a large, faded, black and white photograph of this hotel in its glory days. There is some lettering below the photo, and I look closer: going by the dates, they could have stayed here. But the clincher is the name the hotel bears in this picture: the "Grand New Hotel." And it is dated: 1893, fifteen years before Ruth, Lucy and their mother came to the Holy Land. Of course they would have stayed in this relatively new and "grand" hotel in the wilds of the Middle East.

Forcing myself to speak slowly in case the desk person isn't fluent in English, I tell him, "I think my grandmother stayed here one hundred years ago!"

"Oh! That is very good. Perhaps you would like to see this painting?" and he leads me a little farther down the hall to a large canvas leaning against the wall, ready, I imagine, to be installed in some prominent spot during their renovations.

It is a plain and straightforward rendering of the hotel in pastel colors and in a perspective that is just enough off to lend the work a rather surreal feeling. The fact that everything is depicted as absolutely sparkling clean and native-free is unreal enough. There's not a donkey in sight.

I would guess it was painted in the early 1950s, judging from the three hulking, sausage-shaped cars and the people in the picture. A woman wearing a red, knee-length cape with a matching red hat and bag stands by a light pole. Above her on one of the hotel's narrow, wrought-iron balconies, a man sits at an easel painting a landscape, while another gentleman in a black suit points excitedly at the sky at something beyond the painting's boundaries; what could it be? I'm more concerned with the large, red automobile careening into the picture from the strangely-sloped side street in the right front corner, one menacing headlight and half of a toothed grille just visible.

I'm stoked. This is definitely the place! I'll have to confirm the name in Ruth's diary once we get back to the 3 Arches, but in my heart I know I'm right. I can't believe that we just coincidentally stumbled upon their hotel. I guess the most unlikely of events *do* occur (as we are later to discover again once in Egypt).

Once Richard can tear me away, we head for a photographer's shop Sandy thinks we would be interested in, but as we twist and turn through the alleys (much too narrow for hulking red cars), we happen upon a celebratory procession. Some men are in suits or dress shirts and slacks, but many are wearing red fezzes and short, black vests intricately trimmed with gold braid. Women seem to favor satins; I see red, green and bright gold. All look very sexy with their bare shoulders, loose, thick, black hair and finely applied makeup. Several men are playing strange wind instruments, while others bang drums and tambourines. A tall, lean young man with shoulder-length hair and wearing a T-shirt is filming the whole scene. Everyone is dancing and yelling and happy! A tiny girl in a fluffy white satin dress smiles shyly at us from her father's arms. We stand and gawk with big smiles on our faces, wishing them well in the only way we know how.

Sandy believes it's a wedding procession, probably Armenian, and this is the groom's contingent. Not much farther, and we run into who is definitely the bride and her side of the family. Her dress wreathes her in white satin and tulle. She looks a little like Paula Abdul before she had her nose fixed. She's gorgeous, and she holds her father's elbow, a smiling, tall bald man wearing a green tie. Before them walk three sweet little flower girls, all dressed in white satin with circlets of tiny white flowers crowning their dark hair. More drums and tambourines accompany the festive company. I spot at least one man wearing a yarmulke. It's good to know religion doesn't always trump friendship here.

Another few blocks, and we enter the photographer's small shop lined with wooden drawers and glass cases. An Armenian, Kevork Kahvedjian collects and sells old and rare photographs of Jerusalem's past, mostly those taken by his father, Elia. For many years the negatives of his father's prints lay undiscovered where they were hidden in 1947 in the midst of the post-World War II turmoil. It wasn't until four decades later that Kevork found his father's 1,400 negatives and, a photographer in the family tradition, catalogued and printed this rare, first-hand look into Jerusalem's past. A selection of these prints was put on exhibition and from this arose the book he is now showing Richard.

Sandy urges me to bring out my dog-eared pages of Lucy's postcards. He looks at them intently. He is fascinated.

"Just a minute," he says, and crosses his shop to a drawer from which he pulls a large, sepia-toned photograph. "I think I have this one."

He lays it out on the counter, then places one of my pages next to it. He's right; it's exactly the same shot of the Bedouin warrior. I take a picture of the print and my copy side by side. (It isn't until weeks later that I notice the original is dated 1910. Lucy bought her card in 1908, but by then it's too late to question this discrepancy.)

Then another: the road to Jericho. So this is how these postcards came about. Reduced in size from these elegant prints and transferred to cardboard, in many cases they were hand-colored, although some look as if their color were mechanically applied. We leave the shop, Richard with a copy of the book under his arm, and I with a deeper appreciation for the history of Lucy's postcards.

It's time to meet the girls for dinner. Sandy has made reservations for us on the rooftop of Papa Andreas, a popular Armenian restaurant. By now the sun has dropped in the sky, and the air is some cooler. We pass by the 8th Station on the Via Dolorosa. An Internet cafe is close by, filled with boys busily working the keyboards beneath bars of fluorescent lights. Under the lifeless stares of a pair of pale white mannequins with upswept hairdos, another Armenian restaurant advertises "Happy Hour Special Food From 6-9," and I wonder what "regular" food must be.

Out of the alleys and onto the street, shiny black cars bedecked with blankets of white flowers across their hoods pass us by. It's the wedding party again. In the first car is the bride and groom, the bride all but buried under mounds of white satin and tulle. Unfortunately, a good-sized clump of white tulle has been slammed in the car door. We wave happily at the procession as it passes by.

The girls are waiting for us at the Jaffa Gate, the main entrance to the Old City (I feel good that Liz has gone down this way and can take Katie to it). At Papa Andreas we climb the stairs to the rooftop and find a table where the late sun isn't slanting directly into our eyes.

Liz

The restaurant Sandy chose was on the rooftop of a building and had amazing views in all directions. I could even see the Dome of the Rock, its shining golden crown glowing in the setting sun. I had a wonderful time peering down at all the village activity, unseen from above like a bird on a wire, and taped everything extensively.

On a small side street down below there was a Jewish boy displaying his talents with a particular toy that had rubber cups on a string to a group of captivated Muslim children. Each time he completed a difficult trick they cheered and clapped. They tried their own hands at it, but were unsuccessful and continued to wonder at his long-practiced talent. It was so touching to see such a simple and yet meaningful meeting of cultures.

THIS IS THE FIRST real time Katie has spent with Sandy, who is so larger-than-life in so many ways that I'm wondering what Katie will think.

Menus are produced—ahh, shish kebab, Richard's favorite! It's a slam-dunk order until Sandy clarifies that "shish" and "kebab" are two different things. Really? Are we just too American or what?

"So what's the difference?" we ask.

"Well," she explains in her Southern drawl, "'shish' is just the chunks of meat barbecued on skewers, while a 'kebab' is ground meat that's spiced, molded around a skewer and grilled."

I glance over at a nearby table and see the difference. To be brutally honest, "kebab" looks like dog shit on a stick. But, betting that it's *delicious* shit on a stick, I go with the lamb kebab.

Sandy is excited and happy to be around the girls, and her laughter booms across the rooftop. We ask the girls how their day went. Apparently they judged the pool too chlorinated to swim in and the requisite three-dollar swim caps too expensive, so they spent their time either in the room (what about the urine smell?) reading *O.K.!* magazine, napping in the warmth of the day, or hanging out on the Y's front patio imbibing whatever and getting acquainted with the waiters.

Katie

Dad seemed slightly miffed at my spending, but it wasn't like I bought the most expensive thing on the menu. For once I considered the price before the food unlike what I've been training myself to do.

THE DAY WAS not too strenuous, which I think is good, considering how on the run we've been.

Katie

Sandy's energy was over the top for me. So much more energy and information than I ever needed or wanted. It's a constant barrage, and so I decided not to go with them tomorrow. She's a very *nice* person but just emits too much energy for me. Even over the phone she's a non-stop force.

LIZ HAS ALREADY determined she wants to go with us tomorrow morning to see the Dome of the Rock, so I'm happy she will be well rested.

Liz

And then: the deep soulful call to prayer floating over the rooftops in the dusky air. Captivated, I listened to the sweet, lyrical voice as it moved into harmony with another call echoing from far away. Such a sound cannot even be described; it can only be felt resonating in the body.

Jerusalem, Israel, Sunday, June 22, 2008

THIS MORNING when Sandy picks us up, she is wearing a different hat, a woven straw baseball-type hat with an oversized visor. She is full of resolve that we shall see the remaining sites on my list. I think she knows this will be impossible, but bless her, she's ready to give it a try. Liz is eager to come along, as she wants to see and film the Dome of The Rock, the huge, gold-domed mosque so strikingly visible amidst Jerusalem's landmarks. Katie stays behind, promising to shepherd the luggage down into the baggage room before checkout, and we leave her shekels for lunch and drinks out on the patio.

Katie

Lo and behold, Mom had left both her camera battery, the charger and the adapter in the wall, plus her luggage lock. I knew she couldn't be mad at me for not joining them this morning when I have saved the day for her. I will be excited to whip it out of my bag and calm her frenzied nerves, to be the savior.

WE PILE INTO our taxi that drives us around outside the walls to the southern slopes of the city. We have come to see the Pool of Siloam which appears as a long, rectangular course actually filled with water and lined with cut stone running east to west. Rough, low stone steps border the south side of the site, while all along the north side, the earth has been dug deeply away. Wooden scaffolding supports the excavated earth which reveals the ancient city's ground levels during centuries past.

Liz

Then there was Sandy. Man, that woman really made the day hard! She always wanted us right next to her. No exploring on our own, which is my preferred method of adventure. Once we embarked from the hotel, we were first driven to the Pool of Siloam, or something like that. To be honest, I was really expecting more, like some pools, or something along that line. Unfortunately, there wasn't much to see but some well-worn stone steps.

And then, *oh God*, she made us read Bible verses that talked about them. I thought she was a little more than biased towards her faith, always hinting about how the Jews did or didn't do something *other* religions did, like claim each other's churches or mosques for example. Oh, whatever.

SANDY PULLS OUT her Bible and instructs Richard to read various passages pertinent to this site, although when she sees him helplessly pawing through the pages, she considerately finds the correct pages for him. Something about this pool, and mud and spit being applied to a blind man's eyes, sound familiar: "Here's mud in your eye?" Other than that, it means nothing to me, a religion major in college much too long ago to be of any help.

As Richard stumbles valiantly along, Liz is crawling all over the place, filming every possible angle. A kid comes by wearing an "I Survived Hezekiah's Tunnel" T-shirt—another mystery. Sandy explains that King Hezekiah built an underground aqueduct from the Gihon Spring up the hill from here to the Pool of Siloam to provide the city with water when the pool was still within the city walls. One can wade through foot-deep water from one end of the ancient, pitch-dark aqueduct to the other in about 45 minutes—and it's free! But seeing as how it was constructed in 8 B.C., even for a T-shirt I'm not about to do this.

Enough with Richard as struggling Biblical narrator. Up we climb toward the city walls, passing bracings and sandbags and a long painted mural that is supposed to depict what the Siloam pool looked like during its heyday—clean and pastel. Only later do I find this pool, located in the Arab town of Silwan, is one of those places the guidebook identifies as unsafe "under current political conditions." Frankly, I'm thinking that *any* time in Israel could rate as dangerous "under current political conditions." Before coming to Israel, however, when conversing with Sandy over the Internet, she had assured me that things were pretty quiet presently, and her hearty and familiar exchanges with seemingly everyone in our path is reassuring.

Puffing and sweating away in the already-intense heat, we make the top of the hill, and Sandy is angry to discover that our taxi driver is not waiting for us; instead, he is still mistakenly parked down at the bottom of the hill. She lets him have it over the phone, and so we don't wait long before he speeds into view. We drive back around to the Dung Gate, where we must wait in line to pass through an Israeli checkpoint. A large green metal sign is posted by the "Israeli Police Force—Unit for the Protection of Sacred Sites." Nine strictures are listed, including number seven: "Entry with ritual objects is not permitted." I flash on my six-foot-long Ghanaian talking stick at home; is that the sort of thing that they mean? The list concludes with a polite, "We wish you a pleasant visit."

Me, too, I'm thinking, as after we go through security we pass a phalanx of what I realize are a row of heavy transparent riot shields on our way down past the Western Wall. Then it's another climb up to yet another checkpoint, this one at the entrance to the Temple Mount and the Dome of the Rock. As we wait in line, Sandy notices that the woman ahead of us is wearing a Star of David on a chain. She taps the woman on the shoulder.

"Excuse me, but they'll take that necklace from you if it's showing."

The woman looks at her incredulously. "Oh, I don't think they would do *that*," she responds, and her woman friend looks at us skeptically.

"No, really, they will. Just tuck it down inside your T-shirt or something."

In the end, she does. Phew; no need to start a hassle. I can't help thinking these woman haven't much concept of just how divided Jerusalem is. Once again I'm thankful to be with Sandy with her fifteen years of carefully cultivated friendships with people from all four quarters.

We pass through the checkpoint and are now on the Temple Mount, or Haram es-Sharif, the "Noble Sanctuary." It is huge, flat and rectangular, a space which, aside from its two fabulous mosques, seems remarkable to me for its vast emptiness. But in my mind's eye I can picture it filled wall-to-wall with prayer rugs and kneeling worshipers.

Right in the center of a wide walkway lined by graceful trees leading to the Mosque el-Aksa is a lovely circular fountain, made beautiful by more of that insanely-gorgeous ironwork that here is surrounding and protecting the water. I've never been drawn to ironwork, but I realize that's because I've only seen it used as railings for stairways to cheesy, second-story apartments. This is worlds apart.

Past the fountain is the mosque, which is closed, and it's pretty nice with its dark gray dome, but nothing compared to the breath-taking Dome of the Rock beyond it. My apologies to Notre Dame and Florence's Duomo, but this has got to be the most dazzling structure I've seen so far. Surrounded by so much emptiness and set slightly above ground level by a set of broad and shallow steps, it almost seems to float in space. Richard and Sandy walk over to some shade, but Liz and I are both entranced. The mosque's series of flat sides are covered in an ornate mosaic of primarily sky-blue, tiny tiles, while its majestic dome is solidly gilt with 24-carat gold. Of course it's closed, but the exterior is more than enough to overwhelm me.

Liz is busy with her Handycam filming as much of it as she can, then simply puts the camera down and rests her hands lightly against the cool tile. She can't help it; she is transfixed, exhilarated and filled with an almost holy awe. She stand mesmerized until a guard approaches and asks if she is a Muslim, for if she is not, she is not allowed to touch the mosque. Reluctantly she breaks away, then tells us of this moment as we descend the steps out of the holy precinct. I can only think, I know the feeling.

Liz

The Mount was cool and beautiful and my heart was finally quiet. I spent a blessed ten minutes just soaking in the spirit which filled the place. Call me silly, but I kneeled down on the cool, white stone in front of me and just let the Dome of the Rock overtake me until I felt still inside. I spent a moment with my hand pressed against the smooth wall, but was quietly approached and told if I was not a Muslim that I should not touch the structure. Point taken. Nonetheless, I enjoyed those few minutes of internal stillness greatly.

WE WALK IN THE noontime heat through the streets and alleyways, headed for another excavation site. We pass through a small, covered area solid with colorful spray-painted graffiti. Interesting how one can know no

Arabic or Hebrew, yet still be able to "read" where one is, and here we must still be in the Muslim quarter, for I notice amidst the graffiti simple drawings of what must be the black Kaaba at Mecca. All Muslims feel it's their duty to go on a hajj to Mecca at least once in their lives, so it's not a surprise when a little farther on I spot a sign advertising the services of a man who must be a hajj travel agent. Adorned with graceful and florid Arabic script and two identical photos of the agent, a Koran, pages riffling, is flying over a sea of humanity surrounding the holy site.

Katie
Women here wear sweatpants under their skirts. I don't know how they can stand it with this kind of heat. I was the only one in the dining room to be served. As I sat here, I noticed just how beautiful the YMCA 3 Arches ceiling was. I guess the street was cordoned off because an important man is in town. It is exactly noon.

By now Liz, feeling overwhelmed, is ready to return to the 3 Arches. She has stuck with us admirably, but I'm sure Sandy must be mystified by now as to why she is not accompanying us. Right or not, I feel she is owed an explanation.

While Richard is off getting Liz headed to the YMCA, I start to explain to her about Liz's anxiety disorder, expecting her, as with so many others, to know little about the condition. Instead, I'm surprised that the moment I mention it, her brow furrows and her face fills with concern. She knows about it very well, as she once had a boyfriend who was similarly affected.

"Poor thing. God, I know just how bad it can be. My boyfriend's life was so controlled by it, he could hardly function sometimes. I totally understand."

The dismay and empathy filling her face lead me to sketch for her the outlines of Katie's traumatic assault, her disturbed response, her fear and anxiety about terrorists and how this, coupled with Liz's condition, has altered the path I'd foreseen us taking as a family. Instead of the journey leading us into the past, it has ruthlessly and often harshly revealed to us the realities of the present. Never in all of my daydreams and plans had I even once thought about the potential impact the girls' conditions could have on this journey. I was entranced by a vision—*my* personal vision, not theirs.

Once again I wonder if I should have included my daughters in this journey. Sometimes it seems they have endured rather than enjoyed the duplication of this hundred-year-old reenactment of my grandmother's life. I realize I dearly and selfishly wanted them along because of their proximity in ages to those of Ruth and Lucy. They had expressed their desire to go, but I wonder if they had contemplated in advance the stresses this crazy itinerary would put on them. I just know that if someone had offered me such a trip when I was in my twenties, I would have accepted it without a thought. I can hardly blame them for doing the same.

Unwelcome thoughts of my weeks of treatment in the hospital for depression sixteen years ago and my subsequent struggles with it arise when Sandy confides that she suffers from depression regularly.

"You know," she tells me, "during the three days right before you came, I spent the whole time in my apartment in my nightgown, hardly able to drag myself out of bed. I wasn't even sure if I was going to be able to guide for you, it was that bad. But you know, a friend of mine said, 'Sandy, you need to do this! Being a guide is what makes you happiest and you are so good at it, I'm sure it will help.' And you know, she was right. I've had a great time with you guys."

For so many reasons, I feel as if my heart is going to break. Liz, Katie, Sandy, myself—we all deal with our own devils. As I spot Richard in the distance coming to rejoin us, I tell her quickly about my own times helpless in the grip of that hopeless dark hand. Through the backpack and books and purses and packages, the heat and the sweat, we hug each other tightly in understanding.

Liz

I found the "old town" to be quite pleasant, but after I emerged from its protective walls and reached the park in the new city which I had to cross to return to the hotel, a strange young man began talking to me. He followed me as I crossed the park and tried to pull on my underwear when I bent over to pick something up. I told him sharply not to touch me.

But still he persisted in following me as I continued briskly walking. Finally, at the far edge of the park after he had doggedly followed me in silence, he plucked up his courage and asked me slyly if I shaved.

I wasn't sure I had heard him right and asked, "Shave what? I don't have a beard."

"Between your legs; you know," he answered in an almost embarrassed way, but clearly compelled by some prurient curiosity. I was immediately mortified by this violation of privacy and shouted nonsense at him, then yelled, "Why would you ask me that question?"

As he beat a hasty retreat I put in a final "Shame on you!" and he scurried out of sight. It made me feel uncomfortable and slightly dirty inside, but I figured at least his inappropriate question got rid of him for good so I could walk by myself again.

WE HAVE TO GET back to the 3 Arches soon so we can grab our bags and a bite to eat before heading back out to the airport. But there's just enough time to hit one more excavation, this one of the Old City's wall. A blue and white ruler gives us an idea of just how tall and massive a structure it was. A map on the wall illustrates how over the centuries the boundary of the Old City has shifted, depending on who was the overlord of the century. I remember the Biblical story of the walls of Jericho tumbling down, but they must have been pretty diminutive walls compared to Jerusalem's if they really did "tumble down." Sounds too pretty. I chalk it up to poetic license.

I guess we aren't going to make it to the Church of the Holy Sepulchre, which is supposed to be the big deal of all big deals. Ruth went there and was pretty amazed by all the stuff it held. Never mind; this will give us a "reason to come back," as the old excuse goes. Not that I ever could foresee this happening, but never say never, right?

We make it back to the hotel, where we have a farewell lunch with Sandy out on the front patio. Snap, snap; my camera holds many pictures of our final meal with our excellent guide. The girls later say they felt Sandy to be too biased regarding the region's politics, but I ask them, what did they expect? Anyone who would give up their life in the United States to emigrate to Israel is going to have pretty strong opinions. At least she was professional enough to arrange for us to see the other side of the fence.

Egypt: Cairo

Diary of Ruth K. Crapo, 1907-1908

On board the *Saidich*—Cairo, Egypt, February 18, 1908

We found the sea pretty choppy this morning. In spite of the captain's opinion to the contrary, we all had to be examined by the quarantine doctor at Port Said and so missed two trains to Cairo.

We sat next to the captain at table, and he told us of the Russian pilgrimages to Jerusalem and the Muhammadans to Mecca. Thousands a year go to both. Many die on the way of plague and cholera.

At Port Said we spent the afternoon fooling around. We had a good dinner of ham and eggs at the Hotel Savoy before starting. It was dark when we took the train for Cairo. We were sorry to miss the scenery. The trip was a tiresome one.

Diaries of Holly, Katie and Elizabeth Pierce, 2008

**Jerusalem, Israel—Cairo, Egypt via Amman, Jordan,
Sunday, June 22, 2008**

SINCE OUR FLIGHT is to Egypt via Jordan with all the potential snafus and delays such a trip could entail, we get to the airport at two o'clock this afternoon for the five o'clock Royal Jordanian flight to Amman. Boarding actually begins at five o'clock as promised; a shuttle bus drives us out to our plane, and we climb the stairs from the tarmac to the cabin. It is now, however, 6:20 P.M., and we are just taking off.

The minute we're seated the stewardesses pass out boxes of orange juice, and that's the last we see of them. The seating is two seats on each side of a center aisle, and we take up four seats in one row. In the four seats ahead of us is a family of three children and their mother. She is wearing an "American Embassy School, New Delhi, India" T-shirt, but it's hard to tell what her nationality is.

The mother and her oldest daughter are in front of Liz and me, while across the aisle ahead of Richard and Katie are a little boy and his sister. Both appear to be around six or seven years old, attractive children, the boy with beautiful brown eyes and the girl with an enviable head of thick, shining brown hair.

Too bad they are so insanely out of control. Let's read a book aloud/hide under a blanket/ask to change seats/breathe into the barf bag/open and close the window shade/bang the tray table up and down/wiggle wiggle jabber jabber. Mother has either given up trying to control them or else believes that as long as they don't leave the vicinity, they're under control. She so thoroughly ignores these hyperactive crazy-makers that Liz and I figure she must have taken some sort of sedative.

We hear the older daughter, about ten, calmly ask her mother, "What desert is this?" Good question. Outside all I can see is flat, dun-colored earth stretching interminably into the distance, entirely barren of any features. But either the mother doesn't know or is simply ignoring her daughter, for she remains silent.

At the same time, the other two are playing an old favorite, "Can I bite your boarding pass?" while writhing in their seats. In a fit of frustration Liz grabs her armrest and bangs it up and down a half-dozen times. The noise is so startling and from such an unexpected quarter that Hyperactive and Excitable stare in open-mouthed astonishment at us. Peace at last—at least for thirty seconds. Then it's back to business.

Another country heard from: behind us is another mother and a little girl of about three who decides it's her turn to bang her seat tray up and down. This goes on for a moment or two, when suddenly she begins screaming hysterically. I know this one: she doesn't want to wear her seat belt. (When Liz was two and a half, we went to Hawaii. Being autumn, our girls were the only children on board. Much to the planeload of retirees' disgust, we were not allowed to take off until Elizabeth left her seatbelt on. I knew she was a smart kid, so I shamelessly resorted to telling her that if she didn't keep her belt buckled, the police would come and take her away, a lie that the stewardess vigorously endorsed. It worked.)

The racket subsides after a minute or two, but now Hyperactive, her legs draped over her aisle armrest, is straining to slap hands with her mother. Not wanting to miss a second, her brother is on his knees in high excitement.

"Daniel is trying to kiss me, my little brother," she slyly complains. This doesn't elicit a response, so now she is whipping her hair back and forth in a dervish whirl.

By now the plane is banking over the featureless landscape in its approach to the Amman airport. The outskirts of the city come into view. Buildings are the same dull dun color as the surrounding desert. I've always wanted to see Petra, but if this is any indication of what else Jordan has to offer, I may rethink this wish.

The plane lands. We have twenty minutes to make our connection to Cairo.

At the gate, a clock hanging from the ceiling says it is 6:35. I look at my watch: 7:35. Hmm, perhaps Jordan isn't on Daylight Savings Time? Does Daylight Savings Time even exist in the Middle East?

I go over to the check-in counter and ask the attendant what time it is. He says 7:35. I point to the clock over by our seats. He dismisses it; it is broken. Wow, broken by exactly one hour! I thank him and go sit down.

Thick cigarette smoke swirls over us and around the "No Smoking" sign hanging near the broken clock. A couple of rows over, five well-groomed men smartly clothed are talking and puffing away. After no food and the flight we just endured, my love and tolerance for mankind is zero. Feeling righteous, I stand up and walk calmly over to the men.

"Excuse me, gentlemen, but this is a no-smoking area," I inform them.

They look at me in what I interpret as mock astonishment. "It is?"

I point at the "No Smoking" sign in plain view.

"Oh, we are very sorry!"

"Thank you," I say serenely, and like a queen I return to my seat.

To my surprise, all five men get up and file past, apologizing as they go. I just smile graciously. My family gives me some quiet "Yay, Mom!"s, and I remember with pride when I kept the soccer guys out of our train compartment between Caserta and Bari. How good it feels to receive some genuine praise from my family!

As we collect our bags to board, I see three more men with cigarettes. Drifts of white smoke twine in the light just above them. I hesitate—no, it's not worth it. Then I see them stubbing out their butts in a metal ashcan just slightly smaller than a wine barrel. An ashtray and a "No Smoking" sign? Go figure.

Diary of Ruth K. Crapo, 1907-1908

Cairo, Egypt, February 19, 1908

Many were not feeling well today, so we stayed in bed and rested. Lucy, Miss Blaine and I went out to see about the Nile trip, and after a long discussion, we decided to take the three-week trip and to leave next Monday. We also made inquiries about Algiers and Spain and found that it's going to be hard to find decent boats going there. We may have to give these up.

Cairo so far has not impressed me much. It's foreign in its way, but very dirty. Lucy and Miss Blaine don't like it at all. They went to Shepherds to tea and were much disappointed.

Cairo, Egypt, February 20, 1908

This morning two carriage-loads of us went to the museum, which was filled with mummies and statues of Ramses II as well as beautiful old jewelry found in tombs: scarabs, charms, pottery and trinkets of every old sort.

After lunch we drove to the Mosque of Mahomet Ali in the Citadel. It was here that Mamluk nobles were imprisoned and killed, all but one who made a wonderful leap on horseback over the ramparts.

Cairo, Egypt, February 21, 1908

After an early lunch we drove to the train station, took a car from there and went out to see the Sphinx and pyramids. At the end of the car line we took camels, Mother and we three, and it was a lark. The Sphinx is a peach, though smaller than I expected. At one time English soldiers used its nose as a target, which accounts for its condition.

We had our picture taken on camels. My beast's name was Mark Twain, but he was anything but a joker and easy-going except for mounting and dismounting.

I had my fortune told in the sands of the Sahara.

Cairo, Egypt, February 22, 1908

The streets of Cairo are a regular circus from morning till night. Mother has funny times getting away from vendors who want to sell her beads and postcards. She can't be severe with them, and they follow her for blocks.

I bought a pongee umbrella and a green veil and am now prepared for the tropics and the Nile. The guidebook says that neither is needed. Plenty of strawberries to be had here, but having been advised not to eat them, I am obeying orders.

This is Washington's Birthday. The thought of it makes me quite homesick. We've been a long time from home.

Cairo, Egypt, Sunday, February 23, 1908

The splendid weather continues day after day. My sunshade has already proved useful.

Mother, Lucy and I took a nice walk this morning, stopping and buying on the way a book about the Koran. We found a delightful little park away from the dust and noise and read out loud for a while and watched the natives taking an airing.

We spent the afternoon at the hotel but were entertained all the time by outside attractions. First, two Japanese performers on a trapeze, then jugglers of balls, knives, etc., a bunch of natives praying out loud with a priest, a man and girl with violins who serenaded us, and several processions. There's always something doing in Cairo. I didn't find my Sunday Bible reading very engrossing during the hubbub. Moses' life was tame by comparison.

Diaries of Holly, Katie and Elizabeth Pierce, 2008

Cairo, Egypt, Sunday, June 22, 2008

WE'RE IN CAIRO. Magically, as I walk through the security gate to the outside world, in the sea of howling humanity pressing against the guardrail I spot a cardboard sign with "Holly Pierce" hand-lettered in marking pen. I can hardly believe it; something has gone right! I was so sure that, because we were late, the Hotel Luna wouldn't come through with the taxi to their establishment as arranged in advance.

We go to collect our luggage. Richard, however, finds his bag has once again gone astray. Amazingly, even though it is Royal Jordanian who has left his bag behind in Amman, they insist that he will have to pay for a taxi to go the fifteen kilometers back out to the airport to retrieve it once it comes in on the next flight. As if! We are all righteously outraged. Since we will be in Cairo only for a day before flying to Aswan, we decide we will claim his bag when we hit the airport for that flight. So off to the Hotel Luna, located in the heart of Cairo.

Liz

We did have a driver from our hotel waiting for us. His name was Muhammad (as we rapidly discovered everyone's name is here). He put what would fit into the trunk of the car, and we squished into the backseat, our remaining bags on our laps. He kindly came over to roll my window down, but before the window had nudged down an inch the handle broke right off! I had to swallow a laugh. Muhammad tried to just stick it back on, but it was clearly no use.

As we began our drive to the Hotel Luna, I was immediately reminded that we were back in Africa. Seatbelts? What seatbelts? Lanes? What lanes? Cars swarmed around each other in the dark, dodging bumpers and calmly straddling the faintly-painted white lines.

A RATHER HAIRY drive later, we arrive. The Luna has gotten rave reviews in all the guidebooks, and I have even sprung for the Luna Oasis room, meaning basically that it's on the backside of the hotel rather than facing onto the street with its all-night racket of old Peugeots and yelling and laughing voices ricocheting off the multiple-storied buildings lining Talaat Harb Street.

After shouldering our way through a short passageway lined with shops, we come to a small, circular courtyard entombed by walls rising many floors. We figure out our hotel is on the fifth floor of the building sort of on the left. So up we go in an ancient open cage of an elevator in a country where elevator inspections are most likely at the bottom of its "to-do" list.

Liz

After Mom and Dad had disappeared into the gloom, Katie and I crammed into the corners of the old, creaky machine with Muhammad accompanying us. As the elevator lurched into motion, I noticed Muhammad had blithely left the folding doors wide open so we passed large free-fall gaps between each floor. He was genuinely surprised by my horrified reaction.

THE CAGE DOOR opens into a lobby with dim fluorescent lights which lend it an eerie glow. A dusty glass case offers a variety of Egyptian-themed knick-knacks. Yes, we are expected. We sign in, and a man leads us back through a hallway filled with odd angles that opens into a fluorescent-lit lavender common area with some dusty chairs and one small, low table. Here, we are told, is where the staff will serve us breakfast. Okay, then.

He then unlocks the door to the Luna Oasis room and flips on the light. Egad. The room is entirely painted a deep chartreuse green which glows with a ghastly fluorescence. I guess this is the "oasis" part, like, leafy greenery? I'm not sure what plant would be this color, though. Despite the elderly, wheezing air conditioner, everything is warm; warm, warm, warm. Get used to it. This is Egypt.

Liz

We discovered we were supposed to throw our used toilet paper into the tiny, open trash can provided instead of flushing it down due to water pressure issues inherent with our location on the fifth floor. Well, that was just about enough for Katie, who promptly threw herself onto her bed and started to cry.

Katie

When we got to the Luna Hotel buried in the back of a crowded alleyway and I saw that we couldn't flush the toilet paper down the pipes, I had to cry. All I could imagine was that since the bathroom had no ceiling and its top was open to the room, everyone could hear everything, and it would stink to high heaven.

I told Mom and Dad that after we saw the pyramids of Giza, I wanted to fly home. I had had it. I was *finished,* as they like to say here when something's all gone. I was ready to hop on the next flight home. I had to take a Xanax with my normal medication in order to fall asleep. Dad hugged and cuddled me to try to make me feel better. Mom thanked me for saving her battery and charger. My sister stroked my hair like she does for her boyfriend's child. It was all very considerate and nice.

Liz

I went back to the room to find Katie insisting she was going to leave this country immediately come hell or high water. I think she was done with our repugnant hotel. We weren't sure whether to take her seriously or not. So I stroked her head to help her relax, then fell onto my own bed and tried to force myself to sleep through the piercing hunger in my belly.

AFTER THE GIRLS get settled in with "Angelina Jolie's Baby Bump," Richard and I set out into the hot Egyptian evening to buy him some temporary clothing. No, he can't wear what he wore today; it is all grossly sweaty. Out on the street, people are everywhere, talking, strolling, eating, bargaining. We enter the first store we come to that looks as if it carries men's clothes. Well, yes it does, but Egyptian men's taste in casual shirts is not quite the same as ours. For one thing, shirts are made of colorful nylons and polyesters with some rough cottons thrown in, and for another, they are sized more petitely.

After riffling through the shirt rack, we pick out a few possibilities, and Richard is led into a back room that must serve as a utility room where he tries one on. I take a look—wow, it is really small! And that was an extra-large.

"Excuse me, but do you have this in an extra-extra-large?" I ask politely. The salesman consults stacks of shirts in cubbyholes against the wall.

"Extra-extra-large, that is a hard size," he mutters as he digs around in piles of rustling, plastic-wrapped shirts, but he eventually comes up with one.

I take it back to Richard. It is still too snug under the pits and short in the waist as well. We decide to take the circular staircase upstairs. I'm uncertain if this is still the same shop or not, but what matters is that there are more shirts up here, even if it is stuffier and warmer. And we finally find a shirt, one that he actually wears voluntarily in the future: a light blue with white flowers in a soft Egyptian polished cotton.

Triumphant, Richard carries his XXL shirt back downstairs, where a salesman tries to press a pair of matching nylon dress socks on him. No, thank you; this is all. Richard shells out his Egyptian pounds, and we head back out into the crowds.

Having promised the girls to bring back something to eat, we spot a sort of pastry/sweets/ice cream shop across the way. Now, the guidebooks always say to head for the shops the locals frequent, but this is crazy. The corner store is packed wall to wall with people, all milling and elbowing their way around, waving their chosen wares in the air, calling out to catch a counterperson's attention.

Dismayed, we stand at the edge of the crowd outside the shop until an older gentleman asks us in decent English if we need assistance. He asks us to point out what we would like, then as if by magic, he easily makes the purchase, and we lunge back out to the sidewalk. Obviously he is a well-known local. Short with squiggly gray hair and wire-rimmed spectacles, he is dressed in baggy dress trousers and a white sport shirt. His face looks very kind.

"Come," he directs. "I will take you somewhere quieter where we can talk."

It's been a too-long day, and we are exhausted by travel and heat, so we don't resist. My mind, however, is churning over all the possible sorts of shops to which he might be taking us: carpets? jewelry? the dreaded olivewood? But it's dark and we are walking farther and farther away from the main drag through barely-lit lanes that turn this way and that. If he should leave us here, we'd be lost for sure.

We eventually come into a small, quiet, lamp-lit plaza in which little tables and chairs are scattered about. Across the way a café is open for business. A group of maybe seven young men and women by the door are crowded around several pushed-together tables and are laughing and chatting easily.

"Please sit down," our host instructs us. "What would you like to drink?"

I shrug helplessly. "Just something cool." Richard is equally at sea here.

"Never mind," our guide says. "I will bring us something I know you will like."

While he is gone, Richard and I wonder what we've gotten ourselves into. How naive could we be following a perfect stranger into Cairo's back alleys, no matter how harmless or elderly he looks? What can his game possibly be?

When he returns, he is carrying a tray with cups of fragrant mint tea. He settles into his chair, and we all take refreshing sips. So, what does he want? He is curious about us, about why we are here. A good topic, but I am more determined to know about him.

There is no predatory story here; our man is a social worker who runs a private shelter and works with those people who come to Cairo with only their shirts on their back or have run afoul of the law through their own ignorance. But his work is specialized; he is a Coptic Christian, and his clientele are Copts as well. They are a definite minority in Egypt; only 12% to 15% are Coptic Christian. In this chaotic city of eleven million people, it is good to have someone to turn to if you're in the minority and in trouble.

Across the way I notice the group of seven seems to be indulging in something I've yet to run across in the Middle East. The mouthpiece of a water pipe is being passed around the circle. Being one from the Age of Aquarius, I've only ever associated water pipes with pot. Surely this isn't legal in a country like Egypt?

Our host smilingly explains that the young people are smoking *sheesha*, tobacco mixed with various combinations of spices and fruit essences. The social worker then takes me over to a pair of teenage boys I haven't noticed and asks if I might take their picture. They agree, and I snap a shot of one taking a big toke. Good pic for the folks at home.

Back at our table, our man pulls a worn wallet from his trousers pocket and extracts a much-handled photo of a smiling, curly-haired boy. This is his wife's and his son by adoption, a Coptic Christian boy found abandoned at age seven. Now he looks to be a sturdy twelve-year-old at ease with himself. Without a hint of self-congratulation, the man avows that he and his wife are very proud of him. I'm thinking instead of what a selfless and beautiful thing this couple has done.

The social worker's cell phone rings; it's a call from the jail where someone is in need of help (at a jail in Cairo? I would certainly guess so.) Time to go. We rise and Richard picks up the tab. Despite my feelings of good will, I'm waiting for the closer where he solicits money from us "wealthy foreigners." And indeed, as we near Talaat Harb Street, he does ask if we would like to make a small donation.

As it is, we have little money on us but would like to contribute—perhaps by mail once we reach home? I'm sincere, but he feels us slipping away. Instead of insisting, though, he scribbles the shelter's phone number on a scrap of paper Richard produces, telling us to call should we feel so inclined. Graciously, he shakes our hands, then hurries off to rescue yet another lost soul. He never does write down his name, and so now it, too, is lost to us.

As we hit the corner of Talaat Harb, we come upon a huge display of cheap, boxed toys piled high and garishly lit from the eaves by those hideous fluorescent lights. My eyes idly scan the wares—wait a minute; what's this? Two familiar-looking bubblegum-pink boxes with cellophane fronts catch my eye. Could it really be who I think it is? *Middle East Barbie?*

I grab Rich's elbow, quietly hissing at him to stop a second. We can't look too interested, or we'll have the vendor all over us in the blink of an eye. We look ever so casually.

But no; instead of this being Barbie herself, this is "Fulah," an obvious Barbie knock-off, except—holy smoke, she's covered from head to toe in a black burka. Unbelievable. And just like Barbie, she has accessories, which in this Fulah doll's case are two pairs of ankle-length boots, powder blue and lavender, plus what appear to be two gaudy handbags, orange and turquoise. In between the boots and bags is the pink and white imprimatur, "In Good Taste." I'm guessing this doesn't refer to the accessories themselves but rather to this Fulah being modest enough to be Muslim-approved for play.

The Fulah doll next to her is dressed a little more stylishly. She has on a soft, long-sleeved white dress that has a waistline and a skirt reaching her feet. Then, too, she also has a matching headscarf covering her hair. Her accessories, hung on teeny blue hangers, include an orange, maroon and cream striped top (long-sleeved), with a maroon jacket and a below-the-knee-length skirt. I guess this is the outfit she wears when she goes shopping in some less repressive society with her doll-sized "Fulah" shopping bag. The box also includes a small, peach-colored bottle of what is probably some kind of watery cologne, but does not include the coveted "In Good Taste" label. I guess you take your chances with this one.

Burka Barbie is something I really want, but I simply have no room to carry her without destroying the box, so I decide I must have photos of the two instead. The vendor is still hanging out on the other side of his humongous display, so I have Richard on lookout while I nervously snap pics without a flash of these pseudo-Barbies. In this crummy light, the photos are not sharp, but we beat it out of there anyway. There are more desperate goods needed as it is.

We head back toward the hotel, scanning the rickety tables along the sidewalk piled with cheap wares. I know we will find Richard some underwear here, and so we do. Two young guys are hanging around their table stacked with knock-offs of Nike and Hugo Boss boxer shorts. We're all business, heads down, flipping through the layers of shorts, looking for Richard's size, hoping not to get the hard sell. Ha, ha.

The guys eye us dispassionately. "You want shorts? These are very good shorts."

I pull out a pair that is among the least hideous of designs. "Do you have this in a bigger size? Bigger?" I say straight-faced as I widen the space between my palms. "They are for my husband," and I gesture in Rich's direction. Man, it's that XXL problem again.

"No problem," says one of them. He digs about, then whips out a pair completely different from the pair I hold in my hand. "This will fit." Hardly. They look even smaller.

Heads down, we dig around some more, finally coming up with a pair that should work. "How much?"

"Ten," he says. Ten Egyptian pounds? Bargaining is called for, as is always the case.

"Too much. How about five?"

"Not five. Ten." He's a stubborn dude.

"Five," we insist.

"Okay, eight," he grudgingly replies.

"Six," Rich counters. Then he has an idea. He digs briefly through the piles, then comes up with another identical pair, just in a different color.

"Okay, how about two for ten?"

The guys are momentarily at a loss. We wait for this to sink in, then drop the shorts back on the table. "Okay, thank you," Rich says, and we turn and continue walking down the street. *Whatever you do, don't look back.*

Five feet, ten feet, fifteen feet. Then we hear over the crowd: "Mister! Mister! Okay, two for ten! Two for ten!"

We walk back, smiling now. The bargaining game is over, and we fork over the ten pounds. Never mind that ten Egyptian pounds is the equivalent of about two U.S. dollars; if you don't bargain, you look like a fool, a hick.

Now they're ready to sell us some socks that are over on another table. They're pretty thin and cheesy despite the fake Nike swoosh on the ankle. That's okay; Rich'll only need them for a day or so. We get these at a good price as well.

Off we go, but you know, those guys never did crack a smile, as is supposed to be the accustomed outcome in these dealings. I know things are pretty tough these days in Egypt, and selling and bargaining is taken a little more seriously if one is to make a living. Perhaps we were wrong to drive a hard bargain, but we get our comeuppance shortly thereafter: back in the hotel room we discover the flies in the shorts are sewn shut.

Cairo, Egypt, Monday, June 23, 2008

WE AWAKEN THIS morning in a glowing green aquarium, our Luna Oasis room (the green is especially luminescent because the owner has tinted the pair of tall, narrow windowpanes with watery green paint). It is a decent-sized but dim room, but with walls so high that we find the private bath they have installed in our oasis has no ceiling; thus, everyone is privy to each other's undiluted odors and piddling and plopping sounds.

Pushing open the narrow windows to the outside—the supposedly desirable, quiet backside of the hotel—we look down six stories into a lane so narrow that direct sun must only reach the pavement at high noon. Sitting on a ledge across the way is a row of equally-spaced identical air conditioners chugging their processed air into the building through hoses like those of your old 60s portable hairdryers. This must be another hotel, and I wonder if they, too, tout their rooms to the rear as special. But the overall impression is one of dirt, poverty and slow decay.

Richard, who has been out trying to find some coffee up to his standards, comes in to tell us that our complimentary breakfast has arrived outside our door in the fluorescent-lit lavender room. Through the door I can see that a narrow row of foliage has been stenciled around the room's upper reaches—perhaps an oasis-themed touch? Out on the low table is our repast: hotdog buns and jelly, plus something watery and Tang-like to drink. Now *this* is an all-time low.

Katie

I said I didn't want to "wallow in my own filth" last night, and the feeling persists. I couldn't open the strawberry jam so I stabbed it with a knife and knocked my watery, fake orange juice all over my lap.

As LIZ AND I EAT our squishy buns and jelly in dead silence, I sense movement in the entry to the hall. A tiny woman robed in black peeks around the corner. Obviously she is our server who has come to check that everything is all right. Since the alien Westerners with their indecently uncovered limbs aren't hurling their funky buns against the wall in a fit of dissatisfaction, she scuttles away. It's time to get out of here.

In the dimly-lit lobby we meet our guide for the day: Muhammad el-Katamy, a real breath of fresh air. He is the cousin of Emad, one of TripAdvisor's most coveted of Egyptian guides. Loaded with business as he was when I inquired if we might hire him while in Cairo, Emad has instead set us up with this tall, affable young man dressed in gray slacks and a loose, white cotton collarless shirt. His features are less sharp than those of the Arabs we've seen; he reminds me some of the Berbers I saw in Morocco. His easy grin and manner instantly reassure me.

Liz

We met our guide in the lobby. His name was also Muhammad, and lucky for me, he had a prominent position in Egyptian archeological studies. He had a soft face and good energy, so I felt more confident in this tour than the last.

HE USHERS US (including Katie, for the pyramids were some of the few things she had written she wanted to see) down the creaking cage of a lift we now see is encased in a spiral staircase and out into the tiny courtyard we stumbled through last night. In the light of day we see that this space is actually quite interesting in an "outsider art" kind of way. The walls are densely covered with Diesel jeans posters in various designs, suspended three-dimensional gold stars, tissue paper pennants and fringes in all colors, a woven mat, and all tastefully overlaid with red and black spray-painted graffiti. I stop to take a picture.

Liz

We went down the distressed elevator and found a nice air-conditioned van waiting for us in the street, which we found quite pleasant to ride in. Compared to the chaos of last night, in the morning sun the streets appeared nearly deserted. We met our driver, who was *also* called Muhammad (I sense a trend here. "Jeez-Louise," as Grandma would say). However, we were not at risk of confusing the two, because our driver didn't talk one bit.

AT MUHAMMAD's suggestion, we decide to go to the Museum of Egyptian Antiquities first when it will be less crowded. It safeguards all the most important relics. We are let off in front of an imposing stone block of a building, fronted by a refreshing, rectangular lily pond. A confetti sprinkling of clean, green round pads surround an elevated concrete square box from which a spray of spiky papyrus provides contrast.

Liz
We were driven to the Egyptian Archeology Museum which contained something like 11,000 ancient objects of interest. Man, oh man! I was delighted to find many things straight out of a book I had studied in my Art History class right there in person.

Katie
I was bored in the museum and didn't want to listen to Muhammad who turned out to be twenty-eight.

INSIDE THE UN-AIR-CONDITIONED museum I'm glad we took Muhammad's advice, for it is already warming and filling up. Before going in Muhammad explains his game plan: he will shepherd us around this huge edifice, stopping along the way to discuss the historical and aesthetic significance of one major piece from each period. Then he will give us free time to go back and see whatever interests us. When I see groups of tourists led by droning tour guides inching slowly and painstakingly from one dusty glass case of pottery to another, I can really appreciate Muhammad's approach. Visitors are not allowed to take pictures, which speeds up the viewing process for me considerably.

I recall when the King Tut exhibition came to the De Young Museum in San Francisco before the girls were born. Tickets were expensive and timed so as to allow an even flow of viewers into the museum. We could hardly catch a glimpse of the glorious gold funeral mask of the young king through the massed crowd. Pushing along the outer edges of the exhibit, I instead came upon a case holding everyday items, one being a small alabaster oil lamp. I still remember it, as it most vividly evoked a sense of the time when it must have burned.

Here when I enter the room holding King Tutankhamen's funeral mask and two of his three coffins, the mask happens to be sitting in its protective case in the center of the space, unobserved. Amazing—I can walk right up to it.

Liz

Here is the famed lapis mask in all its glory, along with loads of other carefully crafted things: infinitely detailed collars, giant earrings, shining bracelets, even the very first umbrella ever made, carefully erected in a huge Plexiglas case, and all of them almost perfectly preserved. Most interestingly, archaeologists also recovered and stored the stone marble box and four canopic jars that had held his organs when he was entombed.

VISITORS ARE CIRCLING around the two caskets, one solid gold, the other gilded wood, occasionally stopping to look in momentary wonder at the gold and jewel-laden mask. Poor King Tut; I find I am still most captured by the humble alabaster oil lamps, and now in the next gallery, the trove of gorgeous, paper-thin, beaten-gold jewelry. I've always been a sucker for earrings.

As the museum is so huge, I never do make it to the mummies of which Dearo was so fond. Instead, it is time for a bite to eat in the museum cafeteria before we head on out to the pyramids. They are a distance outside of Cairo and its eleven million people, so it will take awhile to get to the site. One more pass through the gift shop chock-a-block full of mediocre museum reproductions, and we are on our way.

The taxi ride to Giza is an unforgiving Third World landscape. I soak it in. On the main highway we pass a pickup with some black-faced sheep lashed onto a rack above the cab. A long, red, open-bed truck carries seven black cows packed in side-by-side, heads all facing right. At one point we slow, and I see a man bent under the sun assembling woven car seats. There is also a yellow truck parked roadside with an exotic variety of watermelons: pale green, dark green, yellow, striped, some round as bowling balls and others way too huge and capsule-shaped. And motorcycles, and donkey carts. Anything goes.

Eventually, through the palm trees we see flashes of the pyramids. Then we are in the parking lot, shimmering with heat (later we learn it is 115 degrees). There are spots for cars, but more for tour buses; in fact, we step aside as a white and red bus curiously identified in English as the "Santa Claus Transport," complete with a commercial illustration of the jolly old elf himself flying along in his sleigh, belches by. Must be an Egyptian concern, though, as all other printing is in Arabic script.

Of course we must pay to get anywhere near the tombs and go through a security check as well. Egyptians are dead serious in their

War on Terrorism, as tourism is this country's lifeblood. The ubiquitous black-armbanded Egyptian "tourist" police are a result of the bombings in the 1990's by Islamic extremists at the museum we just visited and Queen Hapshetsup's temple in Luxor (where we will be going), and the 2005 attacks at Sharm el-Sheikh. I am happy to comply with their checks.

Then and Now
The pyramids of Giza

Once through security manned by a very bored-looking official in a beige uniform, we trudge along a path cut in the sand toward the pyramid that looks as if it's wearing a coolie hat. This is because the "hat" is what remains of what once was a polished and gleaming limestone sheath encasing the pyramid's exterior. Muhammad tells us the rest of the finished limestone was stripped off in later times for other building projects. I think of how glorious and awe-inspiring these pyramids must have looked centuries ago, shining like solitary massive jewels in the barren desert sands.

Liz

After listening to Muhammad briefly relate the history of the pyramids, I ran right up to one and touched those gigantic blocks of stone with both hands, and suddenly it was as if a lifelong dream had been realized. I was finally there! They were indescribably beautiful, these massive peaks of wonder standing in their grace in the middle of an unforgiving, rocky, dry desert. There was just nothing around them but endless sand, and little shacks full of cheap souvenirs. I made sure to lay my hands on the stones of all three of them. They were truly magnificent, but such a shame that they caused so many deaths; the estimates are absolutely staggering.

It all made me wonder how one of the greatest civilizations in the world had flourished in such a harsh land. My only guess was the careful use of camels, who seemed oddly undisturbed by the harsh heat and cloudless sky.

THE PYRAMIDS ARE STILL massive, but no longer solitary. Looking north, we can easily see the Cairo skyline through a haze of choking, brown smog. It seems clearer here, as if the dirty sky were confined to the city limits, but the land here is bare and unbelievably hot. Again I'm glad we didn't chuck our Chinese parasols; at least they provide thin shade.

Katie

We visited the pyramids, which I had been dying to see for forever, the entire trip, actually. There were three, but the only name I remember was the one that sounded like "girlfriend."

THE HATTED PYRAMID is the Chefren pyramid, second to Cheops in size of the three here at Giza. As we trudge into the sun toward the shady northern side of the pyramid, the sand slopes down to an unexpected shallow, marshy area. It is here that we see what I count as one of the most amazing sights of our entire trip.

"Look! Over there!" Katie excitedly yells, pointing. "See that dog? Watch what it's doing!"

Katie

I caught sight of one of the most bizarre things I have ever seen: a wild dog *fishing* in the still pond in front of the sphinx. I caught the dog in a photograph because I thought she was a hyena at first, but no, just a very clever dog. It was amazing to see.

TRACING HER POINTING finger, we see a medium-sized, dun-colored shepherd mix walking through the shallow water among the patches of sparse reeds and rocks over to the north side of a large boulder, where she settles herself down into the shaded, shallow water. Pretty smart, I think.

But that isn't what has so excited Katie. The mongrel's ears are perked up, and she is looking intently into the water before her. Soon she is pawing and snapping at the water. Then she stands up and trots through the shallow water back to the shoreline, where she climbs the bank partway before partaking of her flopping prize: a fish.

The dog has caught a fish! There, in the hulking presence of one of the Seven Wonders of the Ancient World, we stand in total awe of a dog that fishes.

"I have never seen this before!" exclaims Muhammad. That clinches it. I thought maybe fisher dogs were common to Egypt, but apparently not.

I'd be willing to see this performance again, but the heat drives us on to Chefren's shadow. Not many people are around. Perhaps the tours have ushered them all into the tombs' claustrophobic interiors, something we don't plan to do.

Here we are. It's pretty quiet. The limestone blocks are really, really big, and these stacked blocks rise to a very distant point in the blue sky. I try to feel the overwhelming wonder which I should in this ancient presence, but somehow it's hard to do; I'm not sure why. I could blame it on the tacky little plywood tourist police shack in the distance, or the couple of Arabs lounging in the shade plotting to wangle something out of us. Maybe it's the nearby pyramid guard in his short-sleeved blue shirt with official-looking epaulets or the bright, chemically-dyed pompoms on the camels we'll soon ride, but I know these aren't it.

It's more as if I thought I'd feel some sort of electricity in the air, something that would shake me to the core, but I don't. Instead, the most wondrous thing I've seen here is the fishing dog. Perhaps it's the element of surprise that truly grabs me, of experiencing the amazingly unexpected, something unique and unpredictable. I know I will never forget the rotating toilet seat in Switzerland. Perhaps I've seen so many photographs of the Pyramids, so many PBS or National Geographic documentaries about ancient Egypt that when these tombs are finally confronted, the thrill is hard to muster.

Never mind; I have some Ruth photos to take, Muhammad is off arranging for our requisite camel ride and the Arabs in their djellabas are closing in. Even though a sign posted on the pyramid itself says "No Climbing," I get Richard, Katie and Liz posed on the ground and first level looking disappointed and crabby to contrast with the tinted postcard showing white-robed Egyptians a century ago shoving and hauling a party of heavily-dressed Western travelers up a pyramid's sheer side, block by imposing block. The guard ignores us.

Now one of the Arabs suggests that he will take a photo of all four of us. A nice idea, though I know baksheesh is eventually in order. Click, click. Then they have us each pose with arm upraised, palm down, so that it looks as if we are just touching the top of the Great Pyramid of Cheops over to the northeast. Then there are slanted photos of us, hah, hah, they are having fun now, and what the heck, we go along with it.

When Muhammad shows up ready to take us over to the camels, we shovel out the baksheesh and snap! up go the parasols. Even with the parasols up, the heat hammers us. We trudge over to the camels waiting for their next clients. They are dromedaries, one-humpers, so it's good to see they have sturdy seats with horns to grip both front and back. They are adorned with the above-mentioned pompoms wreathed about their necks and bridles, and saddle blankets are multicolored, one with embroidered Arabic script.

Katie

I felt so much better after seeing the pyramids, I had a big smile plastered on my face, and all the crying from before was forgotten. I got Mom to agree to not bring us back to Hotel Luna when we return to Cairo in a few days. The camels lined up so we could pose for our Ruth picture.

ONCE THE CAMELS are down on the ground, legs folded beneath them, climbing aboard is not difficult, but they complain bitterly with great honking and wheezing as the drivers prod them into standing. With its long, knobby legs, a camel climbing to its feet presents a challenge to the rider: staying on. There's a reason for those saddle knobs fore and aft, one for each hand. First the camel gathers his hind legs beneath himself and hoists his rear up. Once done, the front legs get into the act, unfolding themselves while the animal's long, crescent-shaped neck and ungainly head dip and push forward.

For the mounted, this calls for balance and presence of mind. As the camel's rear rises, the camel driver (not to mention amused family members ready for some action) shout, "Lean back! Lean back!" No kidding; the saddle suddenly pitches forward into a 45-plus-degree angle. This is where those knobs come in handy. Just as you find yourself at this ski-slope angle, the camel driver starts yelling, "Lean forward! Lean forward!" and you find the camel's head and neck heaving upwards toward your face at an astonishing rate. It's back, then forth, then finally on the level, all the while the camels still groaning and braying irritably.

Once we are finally all aboard, the caravan heads out. The camel driver in his white turban and gray djellaba leads two camels through the sand, while a young boy brings up the rear with the other two. I find a camel's walk not unpleasant, just a smooth, swaying gait. Two hands aren't really necessary to keep a grip. I look down over the side of this beast at his feet. Their round flatness reminds me of the lily pads we saw this morning out in front of the museum. Aside from an occasional grumble or the swish of a tail, a camel is a pretty quiet ride.

The riders, though, are a giddy lot. "Take my picture! Take my picture!" we shout back and forth. Cameras even get passed from camel to camel. We laugh, are quiet, and generally relish the ride, even though it's really little different from riding ponies at the fair.

Soon we are as close to the Cheops pyramid as I guess they're going to take us, as the driver and the little boy are wheeling the complaining animals around into a squashed-together row. Posing us for what should be a particularly memorable shot is about the furthest thing from their minds. Muhammad takes our cameras and steps back to catch us all together.

I think about Ruth's large, sepia-toned photo of Dearo, Lucy, herself and a traveling companion. It is sharp and panoramic, with the Sphinx and the Great Pyramid in the background. The camels are spaced well apart with their driver at one end astride a little donkey. They are all so well and formally dressed in their voluminous skirts, little jackets, lacy blouses and traveling hats perched atop these strange beasts! Their hands are tidily folded in their laps, and my grandmother has a bright, excited smile. The photo is mounted on yellowed cardboard with a border of curlicues.

Due to the miracle of the digital age, I can instantly see how Muhammad has captured us. No Sphinx, and the great Cheops pyramid is partially hidden behind the large rise of blinding sand upon which our camels stand. And there we are in living color, dressed in our practical traveling duds, grinning and frantically waving at the camera while the camel driver walks around unconcernedly in the background.

Then and Now
The Crapos and The Pierces
Third from left: Ruth Crapo

What a difference a century makes! It's all a little disappointing but understandable. One hundred years ago with no pocket cameras in existence, having a photograph like this taken was an event. This picture of them on the camels is the only photograph I have that was taken to document their trip. Great care must have been taken to capture this single image—this, in contrast to my four gigs of photos taken at every turn. I'm not sure which I'd rather have.

Once dismounted (same routine, only in reverse: "Lean forward!" "Lean backward!"), we take a different path on the way to the parking lot to see the Sphinx. Somehow this strange creature is not as big as I imagined it to be. But its size is hard to judge, as the area around it is well fenced off, and the ground is scraped flat with buildings and scaffolding cluttering the site. It appears some reconstruction is under way (although I doubt they'll ever redo her nose, which I see as a good thing). We are also now unexpectedly caught up in a perspiring mass of tourists moving with purpose toward the parking lot in anticipation of the air-conditioned comfort of their buses. What with the fences and us trapped in the midst of this hustling crowd, sadly the Sphinx doesn't get its due from us.

Liz
Upon reaching the Sphinx I found many pigeons gathered on the Sphinx's face so as to make the eyes look deeply lidded. Overall I particularly liked the thick, curled tail wrapped around its body.

Not a thousand feet from its base just across the road from the fence surrounding the whole complex was a KFC. It was shocking, really, and saddening to see the depreciation of something of such priceless value.

BACK IN THE parking lot, we wade through the heat toward the mirage that is our taxi. Despite my trusty parasol, my sweaty shirt is stuck to my back. I'm so thirsty. The taxi's air-conditioning is no match for Egypt, and with we three women stuffed in the back seat, we sit in stunned silence.

The taxi jerks out into Giza's main strip, passing a brightly modern, second-story Pizza Hut atop the KFC that contrasts sharply with Giza's endless rows of gray, multi-storied block apartments. It is late afternoon, and the highway to Cairo is heavy with homeward-bound traffic. At least it is flowing, and with all forms of transport. A motorcyclist with a pretty woman in Muslim dress perched sidesaddle weaves carefully in and out of loose lanes of beat-up Peugeots, Citroens and Russian Ladas. A high-sided panel truck pulls alongside loaded with four huge liver and pink cows or water buffaloes; I don't know which they are. They have heavy, dangerous horns with curved-up tips. In the shifting traffic it's hard to get a photo, and I end up capturing only one wildly rolling eye, its pupil bordered by a wide, white crescent. Bicyclists and thin donkeys pulling flat-bedded carts move without fear along the highway's fringes.

Traffic slows as we cross a level concrete bridge spanning the Nile. The river is so wide, smooth, and such a dark green; my heart leaps lightly at its sight. In a flash I sense its commanding power indifferently shaping and controlling multiple generations along its banks. Then the sensation is gone, and I'm back on the bridge amidst the noise and fumes.

As we move into the city's heart, traffic slows to a crawl. It's here where the traffic vendors and beggars walk amidst the stalled cars. A taxi filled with tourists is a magnet, and seated as I am by the right rear window, the lame and halt come to plead their case. I roll up the window, but still they come, mostly women completely robed in black save for their pale, round, moon faces, to beg with silent gestures, often lifting babies and small, thin children to the window, trying to melt my seemingly-indifferent foreign heart.

I don't like being trapped like this, forced to witness this parade of poverty, but I don't know how to make it stop. I try ignoring them, shaking my head "no" at them, until I think I remember an important fact: Muslim women don't like having their pictures taken. In the next moment, a woman holding a child closes in. I lift my camera and take a picture. I'm right; she turns and hurries off. Just lifting the camera now works every time.

Katie

I assured Muhammad my sour mood had nothing to do with him, and he was much relieved. I feel much better now that I'm breaking the rules and throwing a single piece of toilet paper down with every flush. Somehow even that small change makes life bearable again.

Egypt: Aswan

Diary of Ruth K. Crapo, 1907-1908

Cairo, Egypt—On the Nile, February 24, 1908

This morning we went down to the boat, and though at first disappointed at the signs and looks of the little steamer, upon going on board we found it clean and the staterooms very comfortable. Only two Americans besides ourselves, Spalding and Jerome, two young men from Minneapolis on their way around the world.

I can hardly believe I'm in Egypt, the country of the Pharaohs and Moses. We passed the pyramids of Sakkara outlined against a gorgeous sky. The valley on both sides of the river is very fertile with many date palms, just groves of them. I saw both oxen and camels working the queer, antiquated irrigation machines, and caravans ambling by on the skyline. Many native boats with long, curved sails passed us. The evening was warm and starlit, and we are in all enthusiastic.

On the Nile, February 25, 1908

This is Mother's birthday, and a beautiful day it is. Already I've found out that our excitement on board is going to consist chiefly of sticking on sandbars. We've been on at least six or seven today and are now rather blasé about them.

We passed several pretty islands and many mud villages. We also had a visitor on board in the person of a Willy Wagtail, the tamest little bird imaginable that hopped around us and greedily gobbled up the cracker crumbs we managed to find in the dining room. We spent most of the afternoon playing cards—Hearts and poker—with the young men, and the time passed very quickly.

On the Nile, February 26, 1908

Miss Blaine had an early morning discussion with an old Scotch female about American railroads. She thought the Pullman cars beastly, indecent and barbarous, and also said no self-respecting woman would ride in one. Hurray for Scotland.

We finally pulled up at Beni Hasan, and after an awful wrangle with the natives, all managed to get donkeys, each person having two or three dirty attendants. We rode by high limestone cliffs and date palms. There was a fight at the wharf when the men got back from our ride. Stones and mud and clubs were raised.

On the Nile, February 27, 1908

This morning we reached the big locks at Assiut and went through others with a dozen or two other small river craft. Half an hour later we landed at the town, and all got off the boat to go to the bazaars which were supposed to be the best of their kind up the Nile.

Along the way we saw much dirt and filth and several children with their eyes and faces being eaten by flies. The mothers do not lift a hand to prevent it, and it is the cause of so much eye disease.

At the boat it was blazing hot, so we spent the afternoon playing cards—Hearts, poker, Fan-Tan, Old Maid, etc.—on deck. The sailors of the boat gave us a little song and dance about noontime, and it was great fun to watch their dignified performance.

On the Nile, February 28, 1908

Just at sunrise we saw Muhammadans praying on the shore towards Mecca, some standing, arms upraised, others kneeling and still others prostrating themselves. Then at seven A.M. we passed some beautiful lime- or sandstone cliffs, and all hustled into our clothes in order to see more of them. But by the time we got on deck, we had passed them by.

The mud villages were many today, and we made several stops to take on cargo and natives. There were great fields of poppies of varied colors and many herons and sand birds. We passed lowlands with mountains in the distance and witnessed an immense sandstorm on land. The hand irrigation along the Nile is marvelous, and we've seen thousands of men working at it for fifteen cents a day.

We heard our friend Mr. Spalding singing this morning, "Why Do The Nations," etc. He has a fine voice, and it's too bad there is no piano.

On the Nile, February 29, 1908

This morning in Dendera we immediately took donkeys and made haste to the Temple of Hathor, "Eye of the Sun," and a most wonderful piece of architecture. It was built by the last of the Ptolemys; the name of Nero is also to be found there.

We spent the evening playing Puss in the Corner and Grunt. Our sailors also gave us a song and dance, ending the show by eight men jumping into the water.

On the Nile, Sunday, March 1, 1908

We arrived in Luxor early this morning. Eight of the party left the steamer for good, four of them men; too bad.

We had a good look at the Luxor temple before breakfast and afterwards walked out to Karnak to see that wonderful temple, the "noblest architectural work ever designed and executed by human hands." It covers four times the area of Notre Dame in Paris. The pyramids are more stupendous, the Coliseum covers more ground, the Parthenon is more beautiful, but in detail and majestic beauty Karnak exceeds them all.

We sailed with a new crowd on board. We watched the performance of a boxing kangaroo in the evening. An Arab baited him. Weird.

On the Nile, March 2, 1908

The little steamer spent an hour and a half getting through the barrage with difficulty at Esna early this morning. It is not finished, the gates not being hung, and our horsepower was so small that it was a tussle. Parts of the steamer were quite badly damaged.

In the early afternoon we arrived at Edfu and took donkeys to the temple, the most perfectly preserved in all Egypt. It gave one a better idea of what the temples really were like more than anything we've seen. At one time natives had huts inside and on top of the temple, so that the temple's ceilings were ruined by smoke.

Towards evening we saw thousands of migrating cranes on a little island. Each stood on one leg, a wonderful sight. After dinner we had the Southern Cross pointed out to us, four stars very near the horizon.

Diaries of Holly, Katie and Elizabeth Pierce, 2008

Cairo—Aswan, Egypt, Tuesday, June 24, 2008

DARN—TIME to vacate the Luna Oasis room. Richard craftily makes it into the streets where he buys and brings back to the room several large, sweet and flaky pastries from the El Abd sweet shop where we met the Copt social worker the evening we arrived in Cairo. Studiously avoiding the hotdog buns and jelly, we go directly to the desk to check out. All along I've planned that we would stay in the Luna again our last night in Egypt, but already the girls are understandably protesting this idea.

No time for sightseeing this morning; thanks to Royal Jordanian and its cohort EgyptAir, we must instead waste our time at the airport reclaiming Richard's misplaced bag. Our flight to Aswan doesn't leave until noon, but Richard in particular is unwilling to believe this is going to be an easy project.

And he's right. It takes almost a half hour to get to the airport, and once there it is a matter of finding one's way through the bureaucratic tangle of red tape. As there is no point in all of us going along and slowing him down, we three women are parked outside the airport's main doors where the girls are a source of great interest to a gaggle of boys in their mid- and late teens. They lounge around the entrance about fifteen feet away, leaning against a railing, some with their hands stuck in their jeans pockets, a few actually posturing for our benefit. Some display indifference, some shyly sneak peeks, a few boldly stare. Whatever their demeanor, all seven are clearly interested in getting a good look at these tall American girls just standing out here in the open. What are these boys doing here anyway? Nothing constructive that I can see. I think of Katie dying her hair dark and wonder if she has realized by now that it has made no difference in the attention-getting department.

I finally embarrass them away by pulling out my camera and turning the attention on them. I guess it's universal; teenagers just don't like their pictures taken. After a few shots, they mostly self-consciously amble off.

It's been awhile now since Richard entered the airport's maw, and I'm beginning to worry. Maybe a distressed woman would have helped the process along after all. I tell the girls to stay put, that I'm going to see what's going on and will come back promptly if it appears futile.

The airport is packed. I start looking around for an EgyptAir counter and am immediately approached by a gentleman in an airport uniform. He is some kind of facilitator, and for all I can tell, yes, it takes the face of a distressed woman to get some action. Once I tell him I'm looking for my husband who is attempting to reclaim his luggage, he takes me right over to a counter where I describe what Richard looks like and why they might have seen him.

"Oh yes, I know this man," one says. "He was here maybe fifteen minutes ago. He is getting his suitcase now. I am sure he will be here soon."

Okay, then, it's back outside to wait with the anxious girls. At least we know he's in there somewhere and is expected to be back out soon.

"Soon" is about another ten to fifteen minutes later; all told, it's been nearly an hour when he finally heaves into view, bag rolling along behind and with a down-the-rabbit-hole tale of his trek through the bowels of the Cairo airport. There is the ten Egyptian-pound fee that personnel demanded of him for "administrative costs;" an officious little man in a booth who accidentally tears one of the bills Richard has handed him and so spends agonizing minutes carefully Scotch-taping the two pieces together before proceeding; a maze of halls, a ramp and a multitude of tiny offices, each with towering stacks of files on a desk behind which a man sits smoking, drinking tea and staring into space; his bag having to go through a customs search once they find it; a little man who dogs him throughout who Richard can only describe as "Uncle Fester;" and waiting in hallways on plastic chairs for what seems each time an eternity. He is frantic with the absurdity of it all.

But we make it onto the Aswan-bound plane in time. The jet flies south, following the Nile's path. Bodies of unidentified water sit in dark blue tendrils on the pale desert floor. The pilot tells us that it is now 108 degrees in Aswan, but it is a *dry* heat, so it isn't so unbearable. The "dry heat" thing is always supposed to make one feel better, but after a certain point hot is just hot, dry or not.

Katie

We were on Air Egypt, and the flight magazine was called *Horus*, plus they had him on the seatbelt latch. I told Mom that Jesus evolved from Horus, and she rolled her eyes, totally dismissing me. It really made me feel upset since I listen if she talks about Buddhism. All I've studied has led me to believe Christianity got Mary from Isis and Jesus from Horus, and she rolled her eyes as if I didn't take an entire semester's worth of a class on the Gnostic Gospels and I don't know what I'm talking about. It made me feel as if she had reduced me to a child.

I tried to forgive Mom for her rudeness, but she denied being rude. That made me more angry. I was trying to do the Buddhist forgiveness thing so I wouldn't be angry and cause my own suffering, but since she was mean about it, I cried. When Dad asked if I was crying, I said, "Yes, because Mom disrespected me," in a really loud voice so everyone else on the plane could hear.

After crying I felt better. My sister and Dad both patted me. At least I wasn't sitting next to Mom. Dad said we could work it out in therapy, but that didn't help right then.

Diary of Ruth K. Crapo, 1907-1908

Aswan, Egypt, March 3, 1908

We landed at Aswan at eight A.M. and took a walk around, bought some postcards, and in half an hour had run the main part of the town which consisted of the long street on the river and several off of it. Elephantine Island is directly across from the hotel.

In the afternoon we all got donkeys and went out to see the village of the Bishareen, or "Fuzzy Wuzzies," as the English call them. They were black as night with very bushy hair, much jewelry and almost no clothing. For a shilling they performed a few antics for us with spears and shields, and the kids plagued us to death for baksheesh.

I had a short ride into the desert. I rode astride and got a fall in the sand on dismounting.

Aswan, Egypt, March 4, 1908

We had to hustle to leave the hotel for Philos at nine A.M. On reaching the locks we got out and let the boat go through without us. We boarded again and soon came to the barrage, or dam. We went across it in so-called "trolley cars" pushed by the natives and had fine views of the cataract.

We got a boat on the other side and started for the island of Philos and its temple, both submerged in the water. What we could see of the temple was beautiful. The natives carried us around as if we were babes through the water, and where it was too deep we got into a boat and were paddled around. The colorings of the temple on the pillars and ceilings were wonderfully preserved and quite beautiful.

Aswan, Egypt, March 5, 1908

We went to the bazaars early this morning with Miss Coché, who lives in Auckland, New Zealand. We helped her bargain for some Byzantine armor. She was a very nice girl and very marmish.

Afterwards, we went with Johnnie Plumbridge, an Englishman, and Mother to see the Savoy Hotel gardens on Elephantine Island. I had a lemon squash and sniffed the orange blossoms and roses.

Johnnie was rather gay this evening with the light-haired Californian who drives Mother from room to room with her cigarette smoking, and got locked out in the gardens with her. Good one on Johnnie.

Aswan, Egypt, March 6, 1908

Miss Blaine left us this morning in about two minutes' notice and went to Luxor with the Scots trio. We gave her a cool farewell, which she certainly deserved.

Lucy and I went to have a last look at the bazaars this morning. It was hard for Lucy to part with the set of Byzantine armor she had been bargaining for: a shield as big as a wash tub, helmet and small armor, very handsome but hard to manage.

In the afternoon after cleaning up my heavy clothes with ether and smelling up everything, I washed my hair for a change and sewed while it was drying. About 4:30 I dressed and climbed up to the roof of the hotel with Mother to see the beautiful view and the sunset. We recognized a hoopoo bird in one of the trees, the second one I've seen.

Diaries of Holly, Katie and Elizabeth Pierce, 2008

Aswan, Egypt, Tuesday, June 24, 2008

ONCE WE'VE LANDED and gathered our baggage, we step outside to choose a taxi. I say "choose" because there are plenty of them, all with drivers desperate for work. We latch onto an easy-going Nubian who steers us toward his vehicle, but not before the local madman makes a scene. This wild-eyed, crazy-haired old guy insists we are *his* clients. As if; there's no way I'd go anywhere with this maniac at the wheel. Our driver simply guides us carefully onward, telling us to ignore this man's ravings; he is a well-known local fixture and is mentally unbalanced.

Opening the rear hatch of his old Peugeot 504 station wagon, Douli—for that is his name, not Muhammad—packs us and all our stuff in and heads out for central Aswan. Douli's taxi has no air-conditioning and the window handles are broken off, but we've come to expect the lack of such amenities and instead admire his attractive black- and white-spotted fake fur dashboard with a copy of the Koran placed center front.

Liz

Douli, our driver, ended up being quite helpful and didn't try to cheat us a bit after he got to know us. He told us that many people are quite desperate during this time because there is barely any work during the summer as it's the off season for tourism due to the oppressive heat.

OUR DESTINATION IS the Pyramisa Isis Corniche that looks pretty great on the Internet but is actually the run-down predecessor to the new Pyramisa Isis Island, a huge and tony resort smack in the middle of the Nile and of the flavorless variety found worldwide. We arrive at the Corniche, which is perched on the banks of the Nile with stairsteps from level to level and whose layout I never do figure out satisfactorily. We discover that there's some refurbishing going on, tile setting among the more obvious. I know the screech of circular saw on tile is going to drive Katie nuts. She halfway believes all this ear-splitting drilling and whining we've encountered is some kind of a conspiracy to drive her insane, and in a way I don't blame her.

Katie

Pyramisa Isis Hotel, Aswan, is a beautiful hotel with a two-lobed swimming pool. Nice, even though there is jack-hammering nearby.

Of course, we went swimming after an awesome lunch. We had a good time with Hammad, our pool boy. He had pretty eyelashes.

THE PLACE IS pretty deserted. Save for the excellent air-conditioning, our rooms are nothing special, with their only novelty for me being that I can't ever seem to find them. In my searches upstairs and down I'm always running across silent little Arab boys carrying buckets of water or sacks of sand who look at me without emotion with their dark-lashed eyes. Or I'll come around a corner to find a young man bent over under the blazing sun wordlessly setting tiles in the ground. I say, "*Salaam alekum*" with a smile, and they acknowledge me with a nod or even a quiet "*Alekum salaam.*"

They have a swimmable swimming pool here, a first among all the places we've stayed so far, but there are only a few sunbathers in the chaises spaced carefully around the edge. The plan is to hit the pool, then take a felucca, the sharply-triangular-sailed crafts on the Nile since Pharaoh's time, around Elephantine Island, the main isle in the river here. From our perspective it is too large to see it end to end; unless you know how really wide the Nile is, you might mistake it for the river's western bank. The island was once the home of the Savoy Hotel where Ruth went to drink lemon squash in its carefully manicured English gardens. The hotel is gone now, but I'm sure we could find a Sprite or lemon Fanta somewhere.

Liz

I went to get some bottled water from a little café and made about four decent friends in an instant. I didn't have the right change to pay for the water, but the man waved it away and said come back and pay whenever.

BUT AS WE BASK in the luxury of the pool, I begin to worry as an afternoon wind begins to build. Soon it is strong enough that the canvas shades positioned over the chaises are flapping and snapping, and the pool man is tying them back up. By this time Liz has already made friends with yet another Muhammad, this one a short, curly-haired dark Nubian down by the dock who will be our felucca captain. Now, however, his almond eyes look worried.

"The wind is too strong to sail now," he says with regret. "Maybe tomorrow morning."

"What about later this evening?" I ask. I know from where we live that such winds can die down as sunset nears.

"Maybe. We will have to wait and see."

Okay then, we will just have to see the sites in reverse. The plan was to take the felucca this afternoon, then take a boat upriver to the island of Philae tomorrow morning before leaving for Luxor around noon, but that's no longer possible.

But there's still plenty of light; we'll go see the temple now. I don't want to miss this. At the beginning of the twentieth century the temple complex was partially submerged half of every year by floodwater backing up from the then-new Aswan dam downriver. Ruth wrote of floating by boat over underwater sections of the temple and being carried by locals through the shallows. The water was so clear and still, it was like slowly soaring bird-like over the ruins, peering deep into the mysterious and powerful realm of the goddess Isis.

That romantic journey is a thing of the past. In the 1960's the Egyptians decided to build an even larger dam that would have drowned the temple complex completely and permanently. UNESCO to the rescue; the temples were moved stone by stone from the island of Philae to a nearby, flood-proof island where it was meticulously reassembled. Now you can visit Isis' temples, but you have to walk it.

Unless, of course, you want to do this in the evening. We drive out to the dock with Douli and his taxi, only to discover that we are barred from the river by the ancient world's most ubiquitous feature: the light show. Got a cool monument? Get the most out of it by setting up a light show accompanied by a sonorous narration and charging a mint to get in. We skipped the one at the pyramids and know there's one at Karnak in Luxor, but we hadn't planned on one here. The problem is that the show is due to begin in about an hour, and the light show guys at the dock won't let us go out in a boat for fear we might sneak in ahead of time for free.

How, oh how can I make them understand why we need to go now?

"My grandmother, my *nona*, she was here one hundred years ago! Now I am here! I must see the island."

This melts no one's heart. "I am sorry. You cannot go now. Soon there is the light show."

Eff-ing light show. I pull out my tattered pages of copied postcards. "See? Here is the temple, one hundred years ago, in 1908," I say, pointing to the 1908 on the cover page. "Now it is 2008. One hundred years. We must leave tomorrow. This is our only chance to see the island."

Liz

Mom quickly pulled out her pages of printed postcards and began retelling our ancestral story for the fortieth time while we stood in the background acting forlorn.

HMM. THE IMAGES of the old postcards pique some of the minor gatekeepers' interests. They pore over the photos, flipping the pages back and forth.

"Please: we only want to go around the island. We will not go onto the island. We just want a boat to take us around." I circle my finger for effect.

The minor gatekeepers pass the pages over to the boss, who looks them over as well. There is some muttering back and forth. Finally, he relents.

"Okay, you go with this man," he says, indicating a skinny boatman in a gray-striped djellaba, a Nubian who turns out to be named—what else?—Muhammad. "He will take you for one hundred pounds."

One hundred Egyptian pounds, huh? For a personal tour around the island? That's about ten bucks. No impulse to bargain on this score. We walk out on the rough-planked pier to a turquoise and white open boat with a canopied mid-deck which is ridiculously too large for just the four of us. It's going to cost this Nubian a hundred pounds just in gas for this trip. He revs up his outboard motor, and we pull away from the dock, heading south.

Liz

The man was quite intent on making me his wife, often plying me with blunt offers, but tell me, what's the appeal of an eighty-year-old man with half his teeth who you only partially understand? Oh, those men all try, God knows why. If their efforts were half successful, they would already have a dozen American wives, wouldn't they?

OUT ON THE RIVER, the evening is perfect. The melting orange sun is dipping lower, ever closer to the horizon, taking its blistering heat with it. I think of the goddess Nut ready to swallow it once it disappears from sight.

The sky colors from a peachy-yellow in the west to a delicate china blue in the east. The deep green Nile laps up against huge, mashed-together, gray-brown boulders along the eastern shore.

Then: there is the island, now straight ahead, its massive two sets of red granite pylons slicing through the island's width. As we draw closer, I see various many-columned temples between and beyond these sheer, trapezoidal walls. Thick, green foliage punctuated by soaring palms hug the shoreline, drawing a protective curtain across sections of the island.

As the boat motors along the west side of the island, the sun is sinking. Colors are becoming more subtle and subdued. I am truly ecstatic. I stand at the fore of the boat holding a canopy pole with my left hand, my red dress rippling in the temperate evening breezes. Delicate sprays of water gurgle and fly from the boat's prow. Now it's just Ruth and I, witnessing this island devoted to Isis, the all-encompassing, all-powerful goddess worshiped at one time throughout the entire Mediterranean, honored by pharaohs and Roman emperors alike. Their temples on this island attest to their devotion.

"Enjoying yourself?" Richard calls above the rumble of the outboard. The spell is broken; I'm no longer in some Merchant-Ivory movie. That's okay; I'm glad he's here.

"Oh yeah!" I shout back with a big smile. "This is probably the best part of the trip so far!" He grins back.

We've skirted the south end of the island and are moving up the eastern shore. A relatively small temple—four by five columns—stands away from the others. (I suppose I should have brought along a guidebook, but if I had, I'd be too busy reading rather than simply enjoying the spectacle.) I note this little temple's round pillars rise to what look like small artichokes about two-thirds of the way up, then emerge as square columns—an interesting architectural effect. There are also incised friezes on these temples, but twilight and our prudent distance from shore (and the incipient light show) make it difficult to make them out. I resolve that someday Richard and I will come back—but don't I always?

THE RIDE'S OVER, and as we close in on the dock, darned if we don't see two young brown dogs scrambling around in the shallows and up the bank. We don't see them with anything, but I'd bet that hundred Egyptian-pound note in my bag that they're fisher dogs. Crazy.

We are so intensely happy and thankful for this outboard-motor-Muhammad's services that we give him two hundred Egyptian pounds rather than a hundred, for which he is fall-down grateful. We go back through the turnstiles and laud the gatekeepers for allowing us to go. Strangely, however, even though it's getting close to show time, there isn't exactly a bunch of people queuing up for the ride to the island. I can only think that, once again, it's the economy, stupid.

Liz

We waited for Douli and the car. As I sat there staring at the rocky ground my eye was attracted to a little spot of color, and *wouldn't you believe*, I nearly lost my head to discover I had found yet *another* piece of turquoise there on the shore. It was smaller than the first two pieces, but it had the characteristic hole through it just like the others! What could you say to that? I swear, the experience sent the spooks all through me; I barely knew what to do with myself. I will say that after that third discovery I didn't doubt I really *would* return! What a weird thing this whole turquoise business is turning out to be.

Aswan, Egypt, Wednesday, June 25, 2008

Katie

Circular saw this morning.

THIS MORNING the wind from the night before has died to a light breeze. Looking out over the powder pink rooftops of the Pyramisa, I can see the large shoebox-shaped cruise ships (which are quite a bit more funky than the term "cruise ship" would normally conjure) tethered prow to stern along the shore. Over at the island, feluccas rest with their sails tightly furled like so many sharp scimitars slicing the sky. The Nile is cool and unruffled. Looks like a perfect morning for a sail to Elephantine Island.

Liz and I decide to have breakfast in the hotel dining room, which we find is decorated in an unexpected nautical/British pub motif. There are cushioned booths and lots of dark, polished wood with little brass fittings, plus boat helms and other seaworthy paraphernalia on the wall behind a long bar. While eating our un-nautical yogurt, I notice across the hall from the dining room what I assume to be the banquet room, which is equipped with a long table that looks to be made of a piece of plywood on some stick-like legs. Very posh. I can only suppose the hotel has a nice tablecloth to jazz the place up. At least both rooms have nice banks of windows overlooking the Nile.

Dressed in his beige and white-striped djellaba, Muhammad is waiting for us down at the dock with his first mate, a dark, bald man in white "pajamas." The captain helps us board his craft which is painted an enamel white with the words "CAPTIN AHMAD" and "Marhba" hand-lettered above the aft bench seat. I wonder who "Captin" Ahmad is while considering if perhaps "Muhammad" is the equivalent of "guy" in Arabic. Is everyone really named Muhammad?

Liz

We met up with my new friend from yesterday, Muhammad the Seventh (or somewhere thereabouts), who took us out in his nice little felucca on the Nile, or "Neal" as they pronounce it.

OUR SKIPPER UNFURLS the sail, and it snaps into a sharp, white canvas triangle as it catches the breeze. We move away from the shore and are soon scudding across the deep, green-black body of the Nile. Maybe thirty yards starboard a flat, motorized craft passes in the opposite direction. It's the "*SOFIALOREN*," its name boldly capitalized at the prow over a woman's profile with long, wavy brown locks. Elephantine Island looms ahead, steep, sandy and devoid of greenery of any significance except along its base where a small village sits. At the peak of the island is a domed, open-air pavilion sized just for a single person. Muhammad tells us people pray there, and indeed we can see the still silhouette of a worshiper sitting within.

Before we reach the shore, though, we are surprised and tickled by a boy, maybe ten or eleven, with dark, curly hair who is lying stomach down in a very tiny turquoise skiff and using his rubber flip-flops as paddles to propel himself frantically across the river toward us. I'm curious as to what this kid has cooked up. As he nears, I can hear him: he's singing, puffing along and singing.

"*Frere Jacques, Frere Jacques, dormez vous? Dormez vous?*" he pants as he pulls alongside and lunges for our boat with one skinny, brown hand. Now that he is being pulled along, he sits up and in an exhausted monotone belts out his repertoire of old children's songs. Then he is done and looks at us expectantly with his large, dark eyes. Time to dole out the baksheesh, which we do because we admire this kid's entrepreneurial marketing plan: entertain a captive audience.

When we reach the island, we are given a choice: we can continue by boat around the island to the Bishareen village or ride by camel directly across. Katie is not crazy about riding camels, so she opts for the boat, and Richard goes along as well. He's not a big lover of covering any territory atop an animal, so I'm not surprised when he chooses the boat as well. It is only later that I learn he has made this decision because he knows Katie is fearful of traveling by herself among these strangers. Once again I'm struck by what a sensitive and perceptive man he is.

Katie

We took the felucca across the Nile, and it was very relaxing. Mom and my sister took camels, but Dad and I sailed around the island to meet them. On land, a kid bothered me for "baksheesh" and after gentle no's I did my "NO" from the belly, and he ran away. A guy with a Mach 10 gun and an extra clip duct-taped to it escorted us around the Nubian village.

MUHAMMAD EXTENDS to Liz and me a steadying hand as we teeter down a long, rickety gangplank from ship to shore. Then the plank is pulled back, and we wave goodbye as the felucca slowly moves back out into the deep current. Liz and I head up the bank and onto land, where we stop to examine a large chunk of red granite about the size of a compact car. How did this get here? One face of the stone has been sheered flat, and it is deeply etched with an image of Horus on a throne. It seems a kneeling subject is offering him a lamp while a vulture hovers overhead, its great wings fully extended. I probably shouldn't, but since this huge fragment seems to be so casually abandoned here, I lightly run my fingers over the ancient engravings while wondering how many eons ago some anonymous stonemason sweated over these figures.

Liz

This pleasant moment was destroyed by a disgraceful tour guide who was responsible for a group of fat, sunburned British tourists who were clustered nearby and sweating profusely. Well, the tour guide was all worked into a fit and came right over to the nearest camel owner and really ripped him a new one. He was yelling and cursing in this guy's face about how there wasn't "a fucking camel" for everyone and how they'd "paid for one each" blah blah blah for his precious group of clients.

The local camel owner calmly explained to this poor excuse for an ambassador that more were coming, to which the red-faced man said, "They've been coming all morning, haven't they?!"

THE CAMELS EVENTUALLY arrive, and one of the camels is tricked out in a saddle blanket embroidered "ZE CIMARIE—HAPY TRIP." The prospects for that don't seem encouraging.

Liz

Well, some people just really don't get Africa. You can't just come here and demand things to be right here, right now, and this and that. Yelling sure as hell isn't going make the camels get anywhere any faster. Africa runs on its own time, and you have to be patient and just go with it; if you rush things, you will only end up tumbling. As Dad would say, the man was causing his own suffering.

ONCE THE GROUP has shoved off, Liz and I hunker down in the dappled shade. Nearby, a couple of camel men sit smoking and talking quietly. I'm content just to wait. Maybe we can make up for the rude and demanding Brits by not making a fuss. For once we'll be the cool rather than ugly Americans. I also find just sitting here unnoticed a welcome change from that familiar feeling of always having to be "on" as a tourist.

Liz

One of the men produced some fresh-picked limes. When he saw me eyeing them cradled in his palm, he offered us each one, and we happily accepted.

So there we sat, sucking limes on the sandy mat in the morning light. It is this kind of conversation—picking up and dropping off with ease, lilting and casual, blowing through like the breeze—that I enjoy the most. How can I capture the moments that touch your soul? It was incredibly calming not to feel that itchy barrier between the two cultures rubbing against you; you were people all the same, simply sitting, waiting.

EVERY NOW AND AGAIN a camel and rider crest the island's ridge and plunge down the steep, sandy hillside. These awkward-looking animals have a long-legged, loping stride, they are surprisingly swift, and their riders easily sail along. I can see how in Darfur they must be valued by the murderous *janjaweed* for their speed and sure-footedness and how terrified and helpless villagers must feel seeing them coming. Off a lead and unbedecked with silly fringe and pompoms, one can appreciate them as strong and formidable beasts.

I look around. The village isn't much to see, mostly thin-leaved, scrawny trees and thick-walled little mud houses with tiny, square windows and domed roofs. I can tell my blithe assumption yesterday was a mistake. From the looks of it, I'm pretty sure they don't sell Squirt or Fanta in a can, much less serve any lemon squash around here. So much for that Ruth activity.

A weathered Toyota pickup is parked by what I guess is some kind of mini-mosque with a wide blue stripe around its base. A dome sitting atop the square walls looks interestingly like a beehive, as one-brick-sized openings all over the surface give it an almost woven look. Below the dome is a layer faceted with alternating diamond- and cross-shaped windows. At the very top of the dome a sharp crescent moon on a rod identifies the building as Muslim; I remember being in Turkey right after a huge quake there and seeing both the Red Cross and Red Crescent present. I guess I just forgot after seeing so many huge, glamorous mosques that a mosque can also be just your basic mud hut.

The camel guys finally indicate that our two camels are ready to go. Okay, we've had practice getting up on these animals, and I'm beginning to feel like a real pro at staying on the beast while it rises to its feet. No screaming or squealing from us, no sir! I've also noticed how the natives ride with their legs forward and crossed over the camel's curved neck, and it really is more comfortable than straddling the animal's barrel-shaped width. So off we go up the sandy hillside, plodding onward to the Bishareen village and the "Noubian House," their local attraction.

Over the ridge, and we are soon at the village and the Noubian House, where Katie and Richard are waiting for us.

Liz

I was simply grateful that the beautiful, blue-painted Nubian house we were heading to was not the same destination as that of the massive group of horrible tourists. No, this time it was just we four. I dismounted and stepped inside the bright blue walls of the compound to be greeted by red hibiscus tea and a beautiful—no, stunning—Nubian woman with an unforgettable smile.

PAINTING THEIR WALLS with brightly-colored figures of all sorts seems to be the distinguishing thing here. This special Nubian house's exterior walls are lavender with maroon touches and covered with bold paintings of camels, drums, scarabs, fish, crocodiles and even a set of black hands pressed against the smooth, hard mud. Multicolored painted bricks with the words "Sohila Croza" arch over the entrance, while the wooden door itself is carved with six lotus blossoms. A giant painted pair of what look like traditional teardrop-shaped wire earrings bookends the entryway. Of special interest to me is the painting outside of an odd-looking, red-robed figure of a man dressed at first glance like my idea of a Crusader, except he has on a long, elaborate two-part necklace with two crescents, a really odd-looking orange "sunhat" and what appears to be a white veil flowing around his head and shoulders. I'd love to know who this is, but I doubt I could get any definitive answer in English from Muhammad, so I don't ask.

The paintings continue inside in the compact courtyard, with one especially endearing illustration of a boy rolling a hoop followed by a line of lively children. But it's also apparent a family actually lives here, with people like us trooping in and out of their house at all hours of the day. Even for money, how can they stand it? I feel a little awkward as I check out the clay oven by the door and a little handcrafted wire contraption over in the corner that holds four toothbrushes (these people do have marvelous white teeth). A flock of skinny, multicolored chickens are crammed into a too-small homemade wire cage, while two parakeets, green and blue, are housed high on the wall in spacious birdcages. In yet another corner of the tiny courtyard is the requisite and strategically positioned satellite dish.

On a low platform near the oven sits the lady of the house, probably around forty (it's so hard to tell), dressed in the black robe and headscarf that are the Middle Eastern woman's uniform. She smiles shyly with her beautiful white teeth and nods as we express appreciation with simple words and hand gestures for the paintings, the parakeets, the oven, the satellite dish. As for the chickens: "Man, they're really crammed in there, aren't they?" says Liz in a low voice as we bend over the poultry prison. I have to imagine they let them out once the wave of tourists has passed for the day.

"Oh, show them the tortoises!" Katie exclaims, not wanting us to miss these pets. Muhammad reaches far under a bench and hauls out a rectangular tortoise. They're not shaped like ours in Southern California. He sets it down, only to see it make a beeline for its niche under the bench. There's another, smaller one which takes a lot of digging around to find, but we finally do, under a mess of blankets.

Liz

Little colored parakeets call to us from a wicker cage in the corner. I was charmed and desired to stay all day, just us in this sweet, unforgettable moment. Maybe I was born in a place far away from here, but somehow in moments like this my heart reaches out and tells me I belong.

What does this mean? My skin and hair are so different, yet my body and soul desire the simple pleasure of planting, picking and tending. Sometimes I strangely feel as if I want to experience the sun prickle on the back of my neck as I dig in the sand for water-filled tubers. I struggle with this feeling of connection, of snapping into place, that my heart sings in places like these. It calls out to me that this is where I belong.

RICHARD HAS ALREADY paid the price of admission, so after much smiling and goodbye-ing, we set off with Muhammad to return the way we've come. We walk through the quiet village, passing more illustrated houses, most with the beautiful violet-blue doors found in hot climates. One building has a pair of eyes set above its doorway and a painted sign of what I by now recognize as a plane flying to Mecca; this must be the local travel agency. We cross a little irrigation canal which passes through a grove of dusty trees laden with fruit of an unrecognizable kind, and everyone yells at me to "Come on!" when I stop to take a picture of a hand-painted sign of a length of unscrolling purple film overlaid with the words "KodAK FILM." I have yet to see one commercially produced sign around here, not even for Coca-Cola, which should be a slam-dunk.

Back over the ridge by camel, then down to the shore, and we are cutting back across the Nile. The kid with the flip-flops is nowhere in sight; instead, as we approach the shore, a McDonald's comes into view. I suddenly realize this might be my last chance to touch the Nile, and I lean over the side to let my fingertips drift through the cool, green water. The river seems much cleaner than might be expected, but then we are upstream from the cities and trash to come.

Egypt: Luxor

Diary of Ruth K. Crapo, 1907-1908

Aswan—Luxor, Egypt, March 7, 1908

We had a good taste of the heat today in the train. The trains are quite comfortable with the same chairs and blue glass in the windows to deaden the glare, but the sound and dust were so awful that it was hard to breathe. In the dining car we found sand in everything.

We came to the Luxor Hotel and are well pleased with our rooms; Lucy has a single. Miss Blaine had made arrangements for herself and has left our party, though she remains friendly with Mother. The gardens of the hotel are quite lovely with bougainvillea vines and roses, sunflowers, stock, phlox, etc. I'm glad the train trip is over.

Diaries of Holly, Katie and Elizabeth Pierce, 2008

Aswan—Luxor, Egypt, Wednesday, June 25, 2008

THERE IS NOW the question of getting from Aswan to Luxor. When planning, I'd hoped for a romantic journey by felucca between the two cities, but time constraints disallowed that vision. So we are resigned to the alternative: the police-escorted caravan, a boring and dusty drive that takes over three hours in the desert heat.

We have placed ourselves in Douli's hands, and he has lined up his cousin (Muhammad) who owns a van to take us all. As usual, the air-conditioning is faint yet better than nothing. Maybe a dozen vans, mostly white vans, are here at the staging area inside town. I wonder if they have the cool gold fur dashboard this van has.

As there have been attacks along this route, our escorts are in true military attire, khaki uniforms, black berets and gun belts with real guns and semi-automatic rifles. No nifty spotless white outfits with black "Tourist Police" armbands here. There's a good deal of bustling about and walkie-talkie-type preparations as we wait in silence in our van, the idling engine powering the dismal air-conditioning. It seems unreal to me to think they might actually have to use their weapons; this is something I've never had to think about. So I'm both excited and nervous, yet not.

The escort vehicles take up their positions at the front and rear of the convoy, and we roar out of town and into the countryside. At first it's interesting. On the two-lane highway there are donkey carts and minibuses with passengers literally standing on the rear bumpers, clinging to the roof racks. Anonymous dust-brown buildings and fields and clusters of date and palm trees line the road, sometimes breaking to allow us a glimpse off to the right of the Nile itself. Then after a while, it all assumes a dull, sensory-numbing sameness, and we rock along the highway through the clouds of dust stirred up by the vans ahead.

Being expected, we are allowed to speed through the occasional checkpoint marked by blue- and gold-painted oil drums. I see a graveyard as I've seen before in Morocco: jagged, unmarked stones thrust on end into the earth, clustered on level, barren ground. Unless you knew what you were looking at, these burial sites would go unnoticed. I know the Tuareg bury their dead in this way, but I've not heard of these nomads being here in eastern Africa.

About halfway through we make a pit stop at a checkpoint so everyone can get out, stretch their legs and use the bathrooms. It is in the middle of nowhere.

Katie

The convoy travels for two hours before we stop to take a pee break. Douli asks me if I have a "friend," which I later realize is his asking me if I have a boyfriend. I sneak pictures of the soldiers' giant AK-47s. Our signal to get back on the bus and leave is the whoop-whoop of the loud police siren.

WE STAND AROUND in a daze under the blazing sun for about fifteen minutes, then the sudden increase in hubbub means get back in, we're leaving. And on we go, past more and more of the same.

As we near Luxor, the scenery begins to pick up, at least in amount. Here in the outskirts of the city are clusters of squalid, filthy apartment blocks. A train passes us, going in the opposite direction; I wonder if it is the one we would have taken had I bought tickets; in that case I am glad I didn't. The silver and blue railroad cars rock slowly along, their windows wide open to the dust and heat, and they are so beat up it looks as if someone has crafted them by hand, sledgehammering them into shape from the inside out. Occasionally alongside the road are wordless signs bearing portraits of Mubarek, I guess so people won't forget who their President is. Thinking of George W., I wish I could forget who's mine.

As our van makes a turn into Luxor proper, we pass the entrance to a bazaar or flea market where atop a platform stands a mannequin with a head of unruly blond hair dressed in sunglasses and a maroon caftan. She is notable for her raised arm that is actually a leg, she having apparently lost the proper appendage somewhere along the line. Her raised foot-hand gaily beckons to us in vain.

Driving through Luxor, the convoy breaks up, and Douli and his cousin head for the Nefertiti Hotel, passing a sign advertising the "King Dude Restaurant." I wish we could eat there tonight, but once we get to the Nefertiti and give Douli and his cousin our fare and our deepest thanks, I can tell it is not to be.

Diary of Ruth K. Crapo, 1907-1908

Luxor, Egypt, Sunday, March 8, 1908

On the way up from Aswan Miss Merritt and Mr. Delano both had been ill, too much heat and fascination. We spent the morning with them while Mother went to church.

In the afternoon Lucy and I took donkeys and went out to Karnak again. We liked the ruins even better than a week ago when we first saw them. We walked around the sacred lake and startled a fox or wolf at one out-of-the-way place. We hunted up the little temple Mr. Spalding spoke of, very graceful and pretty. A wonderful spot out there, but it makes me boil to think of the terrible destruction the early Christians did. Temples everywhere were devastated by them.

Luxor, Egypt, March 9, 1908

Mr. Plumbridge, Lucy and I got off at about 8:30 A.M. for the tombs of the kings on the other side of the river. My donkey was named Chicago but didn't do credit to his name, as he was not much of a hustler.

We went into three of the tombs in The Valley of The Kings; all of the tombs were built into solid rock. Seti I's was wonderfully fine, with intricate passages, mummy shafts and walls and ceilings marvelously painted and carved. Second was that of Amenophis II; the mummy of the king still lies there in state. The third tomb we entered was that of the richest of all the kings, Ramses III, with much inlay of gold and silver, including treasure rooms.

After lunch we visited the Temple of Queen Hatshepsut, a beautiful temple built right into a hillside of solid rock. The wall painting of the queen still has its gold bracelets and ornaments.

On the way home we passed the Colossi of Memnon, big and ugly. One is supposed to be musically inclined.

Luxor, Egypt, March 10, 1908

We went to Cook's this morning and met Mr. Plumbridge on our way back to the hotel. He took us to his genuine antiques man, where we were granted an audience with the Egyptian. He showed us goods he was about to send to the Metropolitan and British Museums, and I really believe he was all right. I did not find a real scarab I could afford, but ended up buying a royal cartouche of Amenhotep IV, VIIIth Dynasty, 1600 B.C., made of blue porcelain.

We read in the papers of a great blizzard in England and America. Hard to imagine, as today has been most uncomfortably hot and the flies a perfect pest. There was a big lizard on our ceiling last night. Our Arab was not successful in getting it, so we tucked in our netting good and tight.

Diaries of Holly, Katie and Elizabeth Pierce, 2008

Luxor, Egypt, Wednesday, June 25, 2008

KATIE IS RAVENOUSLY hungry and wants to eat this very moment. Exhausted as we are, and despite the Nefertiti immediately being adjudged by our older daughter as having "negative vibrations," we drag ourselves to the rooftop to eat dinner.

Katie

I thought the building rooftop felt sad, and my sister said it felt transient or shifty to her. She is good at reading the energy of a building. If she says it is shifty, I believe her and can see it myself.

ONLINE, THE Nefertiti advertises itself as having a "view of the Nile," and there is one, even if it is that bit of water way off there in the distance. Down below, little kids play in the narrow streets hemmed in by run-down, crumbling concrete buildings, but up here I can see why rooftops in the evening are popular spots. Here the air is no longer so stifling, and to the west the sky is turning a gentle shade of peach. Even our patch of Nile is golden.

I could definitely kick back and relax here, were it not for the latest bone of contention. At my request many months ago, the hotel arranged for a guide for us, who has prudently suggested we leave at seven o'clock tomorrow morning for the Valley of the Kings to beat some of the heat and the monster tour buses. As my mom would've said, this goes over like a lead balloon with Katie, who states she will go nowhere before ten o'clock. Even when we say we will compromise and leave at eight o'clock (and after today, even I'm happy to put off the departure time an hour), she stubbornly refuses.

So it is settled: Richard, Elizabeth and I will leave at eight o'clock, and Katie will stay behind with the luggage that will have to be transferred at some point for our one night at the Old Winter Palace Hotel, a "Ruth stop" and the planned splurge of the trip (even though some past hotels have unexpectedly turned out to be almost as splurge-y).

I'm dismayed and sad that Katie will miss Egypt's Valley of the Kings, home to King Tut's tomb and many other wondrous sites in a spot to which she will probably never return. I think of the West Bank and her fear of terrorists, and I know tourists were murdered here a decade ago—is that it? Or are there other worries preying on her for which she needs to be alone and quiet? Whatever they are, she reacts with hostility to any questions regarding her increasingly common choice to remain sequestered in our hotel rooms. It breaks my heart.

In anticipation of our early departure, Richard decides we should settle the hotel bill tonight instead of tomorrow—smart move. Liz descends the four floors to the desk to inquire about this possibility, as there are no elevators or special amenities in the room like a telephone. But there is a snag: Liz climbs back up to announce the hotel doesn't accept credit cards. Oh dear. Despite the room's cut-rate price, it's not as if we're flush with Egyptian pounds. Dead tired, Richard furiously tears his suitcase and daypack apart trying to scrape up the cash. We women do the same, and with all chipping in, we come up with the pounds.

Liz stamps down the four flights again to hand over the cash, upset by this latest bit of turmoil, and returns with the news that the manager says if we return after noon, we will have to pay for half a day more, the equivalent of ten U.S. dollars. Whoop-dee-do—except that Liz then feels compelled to go downstairs yet again to inform them this is okay by us.

Liz

Somehow I was appointed the point man for the group, so it was up and down four flights of stairs like eighteen times clearing up every kind of business imaginable. First I was settling a time for our guide to meet us, then I was trying to pay for the hotel, which proved to be difficult because I had to figure out how to pay for an extra half day since Katie had declined our morning outing.

However, I had a funny moment when I helped Nasser, the man at the reception desk, with translating a phone call from an old geezer in England who was looking for a blind woman who had stayed in the hotel but had then gone on to Alexandria, and the old man couldn't understand a word Nasser was saying.

Katie

Liz is the only one of us who can speak African pigeon English with all the words mixed up, so the native people can understand her much better than they can us.

WE FINALLY FALL into bed exhausted, with some of us lulled to sleep by the sound of nighttime workers going at it hammer and tongs, refurbishing Luxor in the off season, while another dwells on the curse of the circular saw that seems to be following us the length of this journey.

Katie

I heard the buzz saw tonight for a short time. It's now 9:13, and the call to prayer has started again. Heard it at sunset as well.

My sister did point out something interesting to me today. When I commented that Mom just barges ahead and does what she wants, Katie said I do the same thing sometimes. I never saw that before, but I can see it now, and I think maybe that's why Mom and I butt heads so often.

Luxor, Egypt, Thursday, June 26, 2008

Katie

Circular saw and an old-style car alarm.

THIS MORNING I get to take a more leisurely look around from our chair's-width balcony (the chair is a willow wood armchair covered with chipped and faded purple and turquoise paint) up on the fourth floor. It's pleasant to hear morning noises, heels clacking briskly down the alleyway, store fronts being rolled up, sparrows twittering, a pair of men exchanging pleasantries. At the end of the alley is a sign reading "El daly IZAR" in green above a shop, while a large picture of a bottle of Coke runs the length of a vertical red sign ironically advertising "All Egyptian Meals." A man in white is sitting directly below me at a café table sipping from a little cup, and as I look down a woman's scarved head pops out beyond the railing on the third floor, along with a cleaning rag in hand. Even now before eight o'clock I can tell it's going to be a hot one.

Armed with our parasols, we leave Katie settled in our room and meet our guide for the day at the front desk. What a surprise: his name is Muhammad. Dressed in a yellow polo shirt and khakis, he is rather pale, bearded and has curiously reddish, curly hair. He also speaks very good English. I wonder where he came from, what the story is behind the reddish-brown hair, but I think it would probably be bad manners to drill him on this, so I don't.

From the Nefertiti we cross over the Nile to the western side and the Valley of the Kings. Here was entombed Egypt's long line of pharaohs, including King Tut's. In the past, local grave robbers stripped newly-discovered tombs of artifacts to sell, and enthusiastic western collectors did their own part in this desecration as well (I remember reading about a woman, an archaeologist, who discovered the mummified remains of a missing pharaoh in a little tourist museum outside of Niagara Falls). Now in belated recognition of its significance, the area is well protected from such depredations as we discover at the guard booth at the foot of the valley, the only way to enter.

Muhammad parks our car along a curb, and we pile out and pop up the parasols. It's hot already, yet thankfully the parking lot for the tour buses is still pretty empty. The flat, tan land around us runs up to the base of a long ridge of cliffs rising sharply out of the rocky umber and black scorched earth. The sky is almost devoid of color. Not a bit of even the palest green is present. And it's silent except for the occasional noise of a motor or the faint echo of a voice cutting through the emptiness.

With all this dull sameness it's a relief of sorts to walk past a row of eye-popping decorated motorcycles. Here's one with a shaggy black fur seat cover, purple and pink polka-dotted handgrips and a yellow and green headlight shade. Next to it is a red, low-slung number with a blue bungee net stretched over the chassis and black- and green-striped handgrips. There must be about a dozen of these rides, but here's the one I like: the metallic-red HaoJing 150 with the large, Mylar sparkly sticker of a pink heart overlaid with two blue lovebirds outlined in silver stuck on the plastic dashboard shield and a sultry pair of woman's pale blue eyes painted along the length of the front fender. All of these cycles have chrome extensions out the back to accommodate another rider (girlfriend?); some even have decorated backrests. This is obviously local talent, so I have to wonder, is this really an Egyptian motorcycle club's tour of the Land of the Pharaohs, or do these belong to the workers here in the trinket stands and ticket booth? No answer.

We climb the gradual rise to the ticket kiosk, within which is a rather cool-looking, transparent, three-dimensional plastic model of the Valley, lit from below. I can see where tiny tunnels burrow down to burial chambers, and it would be fun to spend more time with this miniature layout, but we must keep moving. One ticket priced at about three U.S. dollars entitles you to entrance to three tombs, with the exception of King Tut's, which demands a separate charge of about four dollars.

We opt only for the former, having seen Tut's glory in both San Francisco and the Cairo museum. There is also the fact that King Tut's tomb hadn't been discovered yet when Ruth was here, so technically we shouldn't see it anyway. We pore over the map with Muhammad, settling on several that the Crapos entered. We're fortunate these are also close together because this valley is rife with tombs; our map shows about sixty.

There isn't an adequate word to describe the heat out on the flats: searing? blistering? molten? We find out later it is 117 degrees, which sounds impossible except that once you get past a certain point, there's no difference; it could be 125 degrees, but ultimately it's just breathtakingly hot. I try to console myself with the "dry heat" theory with little success. No wonder these mummies never disintegrated; the moisture must have been instantly sucked out of them—poof!—leaving only leathery bits of flesh and hair.

The hike up into the valley is well marked by flat paving stones and a curb; they don't want you wandering off on your own. Once within the valley proper, sections of the path are shaded by the round, rocky cliffs. We pass rectangular entrances to lesser tombs, unnervingly inky-black and silent beyond their sun-seared entries.

Liz

I drank so much water during this time and yet peed so little that I was absolutely flabbergasted to find that our guide was actually fasting during this time—no food *or* water! I would have straight-up passed out from this kind of deprivation, but he simply said he was used to it.

WE HEAD FOR the first tomb on our list, that of Amenophis II. Jeez, how did Ruth get up to this tomb with her bum leg? The entrance is high up the side of a steep ridge, and I can only hope she had some sort of stairway as we do before us. There are steps, then a narrow metal ladder, a landing, then more ladder up to the entry. I'm not crazy about heights, but if Ruth could do it . . . I'm just careful not to look down.

Before entering, Muhammad and the guard at the tomb's entrance warn us that picture-taking is not allowed. That's going to be hard for me to obey. In fact, once we get to the final and main chamber, that tiny Leica in my pocket is itching to get out. It is so unimaginably beautiful! The walls are painted a scroll-figured ocher and are covered with meticulous rows of hieroglyphic text and figures. The tomb's shoulder-high sarcophagus still rests at the far end of the chamber. What enchants me, though, is the ceiling. It is painted a deep lapis blue and covered with rows of asterisk-shaped, yellow-gold stars. The color just knocks me out, still so brilliant after so many centuries!

I am entranced. I know that the repeated flash from cameras is ultimately damaging to these interiors, but what about photography using only the ambient light? Two large and modern rectangular pillars are at the chamber's center, uplit discreetly from below, providing the only source of light. Liz is still here with me; Muhammad and Richard have left.

"Liz!" I hiss. "Watch for the guard. I'm going to take a picture." Reluctantly she agrees.

Click—no flash. I capture the stars in the ceiling. Click again—no flash. I record multiple rows of figures on the far wall. Then—

"Mom!" Liz warns. But it's too late. The guard in his white djellaba has swept into the chamber and wants to see my camera. He holds out his hand.

"Why?" I ask weakly, playing dumb. I quickly assume my enthusiastic-but-clueless tourist persona. Actually, I'm afraid if he gets hold of it, he might accidentally erase the whole chip, which would be a disaster indeed.

"I need to see if you have taken any pictures," he insists. Liz looks on, relishing the scene.

"Well—okay, I did, but only two, and I didn't use the flash," I confess. "I know that the flash is very bad." I figure trying to argue my way out of this is not the way to go; instead, I try the charm.

"It is so very beautiful!" I continue, waving my arm upwards. "I could not help myself." I give him my most beatific, beguiling smile.

His arm slowly lowers. "Yes, it is. But you must understand that cameras are not allowed."

"I do, and I promise not to take any more," I say with what I hope sounds like fervent and utmost sincerity.

I studiously examine some hieroglyphics on the wall, slowly enough to convince him I am serious in my admiration of this ancient art.

The guard is silent. Then—"Come here," he beckons. "Did you look into the sarcophagus?"

Liz and I walk over to the huge quartzite coffin, only now noticing the lid is propped open ever so slightly. The guard takes out a little pocket flashlight and shines it around inside.

"You see the figure of Nut? Her arms are reaching up the side to hold up the sky." We peek inside and it's truly wondrous, this chiseled goddess who appears to be supporting the heavens, and so also the heavy stone lid that once sealed the outer sarcophagus. We point out to each other details not to be missed.

By now a few other tourists have wandered in, and the camera issue is a dead one; in fact, the guard is now our friend, smiling and wishing us a good trip as Liz and I beat a hasty retreat down the corridor to the entrance.

The second we're outside, Liz bellows, "MOM GOT BUSTED!" surely audible to everyone within a three-mile radius. I cringe. Okay, okay; I take my licks from Muhammad and Richard, who I discover has appeased the guard with a little baksheesh on my behalf. So it really wasn't my innate charm after all. I've learned my lesson.

As we set off for our next two tombs, a group of about twenty tourists slog up around a corner on the main path. They are probably German, judging from what we can hear. Most are dressed somewhat protectively, with hats or newspapers over their heads, but one stringy-looking man with wild black hair is wearing only running shoes and the shortest-of-short gym shorts. My God, he is totally medium-rare. We've seen burns, but this one's the worst. On the other hand, we get a few jealous glances at our parasols, and once again I'm so glad we didn't get rid of them.

OVER A GRADUAL rise Queen Hatshepsut's mortuary temple becomes visible. It is still far away, and yet I can tell it is massive. It would be a sacrilege to say this aloud, but this thing is easily as awesome as the pyramids. It sits on a vast, blazing plain, its back against a long, steep range of rock. The parking lot for this monolith lies almost a mile away. Once out of the car, we pay to take a tram closer to the temple, yet we find that there is still a great distance to walk.

Holy crap: this monster temple is unlike anything I'd expect to see in Egypt—or anywhere else. It is so huge the Lincoln Memorial would look like a cloakroom next to it. Unlike all the other pointy tombs, this monolith stretches out horizontally along the mountainside in three tiers with a massive double-laned stairway right up the center which glows white-hot under the naked Egyptian sky. Each tier is comprised

of a colonnade of at least two dozen square stone pillars with some on
the second level replaced by gigantic statues of Hatshepsut as Pharaoh,
arms crossed over her chest. Overall, the straight lines and right angles
of the temple contrast on a sharp and monumental scale with the jagged
mountainside. Okay, so Hatshepsut was the first woman to rule as a king
and a pharaoh, so she has to be strong (ergo, the pharaonic beard) and she
has to dress the part, but this temple is totally over the top.

Liz
I can only imagine what it looked like in its heyday. I read somewhere that
she had loads of plants growing on each tier and spilling out over the sides,
supposedly modeled after the hanging gardens of Babylon. What a sight
that must have been.

BUT BEFORE WE can get up close and personal with this apparition, there
is the matter of making the approach. The area between here and there
is totally covered by the largest, flattest and most reflective paving stones
possible. You would have to have a chin shade along with your hat to
avoid all the UV rays bouncing off this pavement. And of course, the
atmosphere is like an oven. The air is so hot it almost has substance; it's as
if you are gulping down heat in raw, tangible mouthfuls.

No more messing around. With our brave little parasols popped up, it
is time to make Egypt's version of the Bataan Death March. Putting one
foot before the other, I approach a vision that never quite seems to get
any closer. Step. Step. My dress is sticking to my back. Step. Step. I really
begin to understand just how big this temple is. Step. Step. Even with
sunglasses I have to squint. And the Egyptians didn't even *have* sunglasses!
Step. Pause. Step. Everyone is moving at his or her own pace. Where's the
water? Step. There are actually people up on the upper tiers; I see them as
little moving dots.

I finally reach the shade of the first-level colonnade to the right of
the grand staircase. I am last. Muhammad sits to one side, resting quietly.
Richard and Liz are here as well, but there is no one else. I look out over
the valley, white and shimmering. It is a commanding view of a relentless
landscape.

Muhammad tells us that Hatshepsut's carved face was hacked away
by subsequent rulers, probably jealous of her fabulous digs among other
things. But as I begin to look around at the walls behind this first level,

there doesn't seem to be any deliberate destruction, only the toll taken by centuries of weather.

What is left is amazing and delightful. The reddish stone walls are covered with shallow reliefs of daily life. There are little huts on stilts with ladders, palm trees and diagonal bridges with men crossing over them. I begin to make out more and more: cows, bees, hawks, birds, a snake, gaggles of geese and a stork standing in a river amid lotus blossoms. Then there is water, depicted by zigzag lines, and within the water swims a swordfish and a plate-shaped fish with antennae. People are fishing.

It's astounding how much paint remains, especially up high. More stars are there, as is a vulture with wings spread, all still bearing different shades of color. It is thanks to this enduring recipe for paint that I find the most exciting figure of all: a spotted cow, viewed from overhead! Its horns splay outward and its tail swishes around its side. It's as clear as day. Who was this artist who made the daring leap from the conventional and enduring side view? I wish I knew more.

We continue to leisurely examine the carvings while Muhammad fills us in on more Egyptian history. He is very unpushy about it; I like him for this. Finally he says it is time to make a decision: are we going to go up to the next level?

He's kidding, right? There is no way he is getting me up that foot-blistering ramp! Richard feels the same way, but in a miraculous burst of energy, Liz triumphantly goes on to make it to the top tier.

Liz
The final tier of the temple had giant statues in Hatshepsut's likeness, complete with pharaoh gear, though only six or eight full-size statues remained when originally there were many more. At the very top you could walk into the inner courtyard which boasted still more walls covered in carvings, of which I particularly liked a small, carved owl with beautiful yellow paint still on it.

MEANWHILE RICHARD AND I decide to make the arduous trip back to the tram stop and our car. I don't feel as if I've missed out on something; instead, I've had the opportunity to examine these beautiful reliefs with an unhurried intimacy that is worth more to me than slogging past endless rows of columns and giant pharaonic statues.

When the tram drops us off, we doggedly keep walking toward Muhammad's car, parked down by the motorcycles. We trudge past a row of trinket stalls, but it is so hot the vendors make only a half-hearted effort to halt us, one that is quickly squelched when Liz takes an irritable swing at them with her parasol.

Next on Ruth's list: the Ramesseum, one temple among several erected by Ramses II to attest to his eternal might. When Muhammad pulls the car over onto the dirt shoulder, however, we see it to the south in the distance, a low, dark ruin amid a scramble of boulders silhouetted against the high, white horizon. The temple site is surrounded by a barbed wire fence to prevent visitors from approaching it during this designated period of renovation. But sitting in the back seat where it is painful to squint against the glare even in my special Polarized prescription Kate Spade sunglasses, I can tell not a whole lot of restoration is going on here. Nevertheless, I snap the obligatory photo while silently rejoicing in not having to tramp through this hellhole.

Katie

It is 2:30 P.M. and the family still isn't back. Since Tucker Malarky's book has all sorts of death, I am worried that they've been in a terrible car accident or something like that. I don't even know what I would do without them. How I could go on, especially in this foreign country. At what point do I decide to exit my hole and be really worried?

Waiting in worry. Waiting in worry. Waiting in worry. Waiting in worry. As I eat my emergency cashews, I pause every time I hear a hard footstep on the stairs. They had better not be dead, just late as usual. I don't trust anyone here to give me bad news. It is now five minutes to three o'clock, and they were supposed to return around two o'clock at the latest. I take a Xanax.

I will not leave their things in this room unattended. I promised. Now I am just waiting for them and the Xanax to kick in so I won't be so worried minute by minute. It is agonizing to wait and hope they're still alive, knowing anything could happen in this unsafe country. I had never experienced a military escort until I got here. Not even in Israel.

FINAL STOP: the Colossi of Memnon, a pair of huge, rather unattractive, blockish statues of pharaohs seated side by side. They're set without dignity right by the side of the road, much like Stonehenge, except even closer. We pass a deserted RESTAURANT CAFE FOOD GriLL and a gentleman sitting on a little chair in the shade by a large blue and white hand-painted sign alerting us to his "W-C," and in case we don't get it, below is spelled out "WATERCLASS" with a helpful arrow.

Muhammad pulls the car into a small, circular, dirt parking lot, raising a cloud of dust at the feet of the pharaohs. Apparently they once marked the entrance to a huge funerary complex of white sandstone packed with statues and gold and even a floor of solid silver. This pair of seated pharaohs are all that is left, though given that subsequent pharaohs made off with much of its contents to further their own agendas of self-aggrandizement and that it was built on the Nile's floodplain, perhaps it was a feckless bit of planning which gave rise to the famous admonition, "Location, location, location."

I hop out and, using my tattered sheet of postcards as my guide, snap my final Ruth picture of the day. It's definitely time to move on to the promised pleasures of the Old Winter Palace.

Liz

Then we piled into the car for the long drive back, which was really pretty pleasant what with the air conditioning and the interesting talk with our guide, who told us to our surprise that it isn't Americans but Indians that tend to be the worst customers.

BACK AT THE Nefertiti we collect a restive Katie and our baggage, and Muhammad charitably drives us over to and up the circular drive to the Palace. It is colonial Britain at its upper crust best. We say goodbye to Muhammad and thank him for a terrific tour while a bellboy in a dark red jacket and wearing a matching pillbox hat encircled with gold braid loads our grimy bags onto a lacquered brass luggage cart and whisks it away. Empty-handed, we are able to mount with some dignity the left sweep of a pair of stairs which rises gently to the main landing instead of with the huffing and puffing and cursing which usually takes place. A doorman graciously beckons us in.

Katie

We go quickly to the Old Winter Palace and find respite inside its cool arms. We are offered wine glasses without stems filled with cool hibiscus tea. There was a man at the front door with a metal detector and a wand. Five star all the way.

OH MY. WE ARE certainly not in Kansas nor the Luna Oasis anymore. I feel ridiculously underdressed. Next to the entrance is check-in, while across the way is a counter manned by a gentleman whose sole job seems to be to assist guests in any way possible. Richard digs through our "bible" to find our prepaid voucher while the girls and I take a seat within this vast and royal lobby.

I sink into a burgundy velvet armchair with heavy fringe around its base. Sitting on the sofa close by is a bored-looking Asian woman in heels and a tasteful, understated and undoubtedly expensive dress. Watching Liz in her Tevas and striped Indian bedspread sundress over her knee-length black leggings plop down on the facing couch, I pray the girls won't get too goofy. This is not a goofy kind of place.

Instead, this is a place that probably has not changed much since Ruth was here. The entrance opens into a three-story lobby with quiet halls branching off to the left and right. Beyond are carpeted stairs on both sides that rise to a shared landing at the far wall, then continue on, leaving a natural exit underneath to the terrace and gardens. Against the white plaster walls the dramatic, swirling, black iron Art Nouveau balustrades lend the guest a supporting hand; however, should he or she prefer to hug the walls, dark red velvet ropes complete with heavy tassels swing up either side of the stairways. Thick Oriental carpets cover the polished parquet floor while square white pillars with Rococo cornices of curly acanthus leaves draw the eye up to a magnificent chandelier hanging dead center over the lobby.

I get up to stroll around and examine items on a more human scale. There are the groupings of velvet chairs around gilt tables, lamps with pleated silk shades and glass-fronted cabinets holding blue and white Chinese ceramics. There is a portrait hung by a tasseled rope of a white man in Arabic dress, complete with turban, while near the desk hangs a curious little silk banner with the words, "Gaza Sporting Club, Est. 1934, Palestine."

Talk about the British Empire! It's all here, right down to the little shoeshine boy in his tiny uniform sitting at his polished wood and brass post. As he appears to be under ten, I'm silently appalled at such overt exploitation even after reading the sign set nearby supposedly justifying this humiliating gig as a much-coveted job, since it almost invariably opens the way for the child eventually to rise through the hotel ranks.

By now Richard has finished checking us in, and we leave the bored Asian woman still sitting on her velvet sofa. The bellboy leads us to our adjoining rooms on the second floor. Harsh memories of the Luna Oasis room melt away at the sight of our accommodations. Plush beds, thick towels, even a substantial private terrace. On a low table is a little welcome box of bite-sized confections. Did I really once eat squishy hotdog buns for breakfast? It seems so long ago!

Everyone decides that the first order of business is the swimming pool, a luxury I'm certain was not available to the Crapo party. Richard and I stroll through the meticulously groomed garden to the free-form pool only to discover the girls have already beat us there. Set in the middle of one area of the pool is a circular swim-up bar, the benefits of which Katie, wineglass in hand, is already enjoying. Well, I should say so. I think a moment, then order a Campari, which I learned to like back in—Switzerland? France? I'm not sure where. It doesn't matter; the only thing that's important now is this very moment in the late afternoon when I'm floating on my back gazing up beyond the fringed palm trees into the now-blue Egyptian sky.

Katie

Luxor and the Old Winter Palace are truly magnificent. Ruth stayed here. The only danger to the family in the Valley of the Kings was that they nearly melted in the sun. It's 108 degrees in the shade at the pool.

WHEN DOULI AND his cousin had driven us into Luxor, we had passed a sign in the median strip advertising the "King Dude Restaurant." At the time I had wanted to take in the scene at the Dude's this evening, but we are so dead tired from today's forced march that we decide to skip the King and eat here instead.

Not in the dining room, however, where Richard would be hard-pressed to come up with some sort of jacket and tie. Besides, it's hideously expensive, so we opt for the little Italian outdoor café tucked away in the corner of the grounds (and away from the view from the dining room where the fastidious elite won't have to endure seeing us Americans with our shamefully shrunken dollars furtively chowing down). It's mostly pasta, of course—but *ritzy* pasta, right?

Liz

Had the most satisfying salad with avocado and chicken—mmm-mm. I managed to hurt Katie's feelings by making a nasty comment about how she's always complaining—she was complaining extensively about the flies, and I commented that even in the nicest of places she'll find something to complain about—and she stormed off to the room. After much commotion, Dad calmed her down, and I apologized a bunch and, I guess, made it better.

Katie

I went back to the room pissed off and cried because the stress of the day finally caught up, and my sister made a comment that I was complaining when I said I was hungry and didn't like the flies. Dad comforted me, and I felt better. My sister apologized, and we all went to smoke apple *sheesha* in the garden.

AFTER DINNER, INSTEAD of strolling along the Corniche or enjoying the hotel's beautifully planted grounds, I get the task of trying to find a new hotel in which to stay in Cairo. Katie has refused to stay in the Hotel Luna again, not even for one more night, and it's one of those refusals that will turn into a total meltdown should we hold our ground. So down in the lobby I grudgingly seat myself in front of the complimentary computer and bring up my favorite site, TripAdvisor.com. I know I want to be in the east end of the city, nearer the airport.

There is nothing—at least nothing in the price range I will pay in the face of my daughter's obstinacy. I must not be doing this right; most of the hotels recommended are near the Nile, quite close to the Hotel Luna. The setting sun is pouring through the windows behind me, and I am starting to sweat. Come on, I want something nearer the airport. Click. Nothing but two-hundred-dollar-plus rooms. I try Otel.com, the one where you pay in advance and arrive with a voucher guaranteeing your reservation; from my dealings with them, it appears they reserve blocks of rooms at a good rate long in advance. Perhaps a possibility there? Nope.

I work the Internet for maybe a half hour. I'm thoroughly upset, frustrated and despairing. Look at this map: this is a city of over *eleven million people!* How can I possibly think I can find suitable accommodations in such a huge place? It's a needle-in-a-haystack exercise. I hear Richard behind me:

"Okay, just stop now."

"But I can't! I haven't found a place yet! Nothing is coming up! I'm so mad! Why can't we just stay at the Luna like we planned?"

"Look, I found out that the hotel has a travel agent who can find something like this for us, but she won't be in until nine tomorrow. Just let it go until then."

"Fine! But this is now *your* project, and if she can't find anything, we're staying at the Luna, and tough for Katie." I'm practically in tears.

By now the sun has set. In the black mood I'm in, I just want to go up to our room and fume in private. But my more rational side coos, "When do you think you'll be back? Never. You really should see more of this fabulous old hotel you've been anticipating for the past nine months. *Ruth* was here; what would she say?"

So instead of sulking, I wander around and take some more pictures, while Richard and the girls hunt up the area designated for smoking *sheesha*. Nearby is some sort of open-air dance area complete with lounge singer, but the place is pretty much deserted, and the silence of the desert evening predominates.

I fiddle with my camera (discovering yet again another one of its many wondrous but incomprehensible functions) and take a couple of time-lapse photos from the window above the veranda. The success with these lifts my spirits. I decide to find the others, so I pad downstairs and descend from the veranda. They are relaxing in the gathering darkness in some plush lawn furniture under a cluster of palm trees.

They are waiting for their *sheesha*, a small but solid cake of tobacco stuck together by a mixture of molasses and apple essence (*sheesha* tobacco is also sold in other fruit flavors like cherry, melon, strawberry or mixed fruit—rather on the line of Life Savers or Jolly Ranchers). I'm not a smoker, but I'll be happy enough to hang out here and watch my beloveds enjoy themselves.

The *sheesha* eventually comes, and now it is nighttime. Katie and Liz giggle as they pass the pipe's mouthpiece among themselves and their dad. A sweet, mellow aroma fills the air. The girls tease me in vain to try it. Around us, soft lights glow in the darkness: other couples with their water pipes, the tiny lamps lighting the pathways through the Palace grounds, the warm, yellow lights spilling out of the hotel's tall windows.

Leaning back in my chair, I see uplights have been placed beneath the palms whose dim, green fronds radiate over us like the spokes of a wheel. Seeing them this way against the deep desert sky brings on a sudden realization: now I feel I understand why the Egyptians painted their stars they way they did. Unlike my Western concept of five-pointed stars with chunky centers or even the six-pointed solid form of the Star of David, the Egyptian stars I've gotten in trouble for photographing look like six-pointed asterisks. I imagine ancient Egyptian artists sitting around flickering nighttime fires, looking up and gaining inspiration from the asterisk-shaped fronds of the palms outlined against the starry sky. Though I'm probably wrong about this, it gives me pleasure to think I could be right.

Luxor, Egypt, Friday, June 27, 2008

Katie
A pleasant evening last night, bonding over the *sheesha;* makes for fond family memories and good for the Christmas card. I'm glad the family is in one piece, and I hope we make it all home in the same state of togetherness. So close to home and yet so far . . .

Liz
This morning I was heading down to breakfast when a white woman came bursting through the lobby doors and flung herself sobbing onto a couch. I swear, I thought someone had died. I knew we were in a hurry, but no one was helping her, and my heart won't let me leave someone so alone and sad like that.

So I went over to comfort her and ask what was wrong. Well, her story was a strange one, I'll say. I guess she was taking a kind of "second honeymoon" (something about making up for the awful one she had had with her first husband), had paid $10,000 for a seven-day luxury cruise on the Nile and apparently got nothing of what was promised to her, was repeatedly lied to and cheated, etc., etc. Supposedly another couple had gotten everything they were promised and somehow paid half as much. I guess she spent hours and hours on the phone trying to fix the situation, only to be "cheated again" during the move to a bigger boat.

Well, evidently she had been planning this dream trip like forever, and I guess she threw a huge fit and screamed at the people and so got her and her husband thrown off the ship "like rats." And now her husband was enraged because it was pretty much all her fault.

Wow. I didn't want to say "poor little rich girl," but I guess we all have our hard times, and she really appreciated my caring, because everyone was either ignoring her or staring at her.

On the way out, I saw her again in the tearoom and gave her the number of our guide, which cheered her up a bit.

SINCE WE MISSED the big light show north of the Old Winter Palace at Karnak last evening, we decide we must see Karnak this morning before flying off to Cairo in the early afternoon, especially since Lucy's postcards of Karnak are very dramatically rendered watercolor sketches of teensy people dwarfed by massive red sandstone columns and a view showing a partially collapsed column in the moonlight. Katie decides she will come with us, as it's just up the road. Richard unilaterally decides we are going to make the trip along the Corniche by horse and carriage, something I in my heart balk at as an unnecessary and expensive tourist junket of the highest degree, but the girls are excited, so I go along with it. By this time in our journey, I've learned it's just easier in most cases to go with the flow.

Leaving our luggage in the Palace's care, we descend the semicircular driveway to the curb, parasols in hand, where even in the mounting heat of the early morning carriages are lined up waiting for tourists like us. The avenue seems pretty deserted, but the drivers still stake out their spots in front of a hotel with a clientele presumably able to afford this colorful mode of transportation. I guess we're it.

By the time I hit the curb, Richard has already employed a horse and carriage for us. Poor horse; small and brown, he looks kind of bony, but I guess he's lucky enough to be in a line of work where he can't afford to look falling-down starved and ill-kempt. He has a little bag slung under his butt to catch his "road apples," which explains why the streets are devoid of horse manure.

Katie
Aziza was the horse's name, and Dad smoked his Cuban cigar that burned crooked because it had dried out.

THE DRIVER IS effusive—"Come! Come!"—urging us to settle ourselves inside his blue-wheeled carriage shaded by a fold-up black top. The interior bench seat is a becoming marbled red naugahyde with three well-worn stickers of sexy Egyptian pin-up goddesses pasted to the backrest. Liz gets talked into sitting up next to the driver and enjoys the bird's eye view.

Liz
I sat up next to the ancient carriage driver and fended off more marriage proposals.

WE HEAD NORTH, clip-clopping alongside the banks of the Nile. The river's swift, deep, blue-black water reflects the clear morning sky. Vegetation along the opposite riverbank creates a low, green band separating the river's blue and the distant, dust-colored ridges to the west. A simple barred color scheme for a simple, barren land: blue, green, buff, blue. A pretty little iron and stone railing borders the promenade, along with palms, three-globed street lamps, manicured trees—and a sign on a post with the familiar golden arches unapologetically declaring "i'm lovin' it™" with the fast-food chain's Luxor Temple Road location. What a desecration. I have to take a picture.

The Eternal Nile

Clip-clop. We finally reach the Karnak parking lot which is chock-a-block full of tourist buses. They must have arrived long before us in our quaint carriage. Never mind; it turned out to be worth the ride, what with the giddy exhilaration of doing something so patently touristy. We pony up at the ticket booth (did Ruth et al have to pay?), then start down the broad, stone ramp flanked by maybe a dozen identical statues on each side of what look to be reclining lions but with ram's heads. Little pharaoh statues rest wedged beneath the animals' chins.

A pretty spectacular entrance to an even more towering, awesome site. Red stone columns perhaps twelve to fifteen feet in diameter are set row upon row, all incised densely with a multitude of hieroglyphics, with the tallest pillar rising to 140 feet. Papyrus bud capitals top the pillars and connect with other pillars by way of stone lintels carved with geese, bees or wasps, ankhs, feathers, hawks and other symbols, in many cases still bearing their original paint applied centuries ago. I find it's much more rewarding to look up, as otherwise the site is full of huge, amoeba-like clumps of tour groups.

We try to stick together but soon find ourselves on our own within the complex; it's hard to look up and stay together at the same time. After some wandering around, I find the grounds not to be such a madhouse after all. All one has to do is avoid the adhesive clumps. In this way I find myself entirely alone within a stone-yard of partially finished or unplaced works. One pharaoh has lost his head, while another five of varying sizes stand together in what looks like a family group, even though I know they're all probably just the same guy. It is quiet here, with only the wind whining through the deserted stone blocks and tossing the occasional palm fronds like so much hair.

"Missus. Missus. I have something to show you." A short, wizened Arab in a grubby striped djellaba has appeared out of nowhere.

"Wait," I say. "I'm looking for this." I point to Lucy's postcard of the partially collapsed column in the moonlight. "This. Where is this?"

"Come with me," he beckons. I hesitate, but okay, I follow him, not sure if he's taking me to the column or to something else.

After I follow him through a twisting maze of stone blocks, it turns out to be the "something else." He ducks into a small, one-room chamber with only this single entrance. He reaches out his arm and waves it at me. "Come!" he insists.

I realize it's really silent around here. What am I getting into? Given his age and stature and as long as he doesn't have a weapon, I'm pretty sure I could fight him off if I had to. I duck my head as I go through the low doorway.

When I straighten up, I see I'm in a tiny but tall room. The high ceiling has a foot-square opening in the middle, allowing in a shaft of dust-moted light. In the center of the chamber is a waist-high mottled stone block into which has been carved a reptilian-looking scaled limb with a huge claw on the end. It's maybe a foot long and looks as if it's emerging from the rock. What the hell is this anyway?

The guy moves closer, wheedling, "Here. You must touch it." He gestures toward the claw. The room is stifling. It's a little difficult to breathe.

"What *is* this?" I ask. "This—what is it?" I look at the guy, who jabbers away unintelligibly. I can't figure it for certain, but I think it has to do with luck or something. I'm confused.

The stranger touches the claw, then waits for me to do the same. Well, what's the harm? I've never been one to believe in ancient mummy curses or suchlike. I touch the claw. It's smooth and cold and creepy. I don't fall down dead or feel lightning coursing through my body. The little Arab nods his rag-wrapped head vigorously in approval, grinning.

"Can I take a picture?" I ask, holding up my camera. Maybe someday I can find out what this thing is if I have a photo.

"Yes, yes, take picture," he agrees. So I do.

We stoop out through the door, and then comes the inevitable request for baksheesh. I hand him a bill that is never enough, thank him and walk purposefully toward the pillars and people, the strange little Arab trailing behind, rattling along querulously about more baksheesh. Somehow I doubt he's supposed to be onsite, as I've only otherwise seen tourist police with their black armbands. And indeed, he disappears as people begin to come into view.

I still haven't found the collapsed column, but I have an idea. I stroll casually back up the main concourse past gaggles of tourists, listening for a group leader speaking English. This one? Nope; French. This one? Nope; German. Obviously the Japanese group is of no help.

Then I see a group of what must be British tourists in their frumpy khakis and sensible shoes, and indeed, their leader is giving his tour guide spiel of the moment in English. There's a slight break, and I plunge in.

"Excuse me, but can you tell me where this column might be?" I shove the travel-worn photo under his sharp, suntanned nose. The Tilley-hatted Brits watch curiously.

"They've fixed that," he replies tersely and turns back to his group, obviously annoyed at being interrupted by a person wishing at no cost to partake of his vast storehouse of knowledge. Fine, be a twit; at least now I can quit looking for something no longer extant.

Egypt: Return To Cairo

Diary of Ruth K. Crapo, 1907-1908

Luxor-on the Nile, Egypt, March 11, 1908

At noon today, the steamer had not come in, and we had a hot wait in the sun. It was a relief to get on board and get a breeze. At one stop, Mr. Plumbridge bought some big dom palm nuts from a native and gave me one as a curiosity. They are queer-looking things which the natives eat, big, brown, glossy and hard as a stone.

We've already had several little brushes along the numerous sandbars. We had an exciting game of whist with Scottie, Lucy and Miss Blaine, who is becoming quite friendly again. Both Lucy and I were extremely polite.

On the Nile, March 12, 1908

Today we've made a good distance and have gotten stuck on no bars. Peter came today, and so I spent the time reading *Pegasus* by Gertrude Wharton. It was not very good, but better than nothing.

Late in the afternoon we had another game of bridge, still very formal. We passed scenery quite as impressive as our trip going up, with big limestone cliffs, many new birds and a most glorious sunset, the lavender, pink and blue lights being wonderful in the sky. The native boats with their white, graceful sails outlined against such a background made as beautiful a sight as I've ever seen.

On the Nile, March 13, 1908

We spent this entire day on a sand bank. Every effort was made to get us off, but to no purpose; we were on good and tight. Tourist steamers only drawing two-and-a-half to three feet of water passed us serenely by, afraid to help us for fear of grounding themselves. One boat supplied us with bread and meat, so we won't go hungry.

Towards evening, the passengers with a boat to catch from Alexandria on Monday began to fret a bit. There's a queer specimen on board with a dog, an old maid from Canada traveling for the animal's health, who kept us giggling all day long, until she finally got on our nerves.

On the Nile, March 14, 1908

We woke up to find ourselves on another bar this morning. We were a long way out of the channel. The "Monday boat" party could stand the hold up no longer, so after much delay a dirty old sailboat was obtained, the natives turned out, our twelve passengers tucked in, bag and baggage, and off they went to Derout for the train.

After an hour we were off ourselves. At Derout we did not see the party but saw their baggage loaded on camels going towards the city, and we heard later that they had gotten off all right, also that the "lady with the dog" had refused to pay her share of the cost of camels, boat, etc. She lived up to her reputation until the last.

We are to travel all night in the moonlight, and all are praying that we'll not get stuck again. The night before last we ran into a sailing vessel and had the back of the steamer quite badly smashed up. Exciting times, these.

On the Nile, Sunday, March 15, 1908

We had smooth sailing all day; no sandbars, cool and enjoyable. Two parties on board started to play chess, another two, cards, when they were horrified to find that it was Sunday.

Upon landing in Cairo, we drove immediately to the Rossmore House, where very pleasant rooms were ready for us. Being Sunday we couldn't get mail, so we had to be content with a short walk around the city before dinner. Miss Ashley from the steamer came here with us. Miss Blaine has her clinched.

Diaries of Holly, Katie and Elizabeth Pierce, 2008

Luxor-Cairo, Egypt, Friday, June 27, 2008

TIME TO HEAD on out to the airport. Back at the Old Winter Palace I take the few moments left to pad quietly through its Persian-carpeted halls. Colonial British history hangs heavily in the air. Along the corridor, recessed glass-fronted showcases hold polished silver place settings arranged among white porcelain dishware, tea sets and high-necked pitchers painted with the hotel's purple, orange and gold rendering of Karnak's pylons—all probably the very china from which my grandmother was served.

I stop to gaze into a deserted, high-ceilinged sitting room with two large chandeliers, each holding a multitude of small, softly-lit bulbs. Heavy burgundy drapes hang over large, light-filled mullioned windows, and deep leather and velvet chairs are paired with lion-pawed end tables. An uninteresting oil painting in an ornate gilt frame rests on an easel, and potted palms sprout from the chamber's corners. Even though I'm a paying guest here, I somehow expect a hotel employee to pop out of nowhere to scold me should I set foot into such well-preserved genteel luxury. I'm sure Ruth's lace fichu fit in, but my Velcro'd Teva sandals don't belong here.

Farther down the hall is a much darker room, also deserted. Paneled in a deep, cherry-brown wood, it is filled with clusters of ornate, gilt chairs whose round backs and seats are upholstered in a luscious burgundy brocade. Several hanging chandeliers and low table lamps give off the softest golden light which glints off gilt picture frames holding quaint, colored etchings. Sheer voile panels drape two windows, further dimming and enhancing the room's posh ambiance. All it lacks are fat British men in tight waistcoats puffing on cigars while enjoying their tots of brandy.

"May I help you?"

Yikes! At least I *thought* the room was deserted. I now see there is a uniformed Egyptian employee standing in the shadows behind a small bar. He has been busy polishing glassware.

"Oh, oh no, I was just looking about. We stayed here last night," I say to justify what I feel could be construed as snooping.

"I hope you have a very nice stay," the gentleman offers.

"Oh yes, it was *very* nice! But there's so much to see, I just thought I'd look around before we left."

He laughs softly. "Yes, this is a very large hotel. Please let me know if there is anything I can do for you before you leave," he says.

"I certainly will! Goodbye," I say with as much dignity as my Tevas will allow. Then I scram out of there back into the long, silent, carpeted corridor. I pass the first, lighter room, now imagining women in their heavily laced and layered dresses, faces flushed, sipping cups of revitalizing tea after a long, hot day in their carriages exploring the Valley of the Kings. All those dresses and petticoats and shirtwaists Ruth was constantly mending: how could she stand wearing all those layers in Egypt? There's been a definite trade-off between propriety and comfort in the intervening century. I know I should be thankful that I can dress casually and lightly, but there's a masochistic part of me that yearns for the hats and parasols (the real ones, not the Chinese numbers) of yesteryear. Guess it's my love for costumes.

Goodbye, goodbye. We leave the century-old grandeur of the Old Winter Palace for a beat-up taxi with a dashboard nattily covered by spotted black-and-white cowhide which motors us out to the airport for our flight from King Tut Land to Cairo. None of our luggage magically disappears en route.

Diary of Ruth K. Crapo, 1907-1908

Cairo, Egypt, March 16, 1908

We went for the mail first thing this morning and found quite a pile. Letters from home tell of awful zero-degree weather and blizzards. Such climate does not agree with Mother or Ruthie.

We met Mr. Plumbridge, who invited us to tea at Shepheard's. It was a corking place, beautiful dining rooms with bubbling fountains, lovely gardens and much swelldom hanging around. We "watched the pass" for some time there and didn't get home until after dark.

Cairo, Egypt, March 17, 1908

Off to the museum once more, which we found to be much more interesting since we went up the Nile. We could hardly drag Mother away from the mummies and scarabs.

In the afternoon we took a carriage out to the Zoological Gardens along a drive lined on either side with beautiful acacia trees. The gardens were wonderful; there must have been three to four thousand different animals and birds, most of which I'd never seen before: white peacocks, mouse-deer, mongooses . . .

Cairo, Egypt, March 18, 1908

After lunch, Miss Ashley and I drove down into the native quarter to see the Moslem university we'd heard about. It was a wonderful sight with three or four thousand men and boys (we saw two girls) seated on the floors and open courts of the Mosque Al-Azhar. They were in groups with their teachers squatting, too, all studying out loud and swaying back and forth. Students from Sudan, Syria and other countries come to the university and live in quarters of the mosque set apart for them. I accidentally hit one student with my parasol. We were told not to smile or laugh.

Cairo, Egypt-on board the *S.S. Heliopolis,* March 19, 1908

This morning we left the gay city of Cairo and went off to Alexandria. A special train runs for the benefit of the *S.S. Heliopolis.* We went skipping from the train right onto the steamer at Alexandria amidst awful noise and confusion.

In the midst of the din of embarking, an old lady, and an American, too, was terribly frightened by a carriage coming up behind her, and the shock caused her death on the pier just at the foot of the gangway. She was traveling all alone, a thing which a woman of her age (I guessed her age to be about ninety-three) should not have been doing. All of us Americans felt badly to leave her there on the dock without friends or countrymen to look after her, but it had to be done.

Diaries of Holly, Katie and Elizabeth Pierce, 2008

Cairo, Egypt, Friday, June 27, 2008

RICHARD CAME THROUGH. Thanks to the help from the travel agent at the Old Winter Palace, we are now booked into the Al Horeya Hotel in Heliopolis. From my maps I know that Heliopolis is on the east end of town, much closer to the airport than the Hotel Luna and the Nile, where all the hotel rooms go for back-breaking prices and is the area of town that holds the Khan al-Kalili, the huge, everything-goes bazaar. This is the one thing I've been anticipating the whole trip: shopping for crazy, old things, oddities and in particular, a Berber dress.

We arrive at the hotel in the afternoon, and the relentless sun glints off the hotel facade's gold embellishments. This doesn't look too bad, and a porter actually comes out to assist us with our beat-up bags. The girls should like this; they have their own room here.

Liz

We headed to a new hotel in the Heliopolis district called the Ah-Aymwba or something like that instead of staying at the Hotel Luna as originally planned. *Thank God!* This was part of Katie's agreement for staying on the trip, and secretly (or maybe not so secretly) I was glad of it.

UP WE GO to our rooms. The porter unlocks Richard's and my door, *et voila!* another dismal Third World room. Not a picture hangs on the walls. An elderly yet serviceable air conditioner the size of a card table is socked into the outer wall. A single headboard with an electric outlet set in the middle unifies our two beds. Beneath the standard brown and tan spreads are thick polyester fleece blankets of a shocking fluorescent coral, one solid, the other a swirling floral pattern on white. The only light bedside comes from a rickety black standing lamp that casts a feeble glow towards the ceiling. At least there is enough room for all our stuff.

When we go to check on the girls, we find Elizabeth lying curled up, crying and in pain she can only describe as knives twisting in her gut. The rest of us figure the *turistas* have finally caught up with her, but she is deathly afraid her malaria is back.

"Do you feel any chills?"

"Nooo . . ."

"Does your back hurt?"

"Nooo . . ." she exhales in pain.

"Headache?" No headache.

"Do you feel as if you want to throw up?"

"No . . . well, maybe."

I go into the bathroom and retrieve the wastebasket which thankfully is lined with a plastic bag and set it beside her bed. We all work to assure her that she is not in for another bout of malaria but that it is simply traveler's diarrhea, and she begins to believe us.

Taking liquids seems out of the question to her, but after much persuasion, she agrees to take a Cipro. This stays down about five minutes, at which point she leans over and heaves vigorously into the wastebasket. Everything comes up, including obviously the Cipro. Now it's a matter of getting liquids into her, and Katie starts a routine where she cues Liz every minute by her watch to take just a sip of water. Meanwhile I go clean out the wastebasket in the bathroom, using the shower to wash down the sides.

Throwing up has left Liz feeling better, and now that she's convinced she isn't wracked with malaria, she insists that we go on without her. She's got her water, her wastebasket and a card of Pepto Bismol tabs Richard has dug up, and she knows, now that it's late afternoon, Katie is hungry.

Liz

Of course, this meant I didn't get to see a bit more of Cairo, but I guess it's fine because I expect to be returning. I phoned Ryan hoping for some sympathy, but ended up having a horrid conversation which only made me cry. Spent far too much time on the phone, and when I was finished I threw up again. What a wonderful day.

So WITH LIZ settled, we decide to go to the Khan al-Kalili to get in a little last-minute shopping and something to eat. I'm feeling pretty good that back in Luxor I specified that we wished to stay in the bazaar's neighborhood—you know, in Heliopolis. What I didn't realize at the time was that in a city of over eleven million people, "in the neighborhood" is relative. As we speed along the congested freeway, we begin to feel that maybe this taxi driver isn't quite sure where the bazaar is, and this is only confirmed when he stops to ask another cabbie where we're going.

Almost a half hour later he drops us off at the corner of a ragged park by a stanchion attended by several of the tourist police in their smart white uniforms with black armbands. I point on my map to where we want to go—the Naguib Mahfouz Café?—and one vaguely waves us off in the direction of the buildings on the opposite side of the park. No help here. After all, they aren't here to be tour guides but to use their conspicuous machine guns when necessary—a comforting thought.

So we head off toward the opposite corner of the park through the crowds of children trailing mothers shrouded in black holding squalling babies, young men idling time away, couples sneaking in a sweet night out, and when we reach this corner where men sit outside cafés, smoking, drinking hot tea and discussing who knows what, over the noise of this swirl of humanity we hear an unmistakable voice shouting: "Ree-chard! Holl-ee! Kay-tee!"

There, standing on a teetering café chair is Muhammad, our Cairo guide, arms spread wide over the crowd below, a huge grin wreathing his face. He is so happy to see us; we are so stunned to see him. How, in a city of over eleven million people, could we accidentally run into the only person we know? Leaving his friends, he hops off his chair and rushes over to greet us. He is so excited. He must introduce us to an older gentleman, who just happens to be the proprietor of the café here on the corner. Would we like to eat here? What, as if we know a better place?

Muhammad bustles about, shoving chairs around a tiny wooden table to make room for us all, himself included. I marvel at the generosity of this young man willing to give up time off with his friends to hang out with us. The waiter is attentive, and we order the suggested kebabs.

Muhammad talks away happily, asking questions—"Where's Leez?"—and wanting to know about our adventures in Luxor and Aswan. But the noise here is deafening, and so much is going on that my attention wanders. Across the way, sitting on a flight of stone steps is a woman dressed in a plain, full-length, long-sleeved ivory-colored garment. Her head and shoulders are draped in a black cloth with a single small slit for her eyes. Seated on the steps next to her is a portly man in jeans and a maroon polo shirt, and they are sharing a sandwich. To eat, she must ferry her food up under the headpiece to her mouth; I can see her fist bulging at her mouth under the black cloth. I'm fascinated at what this Muslim woman must go through simply to eat in public, what it implies about the restrictions in her life.

Then I think of the women in Afghanistan and Iraq I've seen on TV dressed in full burkas with only a small cloth screen to see through. Obviously, they never eat in public; how could they? They certainly couldn't lift up the hems of their burkas to get to their mouths. At least these shrouds seem to come in a swirl of beautiful colors—small consolation for such a circumscribed way of life.

Just outside the café, however, sits a woman accompanied by a chubby man in a white cotton sport shirt. Seated on an elaborately carved wooden loveseat, they chat while she plays with her cell phone. I think she is younger than the woman with the black headpiece, but I know I'm only assuming that by how old her companion appears. She has a round face with full lips and large, dark eyes, and while she is dressed in black, a pale blue scarf frames her pretty face. She is animated, and she laughs and then leans in to speak more intimately with her companion. I realize that this vivaciousness is what makes her appear young, and that I really have no idea how old any of these women with the slit scarves are. Their drab anonymity just makes them all seem uniformly old to me.

I remember I have to buy something to combat Liz's diarrhea. It's a miracle; there next to the café is a pharmacy. Excusing myself, I walk into its cool, brightly-lit interior. I know no Arabic, but I figure I can get the idea across pretty easily. I mimic gripping stomach pain to the man across the counter, and he doesn't get it. But he calls over a tiny, beautiful woman with a headscarf who turns out to speak well-enunciated English. I explain my problem, and she glides over to a bank of drawers, slides open one, removes a cardboard packet of white pills in blister packs, and explains to me in clear detail how this medication is to be taken. I am so grateful for her kindness and understanding that I could fall on my knees in front of this holy pharmacist, but instead I pay my bill, thanking her profusely all the while.

Back out at the table, Muhammad is just returning from a quick trip somewhere.

"Notice anything different?" he smiles teasingly.

I don't know; he looks the same to me.

"I changed my shirt!"

"You did? But how?"

"I live near here. I went home and changed my shirt!"

Really? It looks like the same orange plaid shirt to me. But it's possible, he does seem a little more spiffed up, and that zit by his lip is gone. I can't decide; either he did go home to clean up in our honor, or he's pulling our leg. Because he's so nice, I decide to believe the former. He's certainly the type to go the extra mile.

Our dinner arrives, skewers on large heaps of now-forbidden lettuce. After watching Liz retching and in pain, we're all being extra-careful now. As we eat, Katie looks down to see a scruffy little cat discreetly hiding under the edge of her chair, ready for any tidbits that might fall from heaven. Aww! Of course we ignorant, soft-hearted Americans are fools for cats and want to feed it, bless its cute little heart. Katie slips a piece of kebab (or is it shish?) under the table to the kitten, who devours it greedily. More? Of course. Here's another little morsel—and here's another little cat!

Katie

There were stray kitties that gathered at our feet, and then more and more, and of course we fed them from our plates. They were adorable, even though I'm sure the owner of the restaurant was pissed we were feeding them. I ended up feeding them half my meal and knocked a bone off onto the floor where the white cat with the hurt eye sat gazing up at me with its paw ready to bat food out of my hand the moment I had it there. So sweet.

By the time we finish our shishes and kebabses, there are maybe five or six little kitties winding their ways around our ankles. We try to make sure each one gets his or her share. They sure are adorable, and I'm sure the owner of the café is gritting his teeth as we attract these scrawny little beggars to his establishment. Oh well, the customer is always right—at least in the U.S.

Eventually we pay our bill and pick up a bagged box of plain cooked rice we ordered for Liz. Now I pull out my map and show Muhammad where I want to go: the alley of Buttons and Trimmings! the lane of Spices, Essences and Perfume! Sikket El Badestan with its amber, antiques and blown glass! Areas marked as sources of gold, silver, alabaster, even belly dancing outfits beckon! This is what I've been waiting for the whole trip! I'm sure my eyes are glazed with that crazed "Shoppers Gone Wild" look.

I'm in for a disappointment. My dream of festive shops crammed with goodies going for a song evaporates as Muhammad takes one look at this sketchy Lonely Planet map and tells us we'll only get lost if we try to follow this. The bazaar is a monstrous, people-eating maze. He can't even tell us where we are at this moment on this map. And it's getting dark, and we're leaving tomorrow morning, and Liz is back at our seedy hotel probably lying in an agony of vomit and diarrhea.

Okay, but can we at least take a look for what I think is a Bedouin dress? I'm specific: it's made of a coarsely-woven dark blue fabric with embroidery about the neck and cuffs. Every time I've seen one on this leg of the trip, there was no time to stop; it's always the old, "We'll find one later" routine. And now is the last "later" we have.

So Muhammad leads us around the corner to a shop he knows of which sells women's traditional clothing. The two shopkeepers unfold dress after dress, pressing me to try this or that one: "Very nice! Good color on you!" But none of these are what I'm looking for; they are of cheap, plain cotton in various colors, and the embroidery is crudely done. I know this shop hasn't what I want, and so does Muhammad.

But the clothes keep coming, along with head scarves and face veils. I am more intrigued at this point by the face veils with eye slits, garishly-colored embroidery and large, cheap metal sequins that glitter in the shop's fluorescent light. They whip out head scarves intended to be worn with the face veils, insisting on tying the scarf and veil combo on me so I will be mesmerized by the effect and buy the whole package.

I'm not in love with the colors on all but one, and that one has no head scarf to match. They insist that the most absurd colors go together, but no, magenta and rust don't do it for me.

"But yes! These go well together!"

"No they don't. This one has green in it, but this only has lavender and blue."

"How can you say that? Now, this looks very nice, very nice." He pushes a fluorescent orange headband against a scarf with red and mint green stitching.

Now Katie joins the fray, supporting me in this battle of the color palettes. Everyone knows these sweating, insistent men just want to clinch the deal, regardless of what insane combination they can press on me. The fact simply is that they don't have the headscarf that goes with the veil. Muhammad stands helplessly to one side while Richard is itching to move on.

The men are digging through what has now turned into a jumbled pile of scarves. They even have the audacity to bring out more dresses which they insist go with the veil.

"But she doesn't want a dress! She just wants the veil," Katie insists.

"But this dress, it is very good with this scarf." He pushes them forward as if bringing them closer will make us magically see something we haven't seen before.

"No, she just wants the veil! No scarf, no dress. This is not the kind of dress she wants anyway." She sure is right about that. I glance at the wall packed solid with bagged thin cotton fabrics in a garish rainbow of colors and patterns.

By now the shop is feeling stuffy, hot and too crowded. I am frantic to get out of there. It's time to cut to the chase. The veil—how much?

One shopkeeper quotes a price in Egyptian pounds that, when converted, makes me gasp: fifty dollars. For this piece of cheap cloth, cotton floss and tin sequins? If they're kidding, I'm not laughing. "No. No good."

"How much? What is your price? Tell me."

"Twenty-five," I declare stonily.

"Twenty-five?" they gasp in unison, expressing their incredulity that I could value this rare and precious veil so little. Nevertheless: "Okay. Let us say forty-five."

"Thirty."

They sigh in distress. Thirty? Surely this can't be so. Richard backs out of the shop. "Best price: forty," they exhale.

Okay, anything to get out of here. "Thirty-five." I begin backing away from the counter.

The shopkeepers eye each other. "Okay. Thirty-five."

Suddenly the tension in the air is gone, and they are all smiles. I unzip my purse and dig out the equivalent of the agreed price in Egyptian pounds. Ha, ha; they flash their white teeth, and I am now their best friend. As they hand me the bagged veil, one shopkeeper makes a final attempt, draping a scarf over my shoulder. "But you are leaving without a scarf?"

No shit. I shrug off the scarf and elbow my way out the door. There is no more magic in the air, only narrow alleyways packed with open-fronted shops filled with harsh light and cheap trinkets. The night is over, and Muhammad apologetically and with concern takes us back through the now-darkened park to the far curb where taxi drivers are lined up, waiting for fares. We are truly sorry to leave Muhammad and promise to stay in touch. He makes sure our taxi driver knows where we are going.

Not surprisingly, it takes perhaps half the time to get back to our hotel as it did to get to the bazaar. Our wrinkled, mustachioed taxi driver knows Cairo, and as we zoom along in the warm night he cheerfully points out various landmarks along the way. There is the opera house! There is the war memorial! There is the parliament building! He is loving his role as extemporaneous tour guide, and his delight rubs off on us, for by the time we arrive at the hotel, our grim mood has vanished.

Upstairs, Liz is asleep, but wakens when we softly open the door to let Katie in and check on the stricken one. Yes, she threw up again once we left, but is feeling some better and gratefully takes the box of mysterious pills the white-scarved pharmacist gave me, along with the box of bland white rice we have been toting with us throughout the evening.

Cairo, Egypt, Saturday, June 28, 2008

Katie

Dad woke me up a half hour earlier than I had requested. I went back to sleep, but he knocked again fifteen minutes later with money for the maids. He finally knocked again at the right time. Between the time we got up and the time we left, both parents knocked countless more times, and then finally two maids barged in on my stretching in front of the mirror. It was as if they couldn't wait for us to leave.

Liz

Farewell, Africa; I will return.

Return To France

Diary of Ruth K. Crapo, 1907-1908

On board the S.S. Heliopolis, March 20, 1908

I was able to get a single cabin, probably that of the old lady who died yesterday. Mother and Lucy are nearby.

I spent a pleasant afternoon on deck reading *Cleopatra* by H. Rider Haggard. Not many Americans are on board, mostly English with a smattering of Germans and French. Seven times around the deck is a mile. Lucy and I did the mile in no time after dinner.

White caps are in evidence this evening, so it's to bed for Ruthie.

On board the S.S. Heliopolis, March 21, 1908

Some Americans with chairs near ours loaned me *A History of Egypt* by Breasted. I found out that Amenhotep IV, whose cartouche I have, was a great old boy after all, Breasted calling him the most remarkable of all the pharaohs and the first individual in human history to thrust aside the religion and gods of his forefathers of thousands of years and set up the one god Aton (the Sun) as the only god for his people. As a ruler and statesman, unfortunately, he was a failure.

On board the S.S. Heliopolis, Sunday, March 22, 1908

We got into Naples at seven o'clock this morning. We didn't get off the boat as she was to sail at ten, but amused ourselves watching the people on the pier. Flower merchants put their bouquets on long sticks and held them up to sell, men and boys dove in the water for coins, and numerous bands of musicians in rowboats were performing for our benefit.

There was card playing, sewing, etc. going on all day. The English are not much for observing Sunday, I find.

Diaries of Holly, Katie and Elizabeth Pierce, 2008

Cairo, Egypt—Nice & Paris, France, Saturday, June 28, 2008

THIS MORNING WE check out of the Al Horeya and head for Cairo's airport. Richard's jet will leave for Paris and his business traveler's hotel near Aéroport Charles de Gaulle at 11:30 A.M. What he will do to while away the hours at this cut-rate hotel next to the runways is anyone's guess. The following morning, Sunday, he will fly from Paris to New York to San Francisco and home. The point for me, however, is that he's leaving me with the girls to fend for myself.

We hug, and while he whispers reassurances, I hold on tightly with fearful desperation. How will I manage my girls without his steadying influence? In the months preceding this journey, he had always joked that he would be the trip's "hod carrier," demoting himself to bag lugger, the "Thomas Cook" to the three women walking in the century-old steps of my ancestors. But how wrong he was! I think back: how many fights did he resolve, feelings did he soothe, euros did he hand out without a whimper? What will I do without my rock?

OUR EGYPTAIR FLIGHT lifts us from Cairo's smog and sand out over the Mediterranean, then up across Italy's boot and the snow-topped Alps to Geneva with its pretty blue lake and tidy, geometric green fields. The disconnect between Egypt's dirt and chaos and Switzerland's cleanliness and order is mind-bending. Egypt is not where you would find rotating toilet seats, nor in Switzerland would you find gaunt ten-year-old boys persistently pushing dog-eared, sun-faded packs of postcards in your face.

Without making a big deal of it, I'm hoping the girls by themselves are absorbing the profound physical, geographical and cultural differences we've encountered so far. Unlike Ruth's tour of famous artworks and stone monuments imperative to the proper cultivation of a young lady a century ago, I see this gradual awakening of the girls' consciousness to the vast and complicated differences in our itinerary's path as their education and preparation for responsibly taking their place in the world a century later. But with Katie's retreat into our hotel rooms and Liz's panic attacks limiting how far she can go before meltdown, I frankly am not sure just how much they have gotten out of this journey.

Katie
They played the movie "27 Dresses" on the tiny screens above our heads. I had to crane my neck to see it clearly, but it ended up being quite enjoyable. I almost cried at the end when they got married since I was fantasizing that the day would come when I would receive such a romantic proposal. It was very sweet, but I didn't want to cry in front of the Europeans I'm sitting next to.

I finally got my giant *O.K.!* magazine—aahh, back to civilization, even though I enjoyed Egypt a lot. I can have my "proper" things again—a flush-force-five toilet and *O.K.!* magazine and a salad I can eat without fear of getting sick.

Diary of Ruth K. Crapo, 1907-1908

On board the *S.S. Heliopolis*—Nice, France, March 23, 1908
We arrived in Marseilles at noon. The Cook's man was late, only arriving five minutes before train time, and we were in quite a stew. He not only turned up late but brought my umbrella broken to bits and Mama's bag split open. *Maybe* we weren't mad, but it did no good. We had to hustle for seats, too.

What we could see of the scenery before dark between Marseille and Nice was very beautiful indeed. After Egypt, this country of trees and flowers and grass seems a paradise. We reached the Isles de la Brittanique hotel recommended by an Englishman.

Nice, France, March 24, 1908
Nice is very clean and gay, with much dressing, many flowers, cafés, theaters, autos, etc., just a great big resort for the giddy rich. However, it's very fascinating even to the sober poor.

And Monte Carlo: such flowers, buildings, scenery and swelldom I never did see, such band-playing, tea-drinking, automobiling and suchlike! The Prince of Monaco gets $1,000,000 yearly rent from his casino. He owns all of Monte Carlo and Monaco. His people are not allowed to gamble. The casino pays all their taxes.

We spent an hour or more in the casino watching the games, cards and the rolling ball. Many more women than men were playing, with heaps of money in sight. Mother didn't want us to play, as we didn't understand the games, but it was a sight well worth seeing.

Nice, France, March 25, 1908

We left Nice at nine o'clock for the Grand Corniche Drive. The day was a perfect one, warm and sunny, the horses were big and fresh, and the people on the coach were jolly. We had a fine view of some washerwomen along the river. Great rocky cliffs, all shades of pink and blue, towered above us, and often as far as we could see were tiers and tiers of mountains.

Menton was a dear little place. We had lunch there and listened to a band concert in the park at noon. We also bought a lot of pretty postcards that I lost.

Nice, France, March 26, 1908

We went to Cook's for tickets this morning, as we are to leave for Paris at 8:15 tomorrow morning and arrive at 10:40 P.M. A bad hour, but the best we could do. Mother wanted to sit up all night and get into Paris at six o'clock the next day. Lucy and I objected.

This afternoon there was a big crowd at the much-advertised "Battle of Flowers" along the seafront. It was a very pretty sight with carriages beautifully decorated for the occasion and flowers being thrown in great profusion by everyone. Bunches of violets, which would cost two dollars at home, were thrown as we'd throw beans on Halloween by the handfuls and bagsful.

Nice—Paris, France, March 27, 1908

We were up at six o'clock this morning for the 8:15 train to Paris. A woman from Canada regaled us with stories of good and bad luck at Monte Carlo, where she had spent some time. At Cannes she met a man who sat in the same car with us. A "friend," she called him. She talked of her husband, and he of his wife, yet she met him by appointment on the train, and they were going as far as London together. Both were very pleasant and agreeable and exceedingly nice to us. One meets queer types, sure enough.

Paris, France, March 28, 1908

After breakfast we got our mail, made arrangements for Mother to go back on the first of April. Then Lucy and I went out again to look at hats. Lucy is hard to please in that line.

We got lost for a while in some side streets, and in the home stretch about six o'clock I lost my watch. As it was almost dark, I didn't go back to look for it, though Lucy did and without success. I will inquire at the Lost and Found department.

Paris, France, March 30, 1908

We went for our mail the first thing this morning and found some letters. We next saw about Mother's steamship accommodations and then went to look her up a new suit. We found one finally at the Magazins Lafayette, but it had to be fitted over and changed.

In the afternoon we shopped some more; we bought three hats, Lucy, one and I, two. Mother wanted us to get them before she left.

Paris, France, March 31, 1908

This morning I took Mother to the shampooers and then went out to do some errands for her. When I got home she had not arrived, and after twelve o'clock had come and gone, I went out to look her up. I found her just coming out of the hairdresser's. She'd spent nearly three hours there, but her coiffure was marvelous to behold.

I feel absolutely lost without my watch, and Mother misses it, too.

Paris, France, April 1, 1908

We were up early this morning, for wasn't Mother to catch a train? Two special trains were carrying the passengers to Cherbourg for the *S.S. Kronprinzessin Cecilie.* We saw Ma off in good shape, and I must say I hated to have her go off alone. I felt blue the rest of the day.

After seeing Mother off, Lucy and I took a good, long walk down to the Hotel de Ville to make inquiries about my watch. They had found no watch, and none had come in, but they are to let me know if mine turns up.

Paris, France, April 2, 1908

There was more rain this morning and more shopping for us. We went to the Louvre stores in the morning where I bought a medicine chest for myself, a case consisting of three bottles and had these filled. I have heard nothing about my lost watch, and I'm beginning to think I'll never see it again.

We have developed a regular "French cake" habit and have spoiled our dinners now for three nights. We must cut it out.

Paris, France, April 3, 1908

It was another dark day, but we were out shopping. The desire to buy is still with me, but the money, gone.

We got ready for our sojourn in the country and packed our duds. It has been packing and unpacking for over six months now, and I am good and tired of it.

Diaries of Holly, Katie and Elizabeth Pierce, 2008

Cairo, Egypt—Nice, France, Saturday, June 28, 2008

THE EASYJET connection from Geneva to Nice goes without a hitch with a perfect landing. The sun is lowering into a reddish-gold horizon. So far, so good. But getting from the Nice airport east into the city proper could mean trouble. The airport is twenty minutes out of town. Guidebooks say to pass up the taxis and their extortive forty-dollar fares and instead take a shuttle which would cost the three of us a total of twelve dollars. In fact, months ago I booked us into a hotel not five minutes' walk away from the bus depot with this in mind.

When I reveal my intention to take the shuttle, the girls go ballistic: "Mom, I'm too tired!" "A taxi will take us directly to the hotel!" "Forty dollars? Dad would take a taxi!" "Mom, come on!"

But "come on;" the shuttle is right there ten steps away, idling at the curb with plenty of room. It's still light out. I move decisively to the shuttle, get on, and so the girls grudgingly follow, complaining the whole way. How I wish Richard were still with us! He would know the right thing to do.

Katie

We arrived, and my sister was very anxious and freaking, but Mom refused to take a taxi so we took a bus. The bus let us off, and then our hour and a half of hell began.

NICE—*MON DIEU!* The shuttle comes to a stop along a street bordered by the bus station and its huge parking structure to the north and some anonymous-looking two-story buildings to the south. I know we're somewhere near the beach, and I have some general directions from Google, but I can't see *exactly* where we are on the map. It's dark now, a Saturday night, and the area is almost deserted. And of course, even with my rudimentary French (*"Où est la Rue Chauvain?"*), the few I find to approach have never heard of this street. It may as well be on Mars, for all these locals know.

By now, Liz has totally gone into meltdown mode. She is hunched down on the median strip with her sweatshirt covering her face, sobbing hysterically, while Katie is shouting invectives at me for not taking the taxi in the first place. To top it off, a French woman slowly driving by disapprovingly wags her finger at us for making a such a loud and untoward public scene. (Bitch; try doing that while passing on foot and we'll see who ends up screaming here.)

So I must find a taxi. A large black man with a round, shiny face at the far end of the parking structure actually calls a taxi dispatcher, but tells me that regrettably, being a Saturday night, no taxis are available. Oh God. So I start off in the other direction, telling the freaking-out girls to stay put. I walk and walk, playing "Hotter, Colder," asking people where the Rue Chauvain or the Hotel Acanthe is. I feel I am closing in on it, and finally I find it. It is only two hundred yards away, a five-minute walk at the most.

There, the night manager, a bald little man in wire spectacles and a light blue polo shirt ensconced behind the front desk, is scornfully unhelpful right from the get-go. When I ask for help with a taxi, he wants to know *exactly* where the girls are. Now, duh; if I knew that, wouldn't they be with me? I try to explain that one of them is *très malade* and so the need for a taxi.

Ah. In an unexpected burst of helpfulness, he scrawls the number of a taxi service on one of my dog-eared pieces of paper and pushes it across the counter.

"Mais, je n'ai pas un telephone," I say. What, someone without a cell phone? *Incroyable.* This seems to irritate him even more. I can tell from his look he feels I'm some incompetent who's just fallen off the turnip truck and that it's against his principles to help this stupid woman out. But finally, grudgingly, he calls the taxi service, and a car is dispatched. All the

while he is protesting that if he calls a taxi, it will come to the hotel, not to where the girls are. No kidding. I detest this little man.

The taxi arrives, a beautiful Mercedes, and off we go to find the girls. Easier said than done. All the streets are one way. We are in the area where they are, but where is the median strip with the map on a pole? The driver is becoming more impatient, chiding me for not having a cell phone nor a specific address.

Eventually we find the spot—but the girls are not there! I decide we must go back to the hotel and see if they have gotten there via another taxi. With many heavings of impatient sighs, the taxi driver ferries this typically dense American back to the hotel. Are the girls there? They are not. Thirty-five dollars down an unpleasant and disdainful drain.

I decide to walk back to the median strip to look for them, and there on the far side of the street is where I find them. They have moved off the strip, and despite her hysteria, Liz has actually found a taxi stand and successfully called for a car!

Liz

I went across the street and begged for help at a bar (no taxis were showing up at the stand), and finally two older men helped me out. One knew some English and told the bouncer what was up, and he called us a taxi. The man was very concerned about my state and acted kind and worried. Finally, I felt as if someone gave a shit.

I RECEIVE A hate-filled, vituperative greeting, and all I can do is humbly apologize, which I do. I should have known that something as logical as the bus into town wouldn't work. And I should have known that Liz was ready to melt when I made them get on the bus; Katie had warned me Liz' "pop-up blockers" were no longer working.

As it turns out, this two-hundred-yard ride to the Hotel Acanthe is quick, direct and only ten dollars. Add that sum to the humiliating thirty-five-dollar search in the Mercedes, and I find my answer: yes, it would have been cheaper and much less stressful to take a taxi in from the airport. That lesson may be learned, but the night is not yet over. We are given Room 351 by the horrible little man, a supposed double with a cot for the third. Add in a cheap wooden table and chair, and there is no floor space at all.

I remove the chair from the room after Liz in her fury first hurls the little table into the hall. The top flies off and the wooden legs take on a crazy angle. I work on banging the legs back into place, as I am not about to be charged for busted-up furniture in this hole. At least there is now maybe five square feet more room.

The cot is wedged into the far corner. In obeisance for my sins, I readily take the doggy cot that immediately collapses into a ski-slope slant. Further investigation reveals that its legs freely bend 180 degrees with no way to make them stay fixed. So down the whole thing goes, and I feel as if I'm on a campout or a sleepover. In fact, a mosquito prompts us to slather ourselves in DEET, which completes the campout aspect.

Liz

I felt so dirty, just filthy, and immediately took a cold shower, still crying. Mom was really sorry, I could tell, for what I went through and took the cot without even saying anything. We all had to sleep the wrong way around because they had pushed the beds so if we slept the right way, we would have hit our heads on these little shelves which were supposed to be next to the beds. Bastards.

LYING ON MY COT in the still, humid air, I can hardly wait to get home and put up on TripAdvisor the scathing review the Hotel Acanthe deserves. The room *could* be a double, but the hotel should be punished for claiming it is capable of being converted to a triple. The beds line up side by side, leaving six inches between them and the wall with the "closet" next to my cot. The room itself is, I believe, trapezoidal, the quaint result of Nice's wedge-shaped city blocks. To do anything in my area of the room I must walk on my cot. Good thing the legs are down—in fact, the only thing to do in this room *is* to lie down. A small, black Telefunken TV is mounted hospital-wise high on the wall, and a partially disassembled light fixture hangs dismally from the ceiling, all of which has been sprayed with a cottage-cheese-like finish, even unto the decorative plate around the light's wire. A Danish-design headboard is glued to the wall, above which is a pseudo-fancy-looking light fixture, two sconces connected by a horizontal rod. Pressing the buttons reveals they don't work, and upon investigation I discover there aren't even bulbs in the fixtures. What a surprise. (We don't dare mess with the button with the bell icon on it.)

Katie

Our room is so small I lay back on my bed, and my sister's butt was right in my face as she was bending over to put something in her suitcase. The bathroom is too small, even at the Sims' standards. Mom doesn't have enough floor space to open her bag to unpack.

THE BATHROOM: what is there to say? The tiny, closet-sized room would be unusable by anyone of substantial girth. The sink sticks its roundness right into the doorway, while to the left the toilet is wedged into a corner. The shower by best estimates is three feet square with a shower pan of two feet. At least the shower head works, as does the hot and cold water.

Did I forget to say that there is no air-conditioning? What a surprise. If we are to breathe, we must open the two French windows wide, pushing the curtains out of the way for the duration. This arrangement puts us on intimate terms with the tenants in the building opposite. On the lower level is a family with at least two very obese members who sleep on the floor, their flab spilling out onto the balcony that is hung with drying laundry and other sundries.

Enduring the heat in the Hôtel Acanthe

Above us a man and woman boldly walk about in few clothes. I have caught the former staring down into our room where the girls in their underwear lie hot and exhausted on their beds. I figure he must see a lot of this sort of thing, and after a while I find I just don't care if someone is looking at me in my *soutaine-gorge*; after all this *is* the Côte d'Azur.

Nice, France, Sunday, June 29, 2008

Katie

Mom was very sweet this morning, barely woke me up when she reached for the key. She brought a breakfast of croissants and real orange juice on a tray to us—so nice! She felt bad about last night, I think, and she ended up spending thirty-five euro for one taxi to look for us and then another taxi just to take us across the street and around the square. The driver looked at us as if we were stupid, but how were we to know?

MORNING COMES, along with more information about our neighbors across the alley than we need to know. Opposite us to the left is an old woman, her gray hair wrapped up in a twist. She is parked in her wheelchair at her breakfast table eating slowly and deliberately. Against the far wall I can see in the dim light a bed with a hanging metal handle used to help hoist her into bed. I'm suddenly reminded of the hoist used by the caregiver to swing my father—Ruth's younger son—into bed. His Parkinson's finally killed him in the early months of 2004, something I don't want to dwell upon.

I turn my attention to the right, where a pretty multicolored cat lives who sits next to its pink and blue litter box on the narrow balcony and stares at the pigeons who shoot through the alleyway. I fleetingly see a middle-aged woman wearing a sleeveless black dress walk by the open French doors.

The girls are waking now, and we see another cat, one that looks part Abyssinian and rubs the balcony railing in ecstasy when we kiss and meow and coo at it. This one belongs to the man who stared at us last night. A rug hangs over the railing which we discover is for the cat to jump up and sharpen its claws on—four stories up.

Liz

The man came out in the morning to smoke his fag, and thanks to his rug, it wasn't until he turned around to go inside that I noticed he was fully nude. Sometimes I would catch his face in one of his window panes looking down on us, trying to get a peek in, no doubt. What a creep, but luckily he left mid-morning and didn't return.

THE GIRLS ARE SO exhausted they decide to stay in, sleeping and reading *O.K.!* magazine the entire day. I am for this; why try to force them to see the sights, especially after last night? I remind them they're entitled to breakfast here, whatever that might be.

So, is there any saving grace to this one-star hotel? Yes: the breakfast. The little room off to the side of the desk is managed by a lovely red-haired woman in her forties who cheerfully brings me buttery croissants, crispy buns, hot chocolate and fresh orange juice with a welcoming smile. It's almost stupefying how different in attitude this lovely day clerk's is to last night's surly little man. The tall windows are wide open to the balmy morning breeze and the bustling passers-by. I wish I could say this makes up for the hellholes they call rooms, but after four weeks, my heart has hardened when it comes to crappy quarters.

I SET OUT WALKING, first deciding to find Ruth's hotel, the Iles de la Brittanique on Rue de la Gare. Okay, "train street:" it's got to be up by the train station. I know the line is to the north, so I start walking away from the seaside.

The town sits on a slope, which could make for a tiring walk. But the sun is mild so far, and I've the whole day, so I take my time. Research back home didn't turn up an "Iles de la Brittanique" hotel, so finding it will require a little detective work and my defective French—just the kind of adventure I like.

After about a mile, I stop a well-dressed older couple to inquire after the Rue de la Gare. They don't recognize the street by this name, but they can tell me how to reach the *gare*: continue on north, then turn left down the street just before the giant, ugly, concrete overpass.

At the giant, ugly, concrete overpass I run into a group of a half-dozen college-aged kids with daypacks milling around in all directions with that dazed look in their eyes that says they're lost. They're speaking American English, and I hesitate to butt in, not wanting to appear to be a meddling old lady. But I keep overhearing "train station," so finally I dive in, asking them if they need help. By now I'm ninety-eight percent sure the station is to the west on what's now the Avenue Thiers. (I wonder why they changed the name; was "Train Station Street" too boring? At least it was helpfully descriptive.) In their confusion they are actually happy to listen to me and take my advice, something by now I'm rarely hearing on this trip.

The Avenue Theirs is very pretty with its large plane trees shading the sidewalks and small stalls. I stop at a fruit stand to ask a man in his sixties if he knows of the Iles de la Brittanique. The older they get, the more they know.

"*Mais oui!* Oh yes! Go past the post office and the train station."

"*Il y èst là?* It is there?" I ask, incredulous at my good luck.

"*Oui!*" he insists, smiling at the dumbfounded look that must be pasted on my face. Off I go, past the block-long, red stone monolith of a post office where I find the most beautiful and ornate building imaginable. It's a pale yellowish-tan with black wrought-iron balconies and topped by a graceful black dome. The building's corner at the intersection of Avenue Thiers and Rue Berlioz is rounded. *Très jolie! Mais*—there is no sign declaring it to be the Iles de la Brittaniques. Nevertheless, I just feel this must be it. Right place, right era, and verified by the fruit stand man. It may not be, but my heart wants it to be, and so I am satisfied.

The building is actually divided now into two hotels which would account for the change in name. The side facing on Avenue Thiers is the Best Western Riviera. It always floors me to see these Best Western hotels all over the world. After all, the chain was originally headquartered in Long Beach, just south of Los Angeles, and I remember it from a child's perspective as the posh place to stay in town.

So of course I go to the Best Western. The lobby is mercifully air-conditioned, as by now it's humid and hot out. At the desk a nice young man in a dark blue shirt and tie chats with me in fluent English. No, he doesn't know of the hotel I seek, and even though I know what the results will be, he obligingly Googles the name to confirm that it no longer exists as an establishment. He is fascinated by my pictures and the tale I have to tell but knows nothing of the building's history. Instead, he directs me to the Musée Masséna on the seaside, suggesting I might find more information there.

Coincidentally, the museum is at the end of the street flanking the other side of the hotel. What luck! Today is my day indeed. By now, however, it's just plain hot and, happy I brought my trusty green parasol, I walk a mile back down the blazing sidewalks to the shore again.

Fortunately, the *musée* is right there, a grand, ivory-colored Belle Époque palace with a sweeping circular drive. Built at the turn of the twentieth century, this lavish, Italianate, fin-de-siècle villa was given to the city by Monsieur Masséna the year before the end of World War I to house local historical memorabilia.

I stagger up the curve of the drive to a bank of steps leading to the entrance, where a tall and official-looking man looks down at me. I smile and start to walk by, but he stops me in my tracks with a question.

"Où est votre billet?"

Hmm. My mind struggles to hearken back to 51A, Conversational French.

"Il est necessaire que vous achetez un billet pour le musée." He gestures back down the drive.

Billet. Oh yeah: ticket. I have to buy a ticket to get in.

"Ah. Oui." I cast him a feeble and apologetic smile and trudge back down the drive to the little booth I'd not noticed on the way in.

"Un, s'il vous plait." One, please. Piece of cake. I puff my way back up the stone driveway. At the top of the stairs the gentleman takes my ticket with an indulgent smile and allows me entrance.

Inside, a surprise. The *musée* is not air-conditioned; instead, tall windows are open to the non-existent breeze off the Mediterranean. But it's a bearable warmth, and it is very quiet and with few other visitors, very pleasant indeed. Here I spend an unhurried afternoon in true bliss, able to stroll and linger without being rushed along by the bored, anxious or hungry.

In one room, surrounded by large posters and embroidered cloths advertising the yearly Nice carnival, is a large glass case holding a tiny scale model of an elaborate yet vaguely bizarre "pleasure palace," the Jetée-Promenade, situated on pilings over the water. I could swear we didn't see anything like that sticking out into the bay.

"Qu'est-ce que c'est?" What's that? I ask a woman guard, gesturing to this confection in a box.

"Il etait un vieux casino, mais—" Oops. I've lost her. Between my lousy French and her dicey English, I get the drift that the Germans supposedly used it as target practice during World War II, and it was never rebuilt. Is this true? I see another old photo of the casino ablaze over the water. Its caption says that it was reconstructed, much to the locals' disgust (apparently the natives were offended by this flamboyant eyesore). Burned? Bombed? I'm not sure what to believe.

I wander on, slightly dazed by the afternoon warmth. Most of the items concern the history and illuminati of the town including Napoleon and Garibaldi, Nice's native son. I respectfully pause to admire a hugely impressive painting of the Masséna family dressed to the nines. What a life it must have been, at least for this one family! But I've seen those paintings of women out pounding their laundry on rocks at the riverside, and from the delicate white hands and kid gloves here, I imagine the Massénas were one of the very few families who personally never had to concern themselves with this activity.

Time drifts by. I suddenly realize I am so hungry I could faint. I momentarily bypass the gift shop and walk down the street to a café specializing in North African food. I order a salad plate, which turns out to be a sort of tomato salsa topped with wedges of boiled egg and kalamata olives and ringed with bits of canned tuna. *Salade Niçoise* perhaps? I also order a canned Lipton tea and press it to my cheeks and throat, which evokes delighted laughter from the cashier, a middle-aged Muslim woman by the look of her dress. It is the perfect-sized lunch, especially with the baklava "cigar" and tiny pistachio goodie with which I finish off the meal.

Back at the gift shop I buy a five-euro book in English for tourists with excellent photos on the history of Nice, in which I discover that in 1883 on the eve of its opening the Jetée-Promenade did indeed burn down, only to be promptly rebuilt. I also find a giclée print of a view of the "Rue de la Gare" dated 1910. It did exist! I must have it. Back at the hotel, I will wrap it around an empty liter water bottle and hope I can somehow get it home without it being totally crushed. What a dreamer.

Katie
Mom left us money so we went to lunch and spent half—fifty euros at Café Le Felix. Enjoyed lunch, the cool sea breeze and the little old ladies chatting in French. Le Felix was good. Mom was still not back so we watched "Veronica Mars" dubbed in French and made up the story line. It was surprisingly hot in Nice, but there were sporadic breezes from off the ocean. We three slept the afternoon away once Mom got back and showed us her pictures.

ONCE BACK AT the hotel, I fall asleep in our stuffy room until eight o'clock that evening. We discover the light above the sink has given up the ghost.

By now the cheerful woman at the desk is gone, and so we must report this to the horrible little man who only shrugs his shoulders and declares he can do *rien* about it. What did we expect?

Katie

Both the headboard lights don't work, and now the bathroom light doesn't work anymore. I think I've seen enough of my sister's butt crack and underwear to last me a lifetime, the shape of her butt and hips with her underwear stretched around them.

THERE'S NOTHING left but to go out for dinner. At an outdoor café, another wallet-emptier: seventy-five euros for three. I guess if the dollar and euro were equal, it would seem somewhat reasonable, but now that it takes over a dollar and a half to buy a euro, it's not.

At the café everyone is concentrating on the big screen and the finals of the European soccer championship, with Germany versus Spain. When Spain scores a point, everyone yells; there's a definite bias here for the Spanish. I guess that's logical, concerning French and German history.

It's not until we finally make it back to the hotel (after a two-hour dinner, most of it spent waiting) that the championship is decided: Spain wins, "and the crowd goes wild!" Outside our window we hear the town erupting with honking horns and wild shouting. Cars with large Spanish flags fluttering out the windows flash by the end of our alleyway, and gleeful cheers ricochet down the narrow lane. On the TV Chancellor Angela Merkel gives each German player a consoling handshake, and the Spanish team is honored like gods with shooting fireworks and a silver loving cup the size of a baby's bathtub. It's too bad that other than the Olympics, the U.S. doesn't have a similar competition with other nations. I feel it would definitely foster goodwill, especially if we lost with grace.

Nice-Franceuil, France, Monday, June 30, 2008

Katie

My sister didn't want to hear me complain about how hungry I was, so she gave me back the roll I secreted for her from breakfast. It's not very flavorful, but it will have to do to tame the unruly beast inside. I get so offended when she's tired of my complaining because I feel as if this whole goddamn trip has been organized daily around her anxiety issues.

I feel as if she has no right to fault me for things that are also out of my control. How patient I have been with all her stopping in the middle of perilous stairways to touch a piece of plastered-on trash. And still, again, her headphones are tinny so that I can hear what she's listening to. I will be glad to get home.

TODAY WE TAKE the train to Chenonceaux, our final destination in our quest to follow Ruth. It will be a pleasure to take the French trains again, except that we must first travel all the way back to Paris before turning around and heading for Tours and the Loire valley and ultimately by taxi to Franceuil.

Liz

In the Paris train station we found our connecting train, with us running, sweaty, and a bit angry because we had waited like fifteen minutes for Katie to pee and buy an Eiffel Tower at the station when we could have been moving.

Katie and I waited on the platform with the luggage while Mom figured out what was going on with the trains because she's the only one who speaks French. I put my observational skills to good use and gave any good cigarette butts I happened to see to a local bum who was wandering around looking for them. He was surprised but pleasantly gracious when I gave them to him.

In Tours, we finally found a taxi to take us to the town. To our surprise the driver was a woman, wearing heels at that.

France: Franceuil

Diary of Ruth K. Crapo, 1907-1908

Franceuil, France, April 4, 1908

Before leaving the hotel this morning, I sent back Bill's fraternity pin by registered mail. I had to do it all in French and also had to run my legs off finding the post office.

We had an uneventful trip to Chenonceaux. It was raining furiously when we arrived. The bus for Franceuil was full, but we squeezed in anyhow, much to the displeasure of its occupants. We were dumped at Franceuil, and a woman directed us to the Garreaus' where it turned out we were not expected, as Lucy's letter was not definite on that point. However, we were hospitably received and think Madame Garreau is charming.

Franceuil, France, Sunday, April 5, 1908

We had no lessons today, instead making a tour after breakfast of the garden, and a fascinating one it is, too, with the promise of many lovely flowers and vegetables. Already the primroses and violets are blooming full blast, and the fruit trees are in blossom. A darling little brook traverses the garden, and all is so spic and span. We took quite a long walk and gathered big bouquets of daisies and violets.

This afternoon Monsieur Garreau took us to see the Chateau de Chenonceau, which had a section built over the River Cher. In the evening he entertained us with his phonograph.

Franceuil, France, April 6, 1908

Our lessons began today, and it's easy to see that they are going to be good, stiff ones. Madame and her husband were both teachers and are themselves wonderfully clever and expect everyone else to be.

Lucy had a hard time today, and this evening she had a good cry, she was so discouraged. It's hard for me, too, but we'll have to stick it out for a while anyway. If the weather would only change! This weird rain and cold is enough to give anyone the blues. Lucy would not have stayed here alone, she said.

Franceuil, France, April 7, 1908

It was Lucy's birthday, and another dismal day as to weather. As her French went better today, she is all right again and thinks she'll stay.

We had a long walk with Madame Garreau this afternoon. An old pupil of Madame Garreau's, a young Englishman, paid her a passing visit and stayed to dinner. Lucy was allowed to speak English, while the rest of us spoke French. He was young, with a brand-new mustache and a bit blasé withal. He departed in the rain.

Franceuil, France, April 8, 1908

Marvelous to relate: the sun appeared again this morning. Lucy had her lesson and immediately after lunch, Madame, their dog, Franca, and the two Crapos started out for our exercise, wishing to get the good of the sunshine. We walked to Chenonceaux and back, and it was perfect out of doors.

When we came back, I had my lesson and a mighty poor one at that, then tea and back to studying again. Each day the lessons get longer and harder, until I'm all in a muddle.

Five new chicks made their debut today. They chose a good day to do so.

Franceuil, France, April 9, 1908

After a morning of study and recitations followed by lunch, Lucy and I took a rambling walk in the fields and gathered marsh marigolds, coo-coo flowers and violets.

There was great excitement in Franceuil today when it became known that a mad dog had been killed nearby. All dogs had to be chained and kept in, and we didn't meet one on our walk this afternoon. Poor Franca was most desolate, whining and groaning all day long. At times I thought she must be mad, too.

Franceuil, France, April 10, 1908

I had no sleep last night and a pain in my side. My room is very damp and cold, and it is necessary to dry out my towels, washrag and brushes in the sun every day.

We spent this morning entertaining young André, the child of the workman in the garden. He is a cunning kid and most independent withal. We had another amble through the fields this afternoon with Madame Garreau. We stop and talk to all the farmers and kids to help us understand the different ways of speaking, a truly exciting pastime.

I've had a headache all day long, but it is some better tonight. . . .

Diaries of Holly, Katie and Elizabeth Pierce, 2008

Franceuil, France, Tuesday, July 1, 2008

WAKING ALONE IN my little chintz-decorated room this morning to a blue, blue sky outside—what heaven. The ski-slope cot seems but a distant memory now. At the front desk the hateful bespectacled troll has been replaced by Laurent, a slender and animated man perhaps in his mid-thirties and ready to assist you in any possible way. The girls suspect he is gay, but I suspect they are wrong; Laurent has graciously offered to drop me off in Francueil once *his wife* returns around noon with the van. He is quite interested in our story and goes so far as to page through the phone book to see if there are still any Garreaus around—and there is, coincidentally, a Laurent Garreau. I write down the address for further investigation.

While the girls' activity for today is simply to relax around this sweet little hotel with its swimming pool and flower boxes burgeoning with purple and pink petunias, my plan is to comb Francueil's cemetery to see if I can find the Garreaus. The town's population is about two hundred, Laurent thinks; Francueil shows up on Google's maps only at the very highest resolution, the one where you can distinguish the chateau's gallery stretching across the river. Surely the cemetery can't be that vast.

Katie

Sick. I had terrible diarrhea last night before bed, again at three o'clock and this morning as well.

Breakfast was at ten o'clock: chocolate croissant, orange juice, yogurt with marmalade and fruit thing, plus hot chocolate. Wish I could have enjoyed it. My sister gave me the magical white pill in the hope it will all go away.

IT'S NOON AND Laurent's wife, a pretty blonde woman, has returned. As we get into the van, Laurent apologizes for its messy state. I assure him it is excellent compared to the taxis we've been in; at least the van has window handles. We putter out the driveway and bump along country roads, passing lush, green fields and dark stands of trees. The land seems refreshingly clear and basic in its colors: blue, green, yellow, white; no grimy tan, wind-weathered red or startling turquoise. It is so simple and restful.

We cross the Cher River. It is a deep, lush green which reflects the blue of the sky. A little way more, and we are at the edge of Francueil. The cemetery, surrounded by a high stone wall and with a solid iron gate, is on the left, and here Laurent drops me off, watching to make sure I can get in before he trundles off on his own errands. And so the search for the Garreaus begins.

I'm right; the square, walled cemetery is not large, but there are enough plots to keep me busy looking for several hours. Some of the stones are quite recent while some go well back into the 1800s, and they vary quite a bit in their state of repair. Old markers are composed of blackish, crumbly granite covered in multicolored lichen that makes the inscriptions difficult if not impossible to read. Elaborate wrought-iron curlicue'd crosses with suffering Christs affixed are all rusted to a mellow reddish-brown. On some, little metal heart-shaped markers on the gravesite bear details regarding the interred.

Newer stones are mostly polished marble slabs, some with enameled photos of the deceased, some with inscriptions in a fancy serif script which seemed to be popular at one point. On some are oversized, pansy-like ceramic flowers in realistic colors, a much nicer solution to the graveyard bouquet dilemma, I think, than the faded silk floral arrangements popular in the U.S. I wish I knew where they came from. I think of my mother's grave sprinkled with some of my dad's ashes by the Blue River in eastern Nebraska's rolling grasslands. Three times a year I always remember to call the floral shop in Crete and order a plain bouquet of real flowers, ungussied with fake butterflies or garish bows, to be delivered to her gravesite at Riverside Cemetery. Moments arise when it's hard for me to think of my parents there, not forgotten certainly, but without anything special to differentiate them from the surrounding dead. I would love to adorn my mom's grave with some of these ceramic flowers. But I suppose there would always be someone with little conscience who would find them unique enough to be carried off.

I'm surprised. I can't believe how many close hits there are on the name Garreau: Garaud, Serreau, Barreau, Garoit—on and on. It's become more frustrating than fun. It's hot now, and under the cloudless blue sky I'm sweating. Once again I'm glad I have my parasol.

While I'm looking, two leathery older men with a backhoe come in by a back gate and begin to work. I walk over to ask if they know of a Garreau in the yard.

"*S'il vous plaît, savez-vous . . . uh . . . où est . . .*" I point to "Garreau" I've printed in my little notebook and wave my arm broadly to encompass the silent graveyard.

Their faces are wrinkled, reddened and damp with exertion, and they squint in the bright sunlight when I point to the name I've written. They scratch their heads, and the younger one walks over to look at some faded paper that I've missed posted on the back gate.

The consensus is that the Garreaus are not here, but the older gent gets across to me that sometimes a body was interred on top of an older, abandoned site *("tombe abandonné")*. They also get the idea over to me that going to the church would probably be fruitless, as no one would be there today.

I continue my search so as to finish what I've started, but even though I look at every single blessed marker in the yard, there is no Garreau. So, to the alternative: the Laurent Garreau listed in the phone book. Naturally, he lives on Rue Chenonceaux, which only make things more confusing, given that our hotel manager is also a Laurent. But where is *la rue?*

I walk on to the center of town that also appears *abandonné*. What a dead town—but cute. There's no one in sight except a man and woman who are leisurely lunching under an awning outside a little café on the corner. When I go to walk in, the man jumps up and follows me; he is the owner.

"*S'il vous plaît, où est la Rue Chenonceaux?*" Oh my, a complete sentence.

"*Ah, oui.*" He hustles me out the door where he and his wife give me clear instructions: "*A la droite*" with a down-and-up hand gesture to the west (okay, "straight ahead"), *"et droite,"* with a hand curving off to the right.

He continues: *"Voici l'auto blanc?"* Yes, I do see a white car turning down there.

"Il est la Rue Chenonceaux?"

"Oui, c'est ça!"

We are all rather pleased with ourselves for successfully negotiating these directions. So with a *"Merci beaucoup,"* I start off down the road. The town seems to be fond of naming their newer streets after French icons, resulting in rues George Sand and Victor Hugo. Only a few cars pass me; otherwise, I'm alone.

Then, after much puffing along under my green parasol up a steeper than anticipated hill, I find Rue Chenonceaux just as directed. Number 2 is a large white rectangle with a red peaked roof set perpendicular to the street and behind a locked gate and driveway. Oh dear, now what?

So, huddled in the shade of a low wall, I take out my little notebook and in my French 51A try to explain how my *grandmère* was possibly a student of his parents or grandparents (who can say how old this man is?) and would like to talk to or correspond with him.

Folding my note around one of our travel cards, I drop it into his mailbox, hoping for the best, a doomed hope, as it were. When I get back to our hotel, I realize I'd written number 8 in my notebook this morning, not 2. How could I make such a stupid mistake? It must have been the heat. Well, I'm certainly not going back, so unless Number 2 drops my little note off at Number 8, I'm out of luck.

After a little wait and rest, I start walking back to Franceuil; I've done all I can do. It's warm, but little breezes come along and cool things down momentarily. Monet's red poppies grow alongside the road, and I pick up a little yellow butterfly, its wings folded in *rigor mortis*, and press it into my little notebook. Thinking of the Impressionists, I feel quite the picture walking along in my stylish red dress with the bright green parasol.

The two gravediggers drive past, and we wave and smile at each other. I stop to take a picture of the hay bales rolled up like so many spools of kite string. I pass through a stately lane of tall sycamores whose crowns create a pale, green tunnel. I take a detour down a dirt road to the banks of the River Cher. From the top of the road I imagine French Impressionists daubing images of pale lavender boats floating downriver against the dark, mossy green of the Cher. Once I reach the shore, however, I can see that under the river's glassy surface it's actually very swift and powerful—even dangerous.

Across the main highway, over the train tracks and into the final stretch into town I go. A man stops his little car in the lane and starts calling out something to me that sounds like the word "Vietnam" is included. I give a quizzical look, and he repeats his Vietnamese message. Finally I just yell, "I'm American!" and he laughs and points, and I realize he's commenting on my parasol! He probably wants to know where I've gotten it. Those poor boys at the Acropolis. If only they knew what a niche in the market is just waiting to be filled!

After stopping off for a bottle of peach Lipton iced tea, I make it to my cozy, air-conditioned room where I strip off my dress and collapse onto the bed. I'm tired, but it's a nice kind of tired. I've made connections and enjoyed myself, something I usually manage to do whenever I'm exploring on my own.

Katie is still in her room suffering from the *turistas*, awakening last night to the feeling of feces running down the sides of her thighs. This entailed getting up to rinse out the sheet and sadly has effectively ruined her day.

Liz, however, invites me for a swim. The pool is perfection; not too hot, not too cold, and all to ourselves. Eventually more people show up, including two little girls whom Liz teaches how to make a "George Washington," as she puts it. A what? I guess you bring your head up face down from underwater, then flip your hair back and it makes a sort of pompadour effect. Why George Washington, I can't say (and why she'd expect these two little French girls to know who George Washington is), but it's so "Liz" to be playing with these girls this way.

Liz

I should be enjoying myself, but the truth is I feel a bit edgy and feel as if there is a stone in my stomach. I think I am nervous about the journey home. So much beauty around me, and yet I seem to feel nothing of it.

EVENING COMES, and we decide to search out dinner in town, as the hotel's *prix fixe* meal is too expensive for us. By now Katie is feeling wobbly but some better, even a little peckish. After perusing the posted menus outside the various restaurants and cafés, we decide on the shaded patio of the Relais Chenonceaux Hotel. There, a resident African gray parrot squawks at us, and even though we keep responding with "co-lor" and "wool," unlike Alex, the famous African gray, he ignores us. Then come my lamb chops, crispy French fries, salad and a chocolate sundae. Chocolate; what better way to end a perfect day?

Katie

I finally went to dinner. I got my French onion soup—so good!—at the restaurant at the hotel across the street. It rivaled the soup in Paris. Also had a bleu cheese, walnut, walnut oil and butter lettuce salad and mint tea.

Favorite Meals of the Trip:

1. French onion soup in Paris and Chenonceaux
2. Thin-sliced beef with balsamic cream-dressed salad in Switzerland
3. Hard-boiled eggs with mayonnaise in Nice
4. Tzaziki with Greek salad in Greece

I asked the girl for mayo three times until my sister kindly boomed out my request for mayo that the girl promptly fulfilled.

Liz

We gave a cheer with our ice cream glasses to the end of a good journey. Katie has professed she won't ever go on a trip with Mom and Dad again, but I wouldn't mind. Certainly this one was insanely hectic, but it's not as if *all* trips are like this one.

WE GET BACK to the hotel around 9:15 under clear, blue skies. It's still light outside. Forty-five minutes later, it's raining! Gray, thick clots of clouds have appeared out of nowhere, and thunder rolls and lightning flashes. Below, I hear clattering and shouting as the staff scurries to move all the dinner's leftover dishware from the outside courtyard back into the kitchen. How strange; we hadn't a clue that rain was coming. But this is Europe. No wonder everything looks so green and fresh here all the time.

Time for bed. Liz and I are going to get up tomorrow and be at the chateau at nine o'clock before the crowds hit. Even she is now convinced this is the way to do it: get there before the herds of tour buses. While she'd like to go, Katie understandably doesn't expect she'll be up for it and tells us not to change our plans on her account. I'm sorry she can't go, but she simply says to take pictures, and she'll enjoy the experience that way.

Franceuil, France, Wednesday, July 2, 2009

TRUE TO HER word, this morning Liz is up and ready to go to the chateau when I am. It's walkable from our little inn, but the rain from last night has hung on, and it is coming down steadily. Nevertheless, we grab our umbrellas (parasols won't do today) and cameras, say *"Au revoir* and get better" to Katie, walk around the corner, then down the road to the chateau's entrance.

Some buses have already arrived, but since it isn't too packed, we decide to stop and have a breakfast snack before entering. A lone girl sits shivering behind a counter inside a three-sided shed, looking none too happy to be there. We try to jolly her up when we buy our yogurt, but she's beyond jollying.

We buy our tickets and trek along an arrow-straight avenue of overarching trees that then passes through broad geometric and curlicue'd-patterned gardens to the chateau's entrance. The rain is serious. Still, without the glare of the sun and harsh shadows, the flowers seem brighter and more lively with their faces washed. People smile in passing, walking along quickly under shared umbrellas. I understand that many of the tourists we see are here on chateau tours, but I can't imagine that chateaus are all that different from each other.

Once inside, we shake ourselves off, then ascend a grand stairway to start exploring the rooms and hallways, stopping momentarily when a nice woman offers to take our picture in front of an old tapestry, this one fronted by a ridiculously huge arrangement of stargazer lilies. Lots of these fresh flower arrangements sit all over the chateau, and I wonder at their absolute perfection, not a wilted bud in the bunch, and who must be changing them every day. The chateau company certainly can't be paying them enough for this tedious chore.

It's hard to imagine living amidst such ostentation. Heavy velvet drapes adorned with braids and tassels frame diamond-patterned mullioned windows. Plaster cupids and saints ornament stairways, and gorgeous but worn majolica tiles cover many of the floors. Room-sized tapestries hide walls in bedrooms, the number of which I lose count. Deeply carved wooden chests, velvet-upholstered and gilt chairs and canopied beds with silk-embroidered coverlets furnish these chambers, each of which has a color theme. The most intriguing is the black bedroom painted with little sperm-like tears by order of the grieving widow Louise of Lorraine; her bed and canopy are also black, but picked out with gold and silver embroidery. All the beds look a little short to me, but I imagine people were shorter back then.

The bedrooms are hung with larger-than-life paintings whose subjects may be real, such as ones of Louis XIV and an unintentionally coy Queen Isabella; the allegorical, embodied in side-by-side paintings of Catherine de Medicis and Diane de Poitiers, both got up as Diana of the Hunt, the latter dressed in a blue and white wispy, impractical hunting costume with lace-up sandals and surrounded by hounds and countless tumbling cherubs; and "mood-enhancing" creations like "The Teaching of Love." Nude, creamy-skinned women are popular. By the bed in one chamber is a life-sized image of a naked woman attended by two bare-assed handmaidens, the woman impassively facing the viewer who is "breast-on." I can't help thinking there's something to be said for subtlety.

What especially fascinates me are the intricately painted crown moldings. In one room I count nine levels of tiny hand-painted and gilded designs running around the ceiling's perimeter. The difference in detail runs from acanthus leaves to twining ribbon, all in tones of red and gold. Another room decorated in greens and golds features cannons in its equally ornate molding. Ceilings are elaborate. Close-set beams run the length of a room and are painted with curling vines and fleurs-de-lis. I keep thinking that the crown molding could be banged out in a workshop, then put in place, but the ceiling beams?

Wow. It is the sheer sumptuousness and workmanship that keep me gawping. Now here, I think, is a working example of the trickle-down theory. You have these few obscenely rich people constantly demanding new decorations, new gardens and gowns, trying to outdo each other, and it all depends on a small army of craftspeople to make it happen. The populace around these chateaus had to have a high rate of employment, no matter how backbreaking the work.

Not having a tour guide, we pick up what we can occasionally by loitering near tour groups. I learn that while the chateau began as a private estate, through some sketchy high-finance maneuvering by King Francois I involving tax penalties, Chenonceau became a royal residence in the form of a "donation" to cancel some tax debt. For me, however, most intriguing is how women played the dominant roles in building up and maintaining the chateau and its carefully tended grounds. Women like the aforementioned Diane de Poitiers, Henri II's mistress; Catherine de Medicis, Henri II's wife, then widow (and so Diane's enemy); Madame Dupin, George Sand's grandmother; and Louise of Lorraine, King Henry III's widow (she of the black bedroom) all seem to overshadow such notables as Louis XIV in this chateau's history.

By the time Liz and I reach the basement kitchen with its rows of menacing cleavers, gleaming copper pots, wooden carving tables dished to hold blood and drippings, and a room-sized fireplace with a pulley-operated spit, we've just about had it. Besides, I have to take the 12:30 bus to Amboise to buy train tickets for the only leg of our journey—a local from Chenonceaux to Tours—for which our rail passes couldn't be used to make reservations. We decide to head back to the hotel, where Liz will keep Katie company while I go buy the tickets.

THE BUS TRIP INTO Amboise leaves me giddy with my ability to carry on a simple conversation in French with the driver and an older gentleman, the only other fare onboard. By now I can use *grandmère, cent ans* and *ici* to get my story across. At least I *think* they're getting it, as they smile and laugh and "ooh" at appropriate moments.

The Amboise bus stop turns out to be a good distance from the train station, but a little hike in a light rain fails to put a damper on my good cheer. It's only when I get to the station's empty waiting room that I begin to worry. A few khaki-clad SNCF employees are bustling around behind the single, tiny, glass ticket window, tinkering with who knows what.

"Bonjour?" I begin tentatively. *"J'ai besoin de billets à Tours pour le demain."* I need tickets to Tours for tomorrow.

They turn toward the window, acting surprised, then impatient seeing me standing there expectantly. They understand me alright, but from what I gather, the news isn't good.

"Non, non, pas de billets aujourd'hui. Il est nécessaire que tu va" etc. etc. I gather that they aren't selling tickets today; I have to go to some other town. They dismiss me to return to their tinkering.

"Mais, je n'ai pas une voiture," I explain helplessly, as if having no car will make tickets magically appear.

Then a darker-skinned, SNCF-shirted young man emerges from the inner sanctum. He speaks English very well, and he tells me the problem is only temporary, an electrical glitch in their computer, and that if I wait five or ten minutes, they'll be back online. Bless him. It may sound racist, but one thing I've learned by now about Europe: if you're having a problem that is going to require some tricky English to solve, just pray for someone around who's dark-skinned, either Indian or African. Almost invariably these immigrants know at least some English, thanks to the British Colonial Empire.

I sit primly in a metal chair directly across the empty room from the ticket window. Minutes tick silently by. I watch the men through the little slot of a window. My cheer has evaporated, and I am cold and exasperated.

After about five minutes, the young man sits in the little booth, snaps up the window smartly and calls me over. After some finagling with the schedules, I have my tickets and the young man kindly calls me a taxi, since the bus won't be back until 3:30. No time to lose, right? except that the taxi costs me sixteen euros as opposed to the bus trip at one and a half.

By the time I get back to the hotel, the rain has let up some, and so Liz and I go back to the chateau to check out the gardens. Tourists in bright raincoats stroll along the raked gravel walks, and on the river a group of kids laugh hysterically as they try in vain to maneuver the green and white kayaks they've rented bankside.

Now: I have an embarrassing admission to make. I watch a TV reality show hosted by a supermodel-turned-superhostess now that she's older. It's not as if I went looking for this program; the girls got me into it. It serves as an experience to share among us. With the manipulation and development by the show's editors of the competitors' characters as mean/corn-fed/pathetic/arrogant, plus its weekly dismissals of weepy model has-beens, it is a story, if a fake one. So the girls and I connect as we root for our favorites and revel in the tragi-comic details of each week's show.

Part of the show involves imparting supposed modeling techniques. One of the keys to attaining supermodel status seems to be mastering looking "fierce." I'm not sure exactly what this means, but striking awkward poses and slitting one's eyes seem to be part of it. Looking *fierce* has become a joke in our family.

It started in the morning when Liz impetuously posed "fiercely" by a pile of logs I was photographing. It continued with her posing fist on hip and head in *fierce* profile between the fairytale paintings of Diane de Poitiers and Catherine de Medici. (At least her black hoodie over her black and coral flowered sundress over her calf-length black leggings and bottoming out at her powder-blue socks and Teva sandals are more practical than the hunting costumes dreamed up by two artists several centuries ago.) We grabbed more of these opportunities, whispering "*Fierce!*" in those split-second moments when a room was devoid of tourists.

Now that we are outside back at the chateau, "fierce" is still with us. Liz poses in a vine-covered gazebo, chin up, leg cocked, then again, cupping a cluster of wisteria in a languid hand while gazing soulfully skyward, all the while looking *fierce*. As I snap a picture of a tree-bordered lane receding infinitely into the distance, Liz unexpectedly comes hurtling across the lens, leg extended, fists clenched, chin jutted, definitely looking *fierce*.

Long beyond the favored fresh and nubile look, I find my own way to express my "inner fierceness." I walk *fiercely* and deliberately through Liz's view as she pans her Handycam across some rose beds. I stick my head out sideways, expression *fierce*, from behind a perfectly-shaped cone of boxwood. By now we're both caring little what people must think of us; as my mom used to say, "We'll never see these people again." This day is undoubtedly one of the most fun and memorable I've had on this trip, not because I love to look *fierce*; rather, because Liz and I are enjoying these moments appreciating each other as silly yet dear equals. Just for today, the "Oh, *Mom*" barrier separating parents from children has come down.

By the time we return to the hotel, I'm famished. Going to Amboise meant skipping lunch, so I take myself down to the restaurant where we'd had dinner and order their inestimable onion soup we'd drooled over the night before. This is true French onion soup, with the crusty cheese bread top and rich onion broth. Even though it's a steep six euros—nine dollars and change—I treat myself after such a great day.

But matters turn ugly when I get back to our hotel. Katie is furious that I didn't tell her I was going out to have the onion soup.

"You *know* that's my favorite! Why didn't you tell me you were going? I would've gone with you!"

"But you and Liz had lunch while I was gone! I went to get the tickets, remember?"

Her face is livid. "You tricked me! You didn't want me to go because you didn't want to buy two bowls! That's just why! You snuck out because you didn't want to spend the money!"

There is truth to this. Nine dollars for a snack? If Richard were here, he would have given her the euros, but since he isn't, we are stuck with my admitted tightfistedness. I *did* offer to take my girls on this journey, all expenses paid; it's just that "all expenses paid" was never clearly defined. When I began to plan this trip almost a year ago, a euro was worth around $1.35; by the time we left a month ago, it was worth $1.55 and steadily rising. The ever-weakening dollar preys on my mind. Richard was given the purse strings on this trip just so I could enjoy myself without constantly thinking about the price.

Katie

Dinner. I got *onion soup* and also a mozzarella and tomato and basil salad, plus my glass of wine, plus a lovely ice cream sundae with caramel sauce and whipped cream. It was delicious to be able to fully "tuck in," as they like to say in London. The Cipro worked like a charm, but I will keep taking it just to make sure the bug is killed.

UNBEKNOWNST to us, however, the onion soup issue will remain a sticking point for months to come.

To Home

Diaries of Holly, Katie and Elizabeth Pierce, 2008

Franceuil, France—Santa Rosa, California, Thursday, July 3, 2008

THE TAXI ARRIVES at 8:15 this morning, ready to take us to the Amboise station. Goodbye, goodbye; I fervently thank Laurent and his sweet wife for all their friendly assistance. I wish I'd found a Garreau, but perhaps my expectations were too high. The sky is a clear china blue with high, white wisps of cloud that later will become burdened with gray, rainy bottoms. I take a deep breath of this fresh, country air and steel myself for what will be our journey's longest and undoubtedly most arduous day. The next time I lay down my head, it will be in my own bed.

WHEN I TOOK that taxi back from Amboise yesterday, the driver charged me sixteen euros—about twenty-five dollars. This morning, however, I begin to suspect this driver is taking us on the scenic route. Not that we don't appreciate it: *"Voila, le grand chateau d'Amboise,"* he says, cheerfully waving his hand at a dour, Gothic-looking structure about a half-mile to the east.

When we finally arrive at the station, we're charged thirty-two euros. Perhaps because there are more of us? Strange; somehow we also managed to cross the Loire River this morning, but I didn't see it yesterday. Perhaps there are two Amboise stations, as this place bears no resemblance to yesterday's tiny room. Who knows? As long as we get on the correct train, I will let this mystery go.

And I do. We have our tickets, no problems with finding seats, and the train leaves punctually. Our reserved seating kicks in at Tours, and the train speeds onward toward Paris, passing ripening fields of wheat and arriving at the Gare d'Austerlitz on the dot—10:50 A.M.—despite stops along the way. Our jet leaves for Boston at 1:30 P.M., so with almost two and a half hours to go, we should make it to the airport in fine time. All we have to do is take a ten-minute walk from the Gare d'Austerlitz over to the Gare de Lyon and catch the Air France shuttle to Charles de Gaulle.

Paris is gray, and it's sprinkling now as we trek across a multi-laned overpass. Traffic is thick and noisy. I start to worry about Liz; by now I know this is the sort of environment that upsets her. I'm in the lead, glancing back occasionally to be sure the girls are with me. I cross with the light at an intersection streaming with cars and motorcycles and buses. When I look back—where are they? They're nowhere in sight.

Moments later, Katie arrives at the corner across the avenue. She is yelling and pointing back the way she came. I can't make out what she's saying, but I fear it isn't good. Yet, her expression: she doesn't seem mad, just excited. I can't figure it out. The light changes, and Katie hurriedly crosses over, her suitcase bumping precariously over the asphalt.

"Mom! Mom! You won't believe what we just saw! Liz videotaped it!" She is wild with excitement. I look across the boulevard, and now there is Liz, a pleased look on her face.

"Road rage! Two men were fighting in the middle of the road, one had a car and the other had a motorcycle! The car guy got the motorcycle guy in his helmet in a choke hold and was trying to push him over the center divider into the cars going the other way! I mean, he was halfway over! It was amazing!" she breathes, her eyes wide at the sight of real-live people going berserk.

I look back at the overpass and see that the median is a line of those waist-high cement dividers. Yikes. By now the light has changed, and Liz is crossing over, shouting to us along the way.

"Wait! The crazy part was that then the guy in the car pulled the motorcycle guy back and then they were talking and then they hugged each other and then the motorcycle guy closed the door for the other guy when he got back in his car! I filmed almost the whole thing!"

Liz

I turned around, and there was another lady stopped on the bridge staring with her mouth open as well. "Hot Blood!" she finally said, and nothing was closer to the truth! What a shocker, I'll say.

Now, EVEN *I* AM pretty impressed by this. Is this the way they handle road rage in Europe? Threaten the guy's life, then kiss and make up? Considering how sometimes it's resolved with gunfire in the U.S., I'm intrigued by this scenario. And, I'm sorry I missed it; the only time I ever saw someone actually punch somebody was in a line at Costco one Christmas. Happily, all this mayhem has put the girls in a grand mood.

THE GARE DE LYON turns out to be a big place, I mean a *really* big place. Inside, I can hardly make out the other end of the station. It is every bit as complicated as any major airport, if not more so. The ancient stone exterior looks elegant with lots of crenellations and curlicues, but inside it has been "modernized," fitting itself around and into the station's old pillars and alcoves. Shops and newsstands and ticket windows are everywhere. Just through the southern portals, those idling sleek, silver trains' hissing and sighing overlie all the echoing chaos. People are hurrying, circled in tight groups, milling about, standing in lines. I can see no one in what would appear to be a station uniform.

I'm not going to panic. I'm not. I start with a ticket window, wasting precious time standing in line.

"*Òu est le autobus d'Air France?*" I enquire when I finally reach the window. The woman shrugs and waves to the next person in line to step forward.

I try a car rental counter, a newsstand, anyone who looks as if they might be familiar with the place. Of course there's no Air France window; this is a train station, after all. One person tells me there are two information booths in *la gare* and heads me in the general direction of the closest one.

It's closed. In fact, they're both closed. Now why in this crush of humanity would an information booth be closed? Does this make sense?

It has become apparent that the best way to handle this situation is to station the girls in one spot while I with my crappy French will scout out the bus stop. It is the old "Hotter, Colder" game again, with me running along, asking anyone "*Òu est le autobus d'Air France?*" Everyone seems to have a general but vague idea—*"À droite, et la gauche"* accompanied by that sweeping but meaningless hand gesture—but we need exact instructions.

A whole hour passes before I can grab the girls and exit out the far end of the station, around the corner and down to the street. There, we finally locate a little kiosk where the precious bus tickets are sold. Better yet, an Air France bus pulls up only moments later. What luck!—except that the driver, a bullet head with a waxed dome and an impatient expression, won't let us on, maintaining that there's no more room. As if! Just look at them empty seats in the back as he pulls away! Damn these French!

Fortunately, another bus comes along about five minutes later, this time with a nicer driver, a slender man with some interesting facial hair. But as we leave the bus stop, it's 12:30, the plane takes off at 1:30, and the traffic is not at all light. I swore I wouldn't panic, but that's not what my armpits are telling me.

The ride to the airport takes thirty-five minutes. At least our driver lets us know we must get off the shuttle at Terminal C2A. We jump off at a run, and it's more "Hotter, Colder." Twenty-five minutes to stand in line, check in our bags, get our boarding passes, go through security, and make it to the plane. But where is the line for American Airlines?

"Boston? Anyone going to Boston?" a young fellow wearing an American Airlines insignia asks. Blesséd be!

"We are! We are!" I shout heedlessly above the hubbub. The young man hustles us past the annoyed line of passengers whose eyes I scrupulously avoid, and we get our bags checked in and our boarding passes. Then it's off to security.

There, a beautiful young Indian woman looking sleek in her uniform ushers us to the head of the line where we have our boarding passes checked. She then directs us to the line designated for persons needing speedy passage. But no—an officious skinhead tells us we must go to the end of the snaking security line along with everyone else. Only fifteen more minutes before the plane takes off. We argue, gesturing back to the Indian woman who looks back at us sympathetically but can do nothing for us.

So back to the end of the line. A girl in black balloon pants and strange-looking black suede shoes that look as if some gnomes in the forest made them, smirks at us. Katie wants to smack her down, and we plan ways to trip her, once past security.

Liz

The bitch! At least she got hers when she had to take off her bunchy-ass shoes at security because they were so overflowing.

The line moves along fairly quickly, though, and soon we pass through security. Then it's off literally at a run to the gate. Balloon Pants has disappeared, so there's no time nor opportunity to exact vengeance. We reach our gate with five minutes to spare.

As we get on the plane, the only thing that keeps Liz centered and in control is when she spots Senator John Kerry sitting in first class.

"Mom! Mom!" she stage-whispers from the opposite aisle as we work our way back along this 767 cattle car (and you can imagine what passes for a stage whisper with her; she may as well have bellowed it). "It's John Kerry! Look! It's John Kerry!" she points frantically. Real subtle.

"I voted for you!" she excitedly informs the senator when edging past. Since the newspaper cart is ahead of me, I have to back up and go around to the far aisle, also past the senator, and I simply say, "Thanks for the hard work."

He doesn't smile or say thank you, but then he looks pretty tired. At least Liz recognized him; kudos for her.

Liz

Boy, were we stoked! That was pretty exciting. Now I can say I flew on the same plane as he did! That is so cool. And boy, do I sound lame!

"Stop it!"

"Stop what?"

"You're getting your hair on me! You know hair creeps me out!" This phobia is Katie's.

"Oooh, sorry. What am I supposed to do?"

"Lean the other way."

"Well, the magazine cart was coming by. What do you want, my head to get sheared off?"

"You should've waited until it went by!"

(Sarcastically.) "You want me to pick it off?"

(Indignantly.) "No, it's too late now—what are you doing?! Stop it!"

"Nothing."

"Yes you are! What are you trying to get?"

(Grunting.) "The card fell out of the magazine."

"Just leave it! They'll get it."

"You know I can't just leave it! Leave me alone!" (More grunting.)

"Ow! You're smashing my knee! Stop it!"

"*You* stop it!"

I sigh and look up the aisle. I look at the strip of Velcro across the back of the seat twelve inches from my face. I try not to look to my right where the bickering continues, this time over the new issue of *O.K.!* magazine which Katie paid seven euros for at a train station newsstand. The ragged issue of *O.K.!* which has been dragged through seven countries is old news now.

"You told me I could see it once we were on the plane."

"No I didn't. I said I'd give you the *old* one once we were on the plane."

"So give it to me. Where is it?"

"It's in my backpack under my seat."

Sarcastically: "Fine." (Grunting begins.)

"What are you doing?? Let *me* get it! I don't want you squashing me!"

"I thought you wanted me to get it!"

"I don't want you grubbing around in my stuff! I'll get it." (More grunting ensues.)

"*Ouch!* You're hurting me!"

By this time we've been in the air approximately ten minutes. Only seven hours and twenty minutes to go. I contemplate what it would be like to sit quietly in the center hole for those seven hours versus seven hours of bickering.

Sigh. "Katie, would you like me to sit in your seat? You guys just aren't getting along."

Indignantly: "Yes. Thank you."

Katie

My sister started her ripping of trash into four pieces and I was through. We got into an argument, and since we three were in a row, Mom had to sit between us so we would stop fighting. I am done with hearing about her period and her old trash things. She's always making noise with plastic bags in the morning. I won't be able to see anyone in the family for about a week after this, or I think I will explode.

I UNFOLD INTO the aisle, let Katie crawl out of the center seat, then twist myself into the center. Katie sits down with a self-satisfied "plump" while Elizabeth sulks. I am in a two-square-foot space. My knees rest against the seatback ahead of me which the occupant has fully reclined. I examine the tight weave of the blue synthetic fabric covering the seatback now maybe eleven inches away and wonder when the last time it was that the fuzz-encrusted Velcro strip was used for its purpose.

Hellhole

After having to take the center hole to shut the girls up, I don't think I'm being selfish using our last five euros to buy myself a small bottle of wine to dull the pain. I really want to use this time to write, but the keyboard is on top of my tiny laptop, and even with that it is almost into my belly. This journey home promises to be long, long, long. No wonder people get deep-leg thrombosis; there is not an inch to spare. At least there's a good amount of turbulence to keep things exciting, since the TV shorts don't. "Ratatouille" looks as if it might be a good little movie, but I refuse to pay two dollars for a pair of earphones when I know I have a free pair from a previous flight in my pack in the bin above. But down here in the hole, that pack may as well be a million miles away.

We're served a meal. I choose beef rather than chicken. My tray holds beef chunks in gravy on one side of a little tin pan along with rice, two tiny broccoli sprigs and machine-molded carrots. That's the hot part. I also have a chilled bun and some type of slaw that is carrot in liquidy white stuff. Dessert is something like shape on top of a tiny layer of white cake with raspberry goo thinly coating the top. I eat it all. (I wonder if John Kerry ate his?)

Katie

Now my sister is busy bothering Mom, singing and jolting Mom's pen while she does Sudoku. It seems the food has given her renewed energy. I'm just glad I'm not sitting next to her anymore, or I think I might pinch her really hard.

AFTER THE "MEAL" I finally manage to beg a Xanax off one of the girls, and that, the bottle of wine, my magenta earplugs plus my jacket sleeves tied around my eyes put me to sleep—almost. Unfortunately, a small boy of about four right behind me keeps kicking my seat (it feels as if he is actually playing in that tiny legroom), and I finally tear off my jacket and turn to the kid's mother and ask if she could possibly keep her child from kicking the seats. As I am doing so, she is hoisting the kid back into his chair, and I feel a little remorseful, as I can easily relate to that crazed-mother look in her eyes.

He doesn't kick much more after that, and I manage to drowse for an undetermined time, but "Scott" is now running up and down the aisles going "Beep! Beep!" in an irritating monotone while his mother is fruitlessly telling him he can't do that. At the same time I feel more kicking going on behind me. I crane my neck to the right, and through a tiny, wedge-shaped space, I see Scott's sister slumped in her seat, swinging her legs fitfully back and forth. She looks to be about six years old with thick, wavy brown hair and matching brown eyes that bug out when I hiss at her, "You stop that kicking! You stop that *right now*!" That works for about five minutes.

Liz

Well, at this point we're a little under an hour from landing in Boston, and I'll tell you I've never been so excited to get back home, pretty damn jazzed to be going back to the comforts of home and the love of my man, not to mention hanging out and talking with people other than my family. I love them all dearly, but I don't want to see any of them for about a week.

WE LAND IN BOSTON, to my mind a far better, more mellow port of entry than JFK. My mom and I had gone through JFK in 1997, and I was carrying a large Moroccan rug carefully rolled in plastic, wrapped and taped. The customs officials were a stern lot. They immediately slashed open the plastic wrapping and pulled apart the rug while I stood by helplessly. Of course there was nothing to find, and we were summarily dismissed with not a move to assist me in repackaging the carpet. Fortunately, I was able to drag this unwieldy mess over to a deserted Air France counter where two employees considerately pulled out rolls of tape and helped me patch up my package.

Only later did I discover that it was my mother they should have been searching; among the items in a large plastic tote bag she was carrying was an antique illuminated page unbound from a Koran of Middle Eastern origin, the sort painted with a camel's eyelash, which I had found in a shop in Marrakech. Unbeknownst to me at the time, importation of any object from that region was strictly forbidden, as was coral, like the kind in the antique necklace I'd gotten in Fez strung with heavy silver moths and rough chunks of—well, you know.

ONCE INTO BOSTON, there's customs to pass, always nerve-wracking, especially since we've been to seven countries and have a grand total of ninety dollars to declare between the three of us (Richard has taken the bulk of our purchases home with him). Mr. Customs, a friendly enough sort, takes a look at the back of our customs form and riffles through our passports and asks us what we were doing in all those countries. I start in with my story: "One hundred years ago my grandmother went on a Grand Tour of Europe and so we decided to follow in her footsteps." At least I don't have to try to say this in French anymore.

Before I can get any further with this potentially long-winded explanation, he just waves us along with a cheerful smile. Later, I learn the girls were in a state of paralysis at that moment trying to think how to explain this strange pattern of travel. For once they are very happy that I have the story down pat.

This last leg we are herded onto a 757, a plane with a little more leg and seat room than the hideous 767; seating is three, aisle, three, rather than two, aisle, three, aisle, two. Graciously, the girls allow me the window seat. No free food on this flight; a sandwich with chips is ten dollars. While Katie decided to eat in the airport, Liz and I have brought on a take-out box of Chinese food with fragrant, heaping helpings of sweet and sour pork, cashew chicken and rice ($6.99) which is enough for both of us. Amusingly, across the aisle an Asian family is breaking open a box of pizza they've brought along. We all chow down along with our free American Airlines plastic cups of water.

I try to sleep again, but the Atlantic doze has taken the edge off the need for sleep. I turn to the passing scenery outside. Try as it may, the jet can't outrace the sun, and the landscape very slowly darkens. Soon I am trying to figure out what that squiggly river is down there, and those lights, and that large body of water (the Great Salt Lake?), but mostly marveling at the vast banks of rolling cloud forms and the black earth of the horizon becoming ever more sharply demarcated, with a sunset that moves from a thin line of fiery red to goldish-orange to the palest wispy pink and into a vibrant cobalt.

Finally all is black, save for the occasional pinpoints of light below, and then we are preparing to land. I see the lights of Oakland below, wondering what kind of crazy approach the pilot is taking until I remember we are landing in San Francisco, not the East Bay. The jet touches down, and we are back home, back to a place unlike any of the other multitude of landscapes we have experienced. For the last time I hoist on my purple backpack, and we are dodging our way past gates, weaving through the flow of outbound travelers moving in streams against us, down the escalators—and there is Ryan, waiting for his girl (Richard has decided to remain at home, allowing Ryan to pick us up, as it's only been days, not weeks, since we've seen each other).

Ryan is calm; why? Where is Liz? I realize now that she has run on ahead of us, in a mad, headlong rush for Ryan, whom she has not stopped talking about for the past month. Beaming, she emerges from a nearby bathroom and snugs up against him, finally, contentedly, at rest.

Bags are claimed, and we head for our cars. Goodbye to Katie, who takes the BART off to Berkeley and her kitties, Sass and Crazy. We find Ryan's '85 Beemer that has just lost its driver's side windshield wiper on the way here. After some unsuccessful fiddling with the wiper, Ryan lightly dismisses the problem with an, "Oh well, I guess I'll be driving blind," and we're off into the San Francisco fog. It's light, though, and the only hang-up from my perspective is that Ryan and Liz don't know how to take the 280 straight to the bridge, so we meander through S.F. on the old 101, unnecessarily wasting time. At this point, though, what does it matter? We've just traveled over 18,000 miles, with over 7,000 of them from London to Aswan, then back to Paris. What difference will a half hour more make?

Two HOURS LATER, and we are finally in Santa Rosa, then on Occidental, on Providence and we're home. It *is* my house, but looks strangely a little alien the way things do after a long absence. But here is Maia, our little orange "greeter" kitty, and she seems happy to see me, not at all stand-offish as is often the case. The final trudge: up the stairs, into the bedroom, and there is my sweetie, asleep in bed despite the bedside lamp brightly shining over his face, relaxed in sleep and with Boy lazily blinking his gold eyes in feline slits.

"Here I am," I whisper as I lean over Rich. His eyes blink halfway open, and then with a grateful sigh, he gathers me into his warm, bare arms. I am home.

Epilogue

TURNING MY HEAD, I looked through the blinds and out over the rooftops of Albany, just north of Berkeley. The room was quiet, save for the occasional tearful sniff from Elizabeth. I thought about the little red diary and of all the time it took to tease out my grandmother's spunky twenty-seven-year-old voice from a century past. I thought of all of the work that had gone into recording our own words throughout our five-week journey, such a wealth of observation and insight. And I thought of my impending sixtieth birthday, only two years away. This last event had been weighing heavily on my mind. Soon I would be old enough to get discounts at Marshall's, at Ross, at theaters and museums, all because I would then be old enough. Elderly enough.

I thought about taking care of my parents through their eighties. At that point they were moving through what some ungraciously call the "twilight years." My father, increasingly suffering the effects of Parkinson's disease, slept longer, got up later and seldom left the house. Those years could not be called productive. What that meant to me was that if I followed in their hereditary footsteps, I really would have only twenty years left during which my body would slow down, pestered by the aches and maladies of old age. Already the topics of conversation among my friends were turning to this or that affliction.

And I thought about the big question: what could I leave behind that would be of interest or value once I was gone? I couldn't be sure, but this book could be my legacy. It would contain the first-hand words and emotions of three generations of women who, although set in worlds a century apart, illustrated how much the same we were at heart. Pleasure and anger, whether on a steamship or an airliner, were felt to the same degree and in the same way. It only seemed to confirm my belief that should our descendants a century from now make the same journey, the same continuity of feelings and emotions would be felt and expressed.

But how is it that we found ourselves in this therapist's office three months following journey's end? Why was it that I might be responsible for a permanent rift between myself and my daughters? How did I get myself into this dilemma?

It was Richard who had gotten us into this pale blue office, that and the French onion soup. The latter was a subject that had longer symbolic legs than I'd imagined; if there were ever a disagreement, somehow Franceuil's French onion soup reared its cheese-encrusted head. After several months of smoldering resentment, there seemed to be only one way to repair the aggrieved and affronted feelings, and that was through family therapy.

Acting on a reliable recommendation, we found our therapist, Nina. We dove into weekly sessions which were fraught with high emotion, yelling, sulking and tears ("How do you handle these live wires!" Nina once quizzed Richard). I came to realize that the girls were right; this journey had been *my* trip, with my family responsible for making this dream a reality. I only needed to recall my moment of clarity in Israel: "I was entranced by a vision—*my* personal vision, not theirs." Somehow, among the nine preparatory months of hotel and flight reservations, train schedules and itinerary manipulations, I had failed to take into account the most critical aspect of this vision: the needs and limitations of my own family members.

And frustratingly, the answers had been there right in front of me all along, yet I only dimly saw them. Before we had left on this trip, I had created a nine-point questionnaire for the four of us to fill out and discuss. What a great idea! I had thought; now we'll leave well-attuned to one another. We wrote our answers out at the kitchen table one bright Saturday afternoon, scribbling them in pencil to the following:

What are your expectations about this trip?

Why do you want to go on this trip? What's important about it to you?

What experiences or places are you most looking forward to?

What don't you want to do?

What are you most afraid of?

How do you see us traveling together daily?

What do you see as your "hot spots?" other people's hot spots?

What would bum you out the most?

What would make you happiest?

Afterwards, we took each question at a time and read aloud our responses. To me at least, many of the answers seemed offered light-heartedly, even tongue-in-cheek: how could "Finding fuzzy leopard pants" in Italy be a high point of the trip? I wasn't joking when I said I feared "Continual snits," but maybe others felt I was being sarcastic as well. Our family does have a well-ingrained facetious streak. But it was at my peril that I ignored this little exercise. And I did; I filed the four pieces of paper into the back of my notebook and forgot about them.

AT ONE THERAPY session we were each asked to come up with one word to describe what was most important to us. For Richard it was harmony. For Katie, authenticity. Liz answered composure. And I in my usual way had to come up with two words: truth and fairness. If I had only thought before the trip to make this one-word query one of the questions, then explored it in relation to each person's answers on the questionnaire, I might have begun to see all of those potential red flags popping up. But I was too busy with trip details. Long after the damage was done, it took a therapist to ask such an important and relevant question, to take us down to the basics.

For Richard, "harmony" meant no fighting or arguing in public or ganging up, children against parents, or in any other configuration. His greatest wish was "to see my family be happy and to explore Europe together." Clearly, that wish wasn't entirely realized, and our venturing into family therapy was his attempt to bring some resolution to ongoing resentments.

Katie desired "authenticity," a term that to me has always been a little fuzzy in meaning and something of a buzz word. But her answers clearly reflected her wish: "getting to know one another anew and as the grown-ups that we are" and that "our trip runs smoothly and any arguments get ironed out so that we know each other better," and "if we all end up with a better understanding of who we are as people."

Liz valued "composure," and if I'd only thought about her history, I should have been more careful in seeing that she was well prepared and up for this trip. She feared that her anxiety would get out of control, that she would find herself "overwhelmed and freaking out," or "angry/isolated from others." Pressure in any form was threatening to her wellbeing, and as Katie often warned when Liz was reaching a melting point, her mental "pop-up blockers" were breaking down. Once that happened, she was at the mercy of her own internal devils.

As for me, "truth and fairness" were all about the motivation, both mine and my family's, behind the journey. So many answers had to do with Ruth and her diary: "Concentrate on the diary;" "Follow in Ruth's footsteps and have my family experience the feelings of personal history it should elicit. Explore her voice." "Fantasy: all together seeking out Ruth's places." But I was also apprehensive of the weight of expectation resting on my shoulders: "Disappointment and feelings of failure if fantasy is unfulfilled," and the desire that they "don't blame me for stuff going wrong." This was a huge and complicated undertaking, and as I wrote, "I could've had a baby in the time I took to plan this."

As could be expected, money was definitely an issue. Richard and I had told the girls that we were taking them on this trip and that we would take care of expenses. Little did I realize how literally they took that. Who wouldn't want an all-expenses-paid trip overseas? Somehow I had thought the girls would take into account what a huge investment this journey was and would be conscious of what even the smallest expenditures meant. After all, at this time the euro at $1.60-plus was at its highest point in recent years, and I often felt as if we were hemorrhaging money. I didn't want "feeling money is getting out of control" or seeing money wasted, and I was the only one who noted this concern. I had taken plastic Target dishes with us so we could have makeshift meals in our hotel rooms, but that plan soon went by the wayside. When people were hungry, they wanted to eat, and eat *now* rather than waiting to go back to the hotel or taking the time to hunt down bread and cheese in a market. Why did it seem it was just me who blanched when a lunch cost seventy-five dollars, or a small bowl of French onion soup went for nine? Casual expenditures for Cokes and snacks soon stressed me to the point where I simply turned over the finances to Richard, who was only too happy to dole out the euros if it meant maintaining harmony among the ranks.

Another issue I had missed noting among the questionnaire's answers was the expressed desire for "alone time." The truth was that I had tried every chance I had to book the cheapest accommodations within reason. This often meant four in a room which resulted in many instances of walking across mattresses to reach the bathroom. How was anyone supposed to eke out a little alone time in such cramped quarters? Why didn't I recognize that "getting too tired" for me also meant needing precious "alone time" to decompress?

While neither Richard nor I had thought of this, the girls were explicit. Katie stated, "I need time alone every day for myself," while Liz simply said, "Time by myself." As the trip progressed, more and more did Katie opt out of going out on excursions in favor of staying behind in the hotel either reading or writing in our room or going out by herself to the hotel's sidewalk café for a cool drink.

At first this was a terrible issue for me; had I taken my daughter on this money-pit-of-a-trip just so she could laze back at the hotel? I was angry. On the other hand, both daughters kept reminding me this was supposed to be a vacation, not a forced march. Then after a while, I simply let the matter be, instead choosing to feel that I could offer Katie these opportunities, and if she didn't take them, so be it.

For a long time I was blind to the reasons behind her choices so clearly delineated that Saturday afternoon. She had penciled down so many fears: getting sick, germs, losing something important, Egypt, Israel and the Gaza Strip, being "hungry, tired, angry, lonely, scared, anxious . . . overexposed to other people's needs, wants," and yes, "terrorists," "joining up with terrorist rebels," or "being held up by terrorists." If she could have anticipated it, I'm sure she would have included the eerie presence of whining circular saws at every turn. Here was a girl who chose to lose herself in the fantasy lives depicted in her tattered *O.K.!* magazine rather than possibly be beset by real-world threats. I had failed her in my lack of sympathy for and validation of those fears.

Elizabeth was another matter. I have always recognized her for the brave and adventurous woman she is. How I relished her scrambling around in the rocks and boulders at the Western Wall so she could get her precious and illicit footage with her Handycam! Her answers to the questionnaire made it clear how much she anticipated filming this adventure: "filming," "filming our experiences," "losing my camera," "making a movie out of it." In London, against Richard's judgment she had gone out in the misty evening alone, mastering travel on the Tube to reach Parliament, Big Ben and the Eye, even having the poise to turn away a man who attempted to proposition her, all so she could take her photos.

But she had her own devils to deal with. Ever since she was a small girl she has been dogged by her anxiety disorder. This has never been a condition she has been comfortable discussing with other people, even her close friends. Instead, she has seen it as something that set her apart from her peers, as if in some way she was broken inside. She felt ashamed by it, as if it were something that should be under her control. Even though everyone else in the family took their own assortment of psychoactive medications, it wasn't enough to convince her that it was a biological disorder rather than a failure of will that was about as shameful as having Type 1 diabetes.

I knew dealing with this was part of her life, but she rarely complained about it. To her parents, the childhood trauma of her inability to deal with her spells of anxiety seemed to be for the most part behind her; she seemed to have her life under control. Yet, interspersed with her enthusiasm for filming the journey were those red-flag comments: "anxiety out of control," "overplanned and stressed out," "rushing me, overwhelmed and freaking out" and the worst for me, "not living up to Mom's expectations." These comments defined the types of external pressures and stresses that would send her under. As a result of our not taking these fears seriously enough, the trip was riddled with stress-related melt-downs.

The inclusion of these episodes in this journal was the sticking point in therapy. Liz adamantly resisted them being included; I couldn't see how this story could be told without them. Thus the therapist's question: "Are you willing to risk alienating your daughter over this?" Because I was determined to birth this book, we had to find an answer.

Katie is a writer. She majored in English with an emphasis in Creative Writing at Mills College. She has written stories all her life, and although she is one of those legions who come to paper their walls with rejection slips, she resolutely sets time aside every day to write. So it was that I found Katie to be my supporter. At one session she exclaimed, "But Liz, Mom has to include you! You're such a juicy character!" I gave her a grateful look for this, as it was something I had wanted to say but felt constrained against doing. Katie knew that reducing Liz to a two-dimensional cardboard character would eviscerate the book. Katie herself would many times not be portrayed in a particularly flattering light, but as a writer she could accept this.

At one session we summed up the book's possible fates. I could just chuck it, quit, give up. I could finish it, add photos and scans of the postcards and keep it as a travel scrapbook for our family's enjoyment. I could write the whole thing as a novel, although how our circle of friends wasn't supposed to be able to figure out who the thinly-disguised characters were, I didn't know. Or I could plow ahead at the risk of the wrath of my children.

All along, though, I knew that the last possibility was the only possibility for me. All of the months spent discovering Grandma Ruth, of mapping our itinerary, making hotel and travel reservations, paying for the whole thing out of my own pocket: this book would be my baby and was destined to be my legacy. So it was that we finally came up with a solution: I would write it, then give the girls editorial license. Parts they found too harsh or embarrassing we would work out together. In truth, I believed they wanted to see this book become a reality as much as I did. All of us knew this was an amazing tale that deserved to see the light.

MONTHS OF THERAPY later, we were through, talked out. Katie's wish had been realized: we had all ended up with a better understanding of who we were as grown-up individuals. Grudges and resentments were resolved for the present, although we came out of our therapy with the understanding that at any given time in the future some issues might rise once again. But at least we would be prepared to spot those red flags and bring understanding to their resolution.

As for Ruth, I felt a deep sense of satisfaction in having finally brought her youthful self alive, when all I could remember from my childhood was her vigorous but old self. Her young voice was as excitable, annoyed and in awe of newly-seen landscapes as was our own. She was as delighted with new tastes—"Tonight had Devonshire cream on our prunes. Great."—as were my daughters: "Had lamb cutlets which were absolutely delectable and savory. Holy crap, they were good." Her naive outlook on potentially dangerous situations—" . . .the boat had sprung a leak . . . We passed the men working on the pumps, and I tell you, it was exciting!"—was much the same for my daughters during the few serious situations we encountered: " . . . we join the convoy that is taking a bunch of tourists to Luxor . . . Sneak pictures of the soldiers' giant AK-47s."

Most gratifying was my daughters' interest in Ruth's journal. Every word was devoured as we made our way along our route. The journey after all had been a success, despite all the tears, protests, and anger. Katie and Liz are now firmly connected through their souls and imaginations to their great-grandmother, previously only an unknown bare branch on the family tree. And they, too, now have their own written tales of their Grand Tour of Europe, just like Ruth's from a century ago.

The path is set, etched twice in the soils of Europe, Asia and Africa. Will there be some descendant in 2108 who will feel compelled to make this journey as well?

Will it even be possible?

Acknowledgments

I give deepest thanks to those without whom this journey would not have been possible, including all the kind and caring strangers along the way, as well as the ladies at the Reggio di Calabria train station, the lovely and most helpful young woman at the front desk of the Condor Hotel, and Laurent who gave me a lift to the cemetery in Francueil; my aunt Frances Johnson, my vital link to the past; Sandra Golden Goodson, for lending me the two precious albums full of postcards; TripAdvisor.com, my trusted and invaluable internet travel agent; our guides, Sandy in Israel, Douli in Egypt, and the multiple Muhammads in both, who expertly crammed so much knowledge into so short a time; Lynn Ostling, for her in-depth knowledge of European art; Jimalee Plank, for her discerning and critical eye; our therapist, Nina Ham, who brought forth meaning out of chaos; my dear daughters, Katie and Elizabeth, who I know will look back on this trip someday and be glad they went; my husband and rock, Richard; and to my paternal grandmother, Ruth Kelsell Crapo Johnson, whose lively voice and indomitable spirit brought this journey into being.